HOW TO
THINK LIKE
SOCRATES

ALSO BY DONALD J. ROBERTSON

The Philosophy of Cognitive-Behavioural Therapy
Stoicism and the Art of Happiness
How to Think Like a Roman Emperor
Verissimus: The Stoic Philosophy of Marcus Aurelius

HOW TO
THINK LIKE
SOCRATES

Ancient Philosophy as a Way of Life
in the Modern World

DONALD J. ROBERTSON

ST. MARTIN'S PRESS
NEW YORK

For Hector, and the virtues of your ancestors

ATHENS *and* PIRAEUS
ca. 400 BCE

N

THE LONG WALLS

THE PIRAEUS

Saronic Gulf

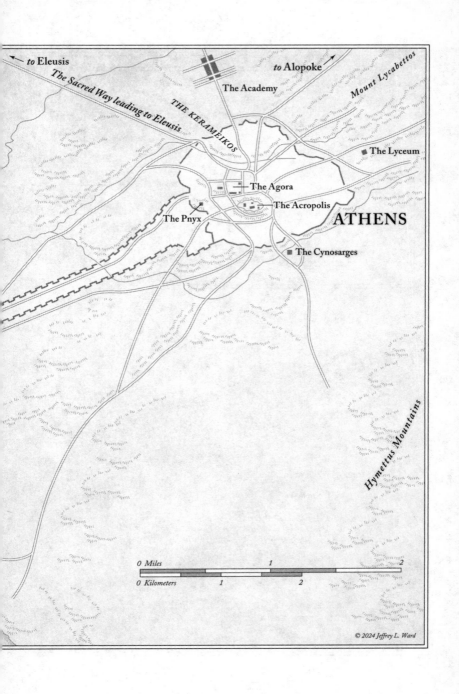

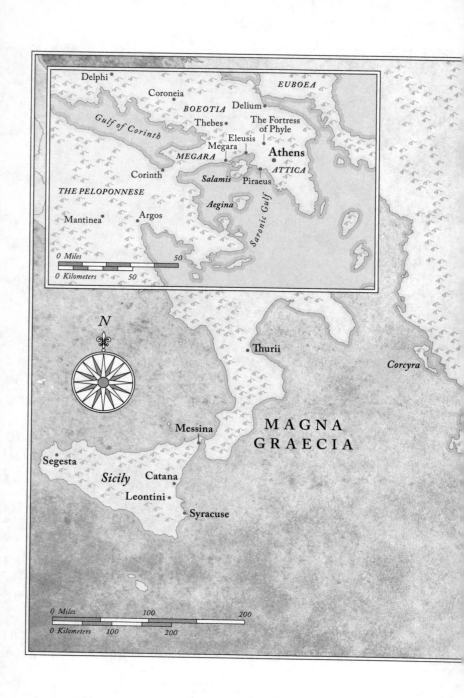

The MEDITERRANEAN
circa 400 BCE

The
Black Sea

THRACE

Byzantium

ACEDONIA

Amphipolis

The Bosphorus

CHALCIDICE

Aegospotami River

Hellespont

Sestos

Lampsacus

Cyzicus

Potidaea

Abydos

PERSIA

THESSALY

Mytilene

— The Arginusae

to PHRYGIA →

Sardis, The court
of Tissaphernes

BOEOTIA

Clazomenae

Athens

IONIA

THE

Notium

Ephesus

PELOPONNESE

Elis

Samos

Miletus

Delos

Area of detail

Sparta LACONIA

ia

Melos

© 2024 Jeffrey L. Ward

CONTENTS

AUTHOR'S NOTE: THE SOCRATIC PROBLEM

The picture of Socrates in Plato's dialogues is not a historically accurate record of scenes, conversations, sayings. *But though it is not a record, it is not mere invention.*

—KARL JASPERS[1]

UNLIKE MOST IMPORTANT HISTORICAL FIGURES, Socrates is known to us mainly through his depiction in literary sources, which are believed to be *semi-fictional*. The Socratic dialogues of Plato and Xenophon were most likely written shortly after Socrates's death. In fact, Plato and Xenophon were both young men when Socrates died, and likely only with him during the last half-dozen years or so. Our earliest source for his life is actually a satirical play written by Aristophanes, called *The Clouds*, performed during Socrates's lifetime, which paints a very different picture of him. There are a few other contemporaneous fragments, mainly of a comedic nature, and many anecdotes, often of doubtful historical value, found in ancient authors writing in subsequent centuries. Socrates was a real person—a famous Athenian philosopher. However, despite a rich tradition of literature, many details concerning his life and thought remain uncertain. The challenge of sorting out truth from fiction in our sources, which has vexed historians throughout the ages, is known as the "Socratic problem."

The philosophical dialogues of Plato, our primary source, contain many conversations between Socrates and other interlocutors. The content is probably made up, or based only loosely on things Socrates really said, although the setting usually involves real people and real places. At times they also make reference, either directly or indirectly, to real historical events. Xenophon's dialogues do too, albeit to a lesser extent. Some scholars believe that the details of Socrates's life and philosophy can be extracted, with due caution, from the dialogues. Others, such as the classicist Robin Waterfield, who has translated many of Plato's and Xenophon's works, are less optimistic:

> The dialogues occupy a fictional universe of Plato's making, set loosely in fifth-century Athens and centering on Socrates but with little attention to the outside world.[2]

Several defining moments are problematic, even the famous pronouncement of the Delphic Oracle that no man is wiser than Socrates. It is impossible to date this for certain, and we don't know whether it happened before or after other key events—some scholars dismiss it as a total fabrication. Nevertheless, it is central to the *story* we are told about Socrates.

We are therefore best to consider the Socratic dialogues of Plato and Xenophon as largely make-believe.[3] They employ the character of Socrates as a literary device, used to imagine what he *might* have said *if* such a conversation had taken place. As the twentieth-century philosopher Karl Jaspers put it, we have inherited such contradictory information that it may simply be impossible to reconstruct an accurate image of the real man. Nevertheless, the anecdotes once told about Socrates deserve to be retold for modern readers who are interested in his philosophy.

This book therefore contains a *dramatized* and *semi-fictional* account of the life of Socrates, designed to make his thought more accessible, while also highlighting connections with modern psychology. I believe that is the best way to help the largest number of people benefit from his story. Even if we must "forgo a historical Socrates," this does not prevent us from continuing to derive immense value from the literary character of "Socrates" passed down to us from ancient sources.

But men of faint heart never yet set up a trophy . . . wherefore you must go forward to your discoursing manfully, and, invoking the aid of Apollo and the Muses, exhibit and celebrate the virtues of your ancient citizens.

—PLATO, *CRITIAS*, 108c

HOW TO
THINK LIKE
SOCRATES

INTRODUCTION

THE YEAR IS 79 BCE. Three centuries have passed since the death of Socrates. A distinguished traveler from Rome, the statesman and philosopher Marcus Tullius Cicero, is visiting the Athenian Academy for an afternoon stroll with his friends.[1] The school founded here by Plato, Socrates's most famous student, is the most important philosophical institute in history—every subsequent *academy* bears its name. For centuries young men had flocked here to hang on the words of great orators and philosophers as they paced up and down brightly painted marble colonnades while athletes trained nearby, wrestling and running on the tracks. When Cicero and his companions arrive, however, *they find the grounds eerily silent and completely deserted.*

As they walk along the vacant pathways, nevertheless, the friends feel a profound connection to the past, stronger than any text could convey. The nearby garden of Plato's house, one says, seems, very vividly, "to bring the actual man before my eyes."

Cicero feels that such places, where great philosophers once explored the nature of wisdom, actually miss the sound of their voices. He imagines the Academy itself mourning the loss. The companions agree that the form of nostalgia they are experiencing can be a healthy sentiment, if it encourages them to follow the example set by men like Plato and Socrates. We should feel inspired not only to know about the great sages of history, in a purely intellectual way, says Cicero, but also to *emulate* their way of living.

Just seven years prior, the Academy area, which lay outside the city walls, had been occupied and despoiled by Roman legionaries during the dictator Sulla's brutal siege of Athens. Its sacred groves were felled to provide timber for war machines, and its shrines and libraries were looted. The Academy may, therefore, have appeared semiderelict to Cicero and his friends. Despite the damage inflicted by Sulla, philosophical studies continued at Athens for several centuries, but the city never recovered its former glory.

Since the end of the classical period, the study of philosophy has shifted from being a practical way of life to being a largely bookish and theoretical pursuit. This change has been lamented by many, such as the British philhellene Lord Byron, who mourned the decline of Athens, and the fading memory of Socrates, the quintessential Athenian philosopher.

As Byron reminisced about watching the Mediterranean sun disappear behind the mountains, he exclaimed:

> On such an eve his palest beam he cast
> When, Athens! here thy Wisest looked his last.
> How watched thy better sons his farewell ray,
> That closed their murdered Sage's latest day![2]

Socrates was, of course, executed not *literally* "murdered" by his fellow citizens—Byron's language is meant to express a sense of terrible injustice and loss. Yet despite Socrates's reputation as one of history's greatest sages, his teachings and the remarkable stories of his life, with which they were entwined, remain unfamiliar to the majority of people. The Socratic dialogues are seldom read today, except by a handful of classical scholars. And Plato's Academy, the cradle of Western philosophy, has lain in ruins for well over a thousand years—*but it does still exist.*

I lay my hand on the grass, close my eyes, and imagine that Socrates and his fellow philosophers are still here. The sun warms my face. I can smell the scorched dust of the paths, mingling with the fragrance of cypress and pine trees. Dogs are barking and I can hear the shrieks of children playing. Young people exercise here, jogging, skipping rope, and practicing martial arts.

The Academy was one of several *gymnasia* or sports grounds in ancient Athens. You can still descend into the ruins of a *palaestra* or wrestling school, in the middle of Akadimia Platonos park, as it's now known. Stray cats saunter through the rubble, instead of famous philosophers. Plato lived near these grounds and taught philosophy here. His house was probably a short walk to the northeast, near the hill of Colonus. After his death his body was entombed somewhere in the vicinity. Perhaps his remains still lie here, somewhere beneath my feet.

Whenever I want to feel a connection to ancient philosophy, I take a leaf out of Cicero's book and come to visit the grounds of the ancient Athenian Academy. I often recollect his remarks about the great thinkers who once walked here. Paradoxically, focusing on their absence somehow makes them feel more present. I imagine Cicero himself could walk around the corner any minute, emerging from behind a copse of trees, in deep conversation with his companions, soon to be followed by Zeno, the founder of Stoicism, Diogenes the Cynic, Aristotle, Plato, or even Socrates—we're told they all set foot here.

Despite laying in ruins, the spirit of the Academy still lingers. It serves as a reminder of a time when philosophy was a shared journey, not just an academic exercise. By offering a contemporary exploration of Socratic wisdom and its practical relevance to our everyday lives, this book seeks to rekindle some sense of what it might once have been like to walk here, conversing with Socrates and his fellow philosophers.

My *first* encounter with philosophy was very different. I was about seventeen years old, living in Scotland, when I chanced upon a copy of Plato's magnum opus, the *Republic*, while nosing through a stranger's bookshelf. It is Plato's longest dialogue featuring Socrates. Spanning ten chapters, this dialogue portrays Socrates discussing the nature of justice, and the ideal political state, with several other "interlocutors" (the term used for participants in the conversation).

The *Republic* opens with Socrates telling an elderly friend that he thinks of life as a journey. We should try to learn as much as we can, he says, from fellow travelers who have already experienced what lies ahead. When I read this, I was eager to learn what Socrates could teach me about navigating my own journey in life. What caught my attention most was the way he focused on fundamental questions about the nature of wisdom and the goal of life. It seemed to me that these are the sort of ideas that most *non*-philosophers avoid thinking about, until they either have a brush with death or lose someone close to them.

That initial encounter with the figure of Socrates, in a Platonic dialogue, shaped the course of my life. A few years later, I was at the University of Aberdeen studying Plato as part of a philosophy degree. After my first degree, I began postgraduate research in psychotherapy. Rather than pursue an academic career, I followed a clinical one, eventually going into practice as a cognitive-behavioral therapist specializing in anxiety disorders. Still under the influence of my initial encounter with Socrates, I began to study the relationship between modern psychotherapy and its ancient precursors, particularly the Stoic philosophers, who emphasized and further developed the therapeutic aspect of Socratic philosophy.

It was from Socrates that Stoicism derived some of its most important ideas. The pioneers of cognitive-behavioral therapy (CBT) frequently quote the famous saying of the Stoic philosopher Epictetus that "people are not upset by events but rather by their opinions about them."[3] The same idea can be found four centuries before Epictetus, though, in the Socratic dialogues.[4] This basic insight into the nature of emotion leads us to the use of reason as a therapeutic technique, as it implies that we should question the assumptions that cause our distress, if we want to get better.

Many different techniques can be used to change our thoughts and beliefs—our "cognitions," as psychologists call them. The goal of CBT, put simply, is to replace irrational and unhealthy cognitions with rational and healthy ones. One obvious way of doing that is by asking questions, such as:

- Where's the evidence for that?
- What are the consequences of that way of looking at things?
- How might other people view that situation differently?

Aaron T. Beck, one of the founders of CBT, said that he initially came across this idea when he was studying Plato's *Republic* for a college philosophy course.[5] "Socratic questioning," of this sort, later became a mainstay of his style of therapy. Countless research studies now show that cognitive therapy techniques of this kind, targeting dysfunctional beliefs, can help people suffering from clinical depression, anxiety disorders, and a host of other emotional problems.

As a young therapist in training, I was astounded, nevertheless, to come across ancient Greek dialogues where Socrates was doing something I can only describe as a precursor of cognitive therapy. He behaved like a relationship counselor or family therapist, at times, by helping his friends, and even his own family members, to resolve their interpersonal conflicts. I wondered why no one had ever told me that Socrates was doing cognitive psychotherapy, of sorts, nearly two and a half thousand years before it was supposedly invented.

On one occasion, for instance, Socrates's teenage son, Lamprocles, was complaining about his notoriously sharp-tongued mother, the philosopher's fiery young wife, Xanthippe.[6] Socrates, it seemed to me, questioned his son in an incredibly skillful manner. He managed to get Lamprocles to concede that Xanthippe was actually a *good* mother, who genuinely cared for him. The boy insisted, however, that he still found her nagging completely intolerable. After some discussion, Socrates asked what struck me as an *ingenious* therapeutic question: *Do actors in tragedies take offense when other characters insult and verbally abuse them?* As Socrates remarked, they say things far worse than anything Xanthippe ever did.

Lamprocles thought it was a silly question. Of course they don't take offense, but that's because they know that despite appearances the other actors do not, in reality, mean them any harm! It's just make-believe. That's correct, replied Socrates, but didn't you admit just a few moments earlier that you don't believe your mother really means you any harm either?

I'll leave you to mull this conversation over. I hope you notice how, with a few simple questions, Socrates helped Lamprocles to examine his anger from a radically different perspective. When assumptions that fuel our anger begin to seem *puzzling* to us, our thinking can become more flexible, and we may begin to break free from the grip of unhealthy emotions. What once seemed obvious, now seems uncertain. Indeed, the brief dialogue that takes place between them encapsulates one of the recurring themes of Socratic philosophy: *How can we distinguish between appearance and reality in our daily lives?*

Socrates exhibited a remarkable ability to carry out psychological therapy with problems as mundane as a teenage boy's irritation toward his nagging mom, while raising much deeper philosophical questions. This fascinated me because, although CBT is certainly very effective, I noticed that many of my clients were left wanting more. Once you realize, for instance, that irrational beliefs play a bigger role in your emotional problems than you had previously assumed, what comes next? Could there be a whole *philosophy of life* based on, or at least consistent with, the fundamental insights of modern psychotherapy?

Socrates, like most ancient philosophers, saw the quest for wisdom and the promise of emotional well-being as two sides of the same coin. He insisted that the mission he undertook, in the name of Apollo, the god of healing, was not only philosophical but also *therapeutic*. His trademark method of questioning was intended as a remedy, to help cure us of a terrible problem: a form of intellectual conceit that blinds and confuses us with regard to our own values. We go through life, for the most part, acting as if we know—or don't need to know—what our goal should be, which things are good and which are bad. Few of us ever take time to critically examine these assumptions.

The approach to self-improvement we find in the Socratic dialogues is therefore unlike that found in modern self-improvement or self-help literature. We usually get self-help *advice* from self-help books. What Socrates bequeathed to us was not so much a series of *answers* but rather a method of asking *questions*, a technique for clarifying our thinking and protecting ourselves from being misled by others, which is known today as the *Socratic method*.

This is not a self-help book in the conventional sense of the word. Indeed, it could be read as a *critique* of what self-help has become. In my experience, most psychotherapists frequently see clients who describe themselves as "self-help junkies" and who have accumulated their own private libraries of best-selling self-help books. They watch videos, read articles, do courses, meditate, keep a journal, and attend workshops, but they still end up in therapy. As we shall see, Socrates met young men who found themselves in a very similar predicament.

Although they may occasionally *feel* better, as a result of all the advice they consume, they're not actually *getting* better. Sometimes they have even gotten worse, despite investing so much time, energy, and money in buying whatever self-improvement gurus are selling them. It would, however, be much better for us to learn how to use reason to actively problem-solve and evaluate different strategies rather than depend on other people for stock advice.

Before we can even begin to *help* ourselves, we need, moreover, to figure out what our goal is. Self-help is no help unless we know what it is we're trying to achieve. First, we need to learn how to focus on the bigger picture and, as Socrates insisted, ask ourselves some difficult questions concerning our values. For instance, should our "self-improvement" be measured in terms of achieving external goals, such as wealth and reputation, or inner ones, such as wisdom and self-mastery? What really constitutes human flourishing or a good life?

The internet is awash with self-help advice. Young people,

in particular, drink from a veritable firehose of opinions about how they should be living. The youth of Athens faced essentially the same problem. Their "influencers" were called the *Sophists*, self-proclaimed "experts" or "wise men." Ancient Athenians attended speeches given by Sophists, who claimed to improve their students, just as today we consume videos by those who profess to be self-improvement experts.

The Sophists charged hefty fees for teaching young men how to become more persuasive speakers, with promises that they would thereby achieve success in public life. Modern influencers often profess to teach us how to succeed in our careers and relationships. Nevertheless, despite being separated by over two thousand years, ancient Sophists and modern-day influencers can, at times, sound uncannily alike. That's because they're often telling their audiences what they want to hear, or what they know will capture their attention—something Socrates described as *pandering*. They compete with their peers for our praise—ancient Sophists for applause; social media influencers for "likes." That inevitably leads them to appeal to our existing prejudices rather than challenge them. *But what if this very relationship does us more harm than good?*

Acquiring our beliefs *passively*, in this way, risks making us dangerously dependent on the opinions of other people, by reducing our ability to think for ourselves. We get opinions—the appearance of knowledge—rather than genuine knowledge. One self-help influencer may tell you to be assertive, another to practice acceptance. Advice or rules that work in one situation—such as "Tidy your room," "Focus on the positive," or "Breathe from your abdomen"—can become a liability if we try to follow them under different circumstances. Rules work until they don't; advice is good until it's not. Even the best advice is no substitute for real wisdom. It's healthier, of course, to be able to adapt your coping style to the demands of whatever situations you encounter. Following someone else's moral or psychological guidance is like following their directions to get through a forest. It only works until you get lost again. You would be much better off, in the long run, if you could learn how to use a map and compass—if, that is, you were guided by reason and your own philosophy of life.

If you depend too much on social media and self-help books for guidance, you risk becoming like those lost souls described by another ancient author. Having gotten into the habit of consulting oracles and diviners before making any decision, they seemed to lose the ability to think for themselves:

> Because of their excessive reverence for omens [or advice], they let the words of others guide them rather than their own heart, and they creep down alleyways picking up advice from other people's remarks, thinking with their ears, so to speak, not with their brains.[7]

Socrates also realized that there's a danger in "thinking" with our ears instead of using reason. We don't acquire wisdom by just listening to other people's opinions. Wisdom requires knowing how to navigate your own path through life by learning to ask other people, and yourself, the right questions.

We will explore some of these questions throughout this book as well as cognitive techniques designed to help us gain related insights. From the outset, though, we should brace ourselves for the possibility that reflecting philosophically on our own deepest values may lead us to question some of the prevailing values of the society in which we live.

As I became more interested in Socrates's life and the period in which he lived, I was struck by how many parallels there are with *recent* history. The Athens of Socrates was a fledgling democracy, in which the basic strengths and weaknesses of that system were laid bare. Their city initially flourished, and built up strong alliances, under the leadership of great statesmen, in whom the people believed wholeheartedly. Following the outbreak of a great war and a devastating pandemic, however, their trust in government was shaken, leading to a split between two political factions that became more extreme and polarized as they fought for control of the state. The political and legal systems of Athens strained under the weight of corruption, as their weaknesses were exploited to the maximum. Demagogues soon realized that populist measures and emotive rhetoric could be used to manipulate the people and to swing votes in the Assembly, by pandering to human weaknesses such as greed, fear, and anger.

Professional advisors, the Sophists, became increasingly famous, and staggeringly wealthy, by teaching politicians the art of persuasion. These men gave celebrated speeches themselves, which often exploited common insecurities and prejudices. A curious hybrid of political and self-improvement rhetoric evolved, which encouraged privileged young men to view contempt for their perceived inferiors as something "strong" and "manly." The violent suppression of foreign nations abroad and total loss of faith in the democratic process at home led, in due course, to armed coups, political purges, and even civil war. Socrates didn't explicitly align himself with any political faction or system of government, but rather his main concern was whether or not those wielding power possessed the wisdom and virtue that might make them competent to be in charge. He was, however, forced to watch as Athenian democracy was first hijacked by demagogues and then reverted to an "oligarchy," or rule by the few, which ultimately collapsed into "tyranny," or what *we* call "authoritarianism."

I will leave it to you to observe more specific parallels between ancient Athens and our modern political landscape. Different people may perhaps draw quite different, and even opposing, conclusions about what lessons we should learn. Most of us can agree, however, that the struggles of Athenian democracy throughout the Peloponnesian War, which marked the main period of Socrates's life with which we are concerned, provide a clear warning to us regarding both the fragility of the democratic system and its vulnerability to abuse. Socrates, if anything, was a *critic* of the Athenian democratic system, particularly the ease with which speakers could sway votes by pandering to the worst tendencies, or vices, of the people. Nevertheless, the ability to reason well and maintain self-awareness, then as now, may be our best defense against the rhetoric of fear and anger that threatens to tear *our* democracy apart, as it once tore apart that of Athens.

THE SOCRATIC DIALOGUES

AS MY APPRECIATION OF THE Socratic dialogues deepened, over the years, I wondered what sort of book might help my cognitive therapy clients to benefit from Socratic philosophy. I also wondered how, if I could go back in time, I would introduce the wisdom of Socrates to my teenage self? This book is my answer to those questions. It reflects my own journey and my hope to throw open the doors of ancient Greek philosophy for others.

The following chapters will take you back to ancient Athens and allow you to experience Socrates in dialogue with his students. The dialogues you will encounter are drawn from original sources that have been preserved for around twenty-four centuries, for the simple reason that they're considered to be of exceptional literary and philosophical value. Fortunately, despite the loss of so much ancient literature, the complete works ascribed to Plato survive today, including all thirty-five of his dialogues featuring Socrates. We also have about forty, mostly quite short, dialogues from Xenophon, another friend and student of Socrates. Countless more were written by their contemporaries but none of them survive, except a few fragments from another philosopher called Aeschines. It was, first and foremost, by studying these dialogues, and following their example, that ancient philosophers began to learn how to think like Socrates.

I've adapted several of the ancient dialogues for this book. To make the ideas they contain more accessible to modern readers, I've excerpted key parts from longer dialogues, simplified arguments, clarified terminology, combined elements from different texts and sometimes different authors, and modified them in countless other ways. Where it seemed to work better, I've adapted dialogue spoken by one character and attributed it to another.[8] I've created entirely new passages of dialogue in a few places, loosely based on the available information about Socrates and his companions. I've also provided information about some of the main interlocutors, events, and settings, which Plato and Xenophon assumed their audience already knew.

These dialogues, I must emphasize, are not intended to be historically accurate representations of conversations the real Socrates ever had—but neither are the ones written by Plato and Xenophon. This book is based on historical sources, nevertheless, and aims to capture Socrates's style and the substance of his ideas and questions. In other words, I intend to remain faithful to the philosophical views attributed to Socrates.

While you are reading Socratic dialogues, whether it's the ancient ones or the adapted versions in the following chapters, you have the opportunity to accompany the participants on an adventure, both philosophical and psychological in nature. You may—albeit temporarily—*become* Socrates and his interlocutors and take part in a sort of philosophical psychodrama. You may agree or disagree with what Socrates says, be stumped by his questions, have your cherished beliefs refuted, feel confused, or glimpse flashes of insight—so-called *aha!* moments.

At first, this can be unsettling. Whereas some individuals were thrilled to be questioned by Socrates and found the experience addictive, others grew infuriated, indignant, and ashamed when their hidden confusion was exposed. Can *you* recall a time when you were made to realize that you had been guilty of some grave mistake? It requires patience and tolerance to willingly subject your deepest beliefs to cross-examination. Often, we're left knowing less about life than we *believed* we knew at the beginning. Greek philosophers called this *aporia*, meaning a state of profound confusion and disorientation. Plato said that after having been questioned by Socrates his interlocutors sometimes felt as though they'd brushed against a "torpedo fish," an electric ray, and received a powerful jolt that left them temporarily stunned.

Why, in the name of heaven, would anyone want to experience the notoriously painful sting delivered by this fellow Socrates? Our moral certainty can function like a security blanket that we cling to for reassurance. Even if that sense of comfort is based on an illusion, it can be a cherished one, and we may feel anxiety if someone threatens to rip it away from us. We prefer it when experts, like the Sophists or their modern descendants, pander to us because it's easier for us. What we stand to gain from being challenged by Socrates is something less tangible and harder to define, because it's more about learning to use a philosophical method than simply "learning" to memorize the content of specific doctrines.

Plato famously compared the benefit of philosophy to the experience of someone who has spent their life chained in a cave, observing shadows cast on the wall.⁹ One day, let's suppose, the prisoner escapes and glimpses the real world outside of the cave. Dazzled at first by the light, he returns to explain to his fellow captives that what they're looking at are merely shadows cast by various objects. They, of course, think he's lost his mind. This is the experience of anyone who has seen through a common illusion. Socrates is trying to snap us out of a trance by asking questions, but the benefits of awakening can be difficult to describe to those who are still entranced. The promised goal that awaits us, though, can be said to consist in *greater freedom*. It is my belief that this Socratic freedom resembled what modern psychologists call "cognitive flexibility," or openness to exploring alternative perspectives, a trait that has the potential to improve mental health and emotional resilience.

The Socratic dialogues that lead the way there can be thought of as a philosophical "assault course," where our beliefs about life are put through their paces. When we read them in the right way, we're using our imaginations to mentally rehearse *being there* in conversation with Socrates and his companions. We may thereby develop thinking skills that benefit us in the real world and free us from common mistakes. Imagine, for example, becoming the venerable Sophist Protagoras for a while, or the charismatic young nobleman Alcibiades, by allowing the drama of the dialogue to unfold in your own mind. If you can genuinely experience the impact of Socrates's questions, you may learn to think more critically and reflectively. These skills can help you when faced with the pronouncements of modern-day Sophists on the internet, or authority figures in other walks of life. It does take practice, though. Each dialogue is therefore best approached as a different mental *palaestra* or training-ground where we can practice the Socratic method.

Socrates is important not only because he is the source from which most philosophy, as we know it today, originated but also because much of our modern literature on self-improvement is, ultimately, indebted to him. In a sense, Socrates is the great-grandfather of modern self-help and psychotherapy. In some cases, the philosophical and therapeutic tradition he initiated has, inevitably, degenerated back into the "pandering" of the Sophists. By returning to his original method, however, we gain insight into everything that followed and may learn how to find our own way through the forest of self-improvement advice. If we can imagine Socrates in a way that makes his philosophy come alive, we can walk in his footsteps for a short while, learn to ask some of the questions that he asked, and think about our lives more deeply than we have become used to doing. What that promises is something more than modern self-help literature can typically offer: *a way of living, guided by our own reason rather than the advice of others, which can lead us toward freedom and genuine fulfillment.*

This book tells the story of Socrates's life, as a philosophical journey. It is a *dramatized* account, which treats Socrates as a literary character in order to explore the connection between his thought and life. I hope you feel, at times, as though you're reading a historical biography but, in fact, more than half of this book consists of dialogues applying philosophical concepts, derived from classical texts. Think of it as an invitation for you to engage with philosophy not as a bookish and abstract subject but as a practical guide for living. Socrates, as Plutarch puts it, was the first to show that philosophy is applicable to our lives at all times and in all aspects, and to every one of our experiences and activities.[10]

We may not have a very reliable account of Socrates's life, but what we do have are stories about him and conversations attributed to him by his students. What matters most isn't whether Socrates *actually* did or said certain things but whether you and I can benefit today from the ideas attributed to him, or gain insight from the sort of questions he's said to have asked. According to Plato, for instance, we're told that Socrates himself would have told us:

> If you take my advice, you'll care little for Socrates but much more for the truth. If you think I'm speaking the truth, agree with me; but if not, resist me with every argument you can muster.[11]

We will never know the real Socrates. The literary figure of "Socrates," found in the dialogues, tells us, nevertheless, that we must learn to know *ourselves*. Perhaps, even if his story does blend fact and fiction, by retelling it in a way that highlights certain questions, and their relevance to self-improvement, he may still help us to glimpse the truth about ourselves today and free us from certain errors that may otherwise blind and imprison us.

I

THE TRIAL

"I CANNOT SAY FOR CERTAIN, fellow Athenians, how you have been affected by the words of my accusers. What I do know is that they spoke so persuasively they almost made me forget who I was."[1]

The year is 399 BCE. The philosopher Socrates, barefoot as usual and dressed in his threadbare cloak, has risen to address a jury of several hundred Athenian men crammed into a courtroom before him. They are in the Agora, the city center of Athens. Many of those present can barely contain their rage. What he says next only provokes them further.

"Some of you may think I am joking; I promise you I am not. It is my contention that I gained such a bad reputation among you precisely because of the *wisdom* I possess." The courtroom remains quiet, but only because its occupants are momentarily stunned by this remark.

Socrates continues: "The philosophers who preceded me, and to whom I have been falsely compared, laid claim to a *superhuman* wisdom. They professed to know things that no man knows for certain: concerning the nature of the sun and moon and other such things. The wisdom that I acquired, by contrast, was the sort wholly appropriate to mortals. You have heard me say many times in the past that my own investigations have nothing to do with what is beneath the ground, in Hades, or high above us in the celestial realm of the gods. *I am not that sort of philosopher.*" With his bulging eyes, snub nose, balding head, and thick lips protruding through his beard, he reminds them of an oafish comedy character, or the bestial satyrs of legend—they don't like the look of him and don't trust him. Despite this, he glares at them and speaks with unapologetic self-assurance: "I have concerned myself with something much closer to home: 'Whatsoever,' to borrow a phrase from Homer, 'is good or evil in a house.' It is in this, the field of knowledge most appropriate to mortal life, that I do indeed call myself *wise*."

Enraged jury members press against the railing, eyes blazing, as they noisily spit insults at the accused philosopher. A few even begin fighting among themselves. Socrates, though now in his seventies, is completely unfazed. He must pause, nevertheless, while the court officers, with some effort, restore order. His young wife, Xanthippe, and their children are not present. Nobody was surprised when he insisted they remain at home. Everyone, however, feels the absence of Chaerephon, Socrates's childhood friend and fellow philosopher, who recently passed away. One of Socrates's young students, Xenophon, who would go on to make a name for himself, is absent on military service. Most of his other friends are here: Crito, his lifelong companion, a wealthy agriculturalist who grew up in Alopece, the same Athenian deme (suburb) as Socrates; Phaedo of Elis, the beautiful young nobleman whom Socrates had rescued from a life of slavery after he was captured and sold to an Athenian brothel; Plato, one of Socrates's wealthy young aristocratic students, who would one day become Athens's most famous philosopher.

Each one of them looks deeply concerned at the mounting hostility of the crowd.

A few days earlier, Meletus, a young aspiring poet, unknown to Socrates, with a long nose, unkempt beard, and lank hair, had nervously delivered a verbal summons to him. The streets of Athens were abuzz with talk of the charges. Five hundred jurors, plus one more to prevent a tied vote, had filed into the Heliaia, or supreme court, on the morning of the trial. They took their seats on benches before the litigants, separated from them by a sacred wooden railing, which helped to stop brawling. Hundreds of observers also crammed into the courtroom. The sun bore down cruelly on its occupants through an open roof. Above them, in the distance, atop the Acropolis, a colossal bronze statue of the goddess Athena watches over proceedings from beside the Parthenon, her temple.

The jury was composed only of male Athenian citizens above the age of thirty. Although chosen by lot, and therefore potentially from different walks of life, most were veterans of the Peloponnesian War, grateful for the three obols per day the state paid them to be here. Prayers were made and sacrifices offered to sanctify the proceedings. The air in the building was soon filled with sweet-smelling and musky incense smoke, which lingered throughout the day, reminding everyone of their oath to the gods. It also helped to cover the smell of hundreds of sweating bodies packed close together.

"I will vote according to the laws," they pledged. "Concerning matters about which there are no laws," the oath continued, "I will cast my vote according to the most just understanding of things, and not out of favor or enmity." They promised to give the accusers and defendants equal hearing and to exclude from consideration any matters not bearing on the prosecution's case. "I swear these things by Zeus, Apollo, and Demeter," they murmured. In addition, they affirmed that the gods should bless them if they kept their word but curse them if it was broken.

Despite the solemn oath they took, one contemporary satirist claimed that many jurors were far too petty-minded to cast their votes dispassionately. They became intoxicated with self-importance, he said, at having the great and good of Athens cowering at their feet, particularly smug intellectuals like Socrates. According to Aristophanes, begging some of these jurymen for mercy would be as pointless as trying to cook a stone.[2] He compared them to an angry swarm of wasps, who delighted in being able to inflict great pain. He also claimed that the court officials who oversaw proceedings were easily bribed. Jurors in Athens can't all have resembled the embittered old busybodies he pours scorn upon, but his caricatures must have been recognizable to the theatergoers who laughed at them. The jurors perhaps also saw something of themselves in the lead character of another of Aristophanes's plays, *The Clouds*, who ends up trying to teach Socrates a lesson by burning his school to the ground. From the outset, Athens's most controversial philosopher was unlikely to receive a fair hearing.

The herald had formally announced the charges. "The following complaint was lodged under oath," he stated, "by Meletus, son of Meletus of Pitthos, against Socrates, son of Sophroniscus of Alopece." He read aloud the affidavit: "Socrates breaks the law because he does not recognize the gods recognized by the city, and because he introduces other new divinities; and he breaks the law because he corrupts the youth."[3] The jury then listened to Meletus speak, followed by Anytus and Lycon, the witnesses he called for the prosecution. Anytus, the most famous of the three, had inherited a prosperous tannery. Claiming to represent the interests of other craftsmen, he became a leading Democrat politician. As he had been accused of bribing an entire jury in the past, he asked or, according to one source, *paid* his friend Meletus to file today's charges in his place. They were aided by Lycon, a rabble-rousing orator—we know little else about this man. Socrates claimed that the witnesses had perjured themselves by bearing false testimony against him. The jury were at last listening to the philosopher speak in his own defense before voting on his guilt and the death sentence that Meletus had officially requested.

Socrates, who had been pacing back and forth on the rostrum, now halts and turns toward the jurymen as he patiently requests not to be interrupted. "Some of you, I can see, are growing angry, but although it may seem like a presumptuous claim, *wisdom* was not the word chosen by me, but by Apollo, god of Delphi." As soon as he mentions the god, the courtroom falls silent once more, except for the relentless trickling of the water clock beside the entrance, timing the proceedings. For a while, Socrates becomes motionless, his face frozen, brow furrowed. Lost in contemplation, he gazes into the distance over the heads of the jurymen. It was an expression very familiar to his friends, one that meant he was lost in deep contemplation. Watching him, some of them recalled a scene from decades ago, before an otherworldly temple, on the slopes of Mount Parnassus. That was where his story really began, or so he liked to say. His boyhood friend, Chaerephon, was with him at the time, flapping his long, thin arms, as they both spoke excitedly about two famous words, inscribed upon a pillar by the threshold of Apollo's temple.[4]

Delphi is several days' trek northwest of Athens, on the mountain slopes where Apollo, the son of Zeus, had reputedly slain a dragon called Python. According to legend, Zeus had also cast down a great stone there, called the Omphalos or navel, because it marked the very center of the universe. This sacred boulder lay within the precinct of the Delphic temple of Apollo. Greeks from all around the Mediterranean would travel there every four years, to attend the Pythian Games, in honor of Apollo's victory over the dragon. It was a mysterious place, full of treasures from distant lands. From this hallowed vantage point, in the mountains, worldly troubles seemed relatively fleeting and unimportant. One could almost believe that this was, indeed, the center of the universe. The temple also lay at the very center of philosophy—it was, in a sense, the birthplace of Greek wisdom.

There were two very important maxims inscribed at Delphi. The first, and by far the most famous, said: *Gnothi Seauton*, "Know thyself."[5] Socrates loved, and often referenced, this inscription, which he'd studied with his own eyes. For centuries to come, books many volumes long would be written by philosophers trying to interpret these two words. Standing at the entrance to the immortal god's abode, the most obvious meaning was that we should remember that we are mortal and act accordingly—to know yourself is to know that you, unlike the gods, must die.[6] Socrates considered philosophy to be, in a sense, a lifelong meditation on death. Having long reconciled himself to his own mortality, he is completely unperturbed by the threat of execution now looming over him.

"Most of you here knew Chaerephon," says Socrates softly, breaking the silence. He turns his gaze once again toward his audience, slowly scanning the room, as he continues. "He had been my friend since childhood. He was your friend too. He went into exile with the people and returned to Athens after the Thirty Tyrants were defeated." Many nod, and the courtroom remains quiet, although some expressions darken further still. Socrates continues: "A most impetuous man, he made the journey to Delphi and asked—" Several members of the jury abruptly resume their shouting, causing a disturbance and forcing him to wait while order is restored. Again, he politely requests not to be interrupted but has to raise his voice to be heard above the disgruntled murmurs.

"He asked—" Despite more angry cries from the jurymen, Socrates continues: "*He asked* the Oracle whether anyone was wiser than me. The god Apollo, spoke through the mouth of his priestess, replying that no man is wiser than Socrates." Some jurymen begin to heckle him but are restrained by others, who urge them to hear the defendant out. Socrates gestures to the gallery. "Although my friend, Chaerephon, is no longer with us, his younger brother, Chaerecrates, is in court today and will confirm that every word I have just said is the truth." At this, Chaerecrates nods slowly, his gaze fixed on Socrates—his eyes are already tearful because it seems clear to him how the day will end.

"Why mention this?" asks Socrates, leaning forward. He can see that bringing up the subject has upset many in the courtroom. "In order," he says, lowering his voice and staring directly toward the most enraged, "to explain how I earned such a *bad reputation*." Socrates waits for their murmurs to die down before beginning his story . . .

"When the Oracle's pronouncement reached my ears, I was puzzled, and immediately asked myself: 'What can Apollo possibly have meant by saying that I, Socrates, was the wisest of all men?' That was a riddle to which I had as yet no answer. For I knew that I possessed no wisdom whatsoever, great or small. Nevertheless, Apollo is a god, and so it would go against his nature to speak falsely." Indeed, as everyone present realizes, it would have been an outrage for Socrates to have stood in court and accused the god of lying.

"After thinking about this for a long time, I came up with a method of testing his answer. I realized that if I could find someone wiser than myself, I would be able to return to Delphi and present the god with contrary evidence. By pointing out an apparent exception to his claim, I would force him to clarify his meaning. Indeed, I would proceed somewhat as one might here, in court, when challenging the testimony of a witness. I would say: 'You stated that I am the wisest of all men but here is a man who is obviously wiser than me.'[7] I therefore went straight to someone who had an outstanding reputation for wisdom, a famous statesman, whose name I need not mention.[8] Once I began to talk with him in person, it became impossible for me to believe that he was really wise, although he was thought to be so by a great many people, most of all by himself.

"I tried to show him that though he believed himself to be extremely wise," says Socrates, "he was mistaken. As a result, he grew to resent me, and his hatred was shared by several of his friends who overheard our conversation. As I left their company, I began thinking to myself that although I could not believe that either of us knew anything genuinely important about 'the good,' or the goal of life, I was better off than him. Despite knowing nothing, he mistakenly believed that he knew things of great importance. I, on the other hand, neither knew nor believed that I knew such things. In this regard alone, therefore, I appeared to have an advantage over these sorts of men: I *realized* that I was ignorant concerning the true nature of goodness, beauty, and other such things.

"So I continued my search, going from one man to another, testing those who had pretensions of wisdom in the same way. As I did so, many others turned against me. Some spread rumors, others berated me, and a few even assaulted me with their fists in the street. All this I endured without complaint. To become angry with my attackers seemed as pointless to me as blaming an ass for kicking me or a dog for barking at me. At first, I was quite concerned about the animosity that my questions provoked. I felt, however, that my only choice was to persevere. The word of Apollo was more important than my own reputation. I was committed to seeking out anyone who appeared to have knowledge, in order to solve the riddle of his oracle.

"These were the mighty *Labors of Heracles* that I undertook. I wandered from one place to another, in search of a wise man. And I swear by the dog, citizens of Athens, that I must tell you the truth about my mission's outcome. What I discovered, after much investigation, was that the men with the greatest reputation for wisdom were often the most foolish. Others whom the majority held in lower esteem were, in fact, much wiser and better men." This draws murmurs from the jury, not all of whom take issue with Socrates's remark.

"My labors caused me to acquire enemies, many of whom were influential men, and this is the sole reason for my current predicament. I am called 'wise' by those who imagine that I possess the wisdom I find lacking in others. The truth is, however, that only God is wise. What Apollo meant to show through his pronouncement was that the wisdom of men is of little or no value by comparison. When he used my name it was as an example of a more general truth, as if he were saying, 'He is the wisest, who, like Socrates, realizes that his apparent wisdom is worth nothing.' After all these efforts, therefore, I was forced to conclude that the Oracle's pronouncement could not be refuted, but I also believed that I was closer to understanding its meaning."

Socrates was not behaving as a man on trial was expected to behave. These words, in particular, rubbed many jurors the wrong way, as he appeared to have called into question their own wisdom. Since there were no judges in Athenian courts, everything had to be addressed to the jurymen. Socrates went against convention by referring to them simply as his fellow Athenians rather than more formally as "men of the jury"—he did not seem to regard them as his judges.

"So I go about the world, in obedience to the god," he continues, "searching for signs of genuine wisdom in those, whether citizens or foreigners, who appear to be wise. If they are shown to be lacking in wisdom, the oracle is vindicated. This calling has consumed my life so much that I have no spare time for any matters of public interest, or any private concerns of my own. In fact, I find myself living in poverty because of my devotion to philosophy and my service to Apollo."

Socrates had a way of striding around, fixing his gaze intently on those to whom he was speaking, which made some of the jurymen feel like sprats being stalked by a hungry pelican. Many were aggrieved by the sense that *they* were the ones being placed on trial by the accused. Despite their hostile looks, he continues: "Some of you will say: 'Are you not ashamed, Socrates, to have followed a path in life that is bound to lead you to an untimely death?' You are mistaken, though, if you believe that a good man should make his decisions by calculating the chances of living or dying. He ought to consider only whether he is doing right or wrong. Otherwise, by your standard, we must suppose Achilles and the other heroes who fell at Troy to have been worthless individuals. For they risked their lives, according to Homer, despising dishonor more than they feared danger. Indeed, wherever a man's place is, whether through his own choice or at the behest of his commander, there he ought to remain. Even in the hour of greatest danger, he should stand his ground, paying heed only to his honor and not, for one moment, fearing death.

"I was ordered, along with the other soldiers, to remain at my post and look death in the face by the generals you elected to command us at Potidaea, Delium, and Amphipolis. Would it not be strange, therefore, men of Athens, if I now did the opposite and fled from danger? Apollo has ordered me, as I understand it, to follow the mission of a philosopher rather than that of a soldier. The path of philosophy has led me to this courtroom, where I now face the threat of execution. It would be both strange and contradictory of you to praise me for facing death in order to protect our city but blame me for doing so in order to preserve the character of its citizens. Of what value, indeed, are the city walls if the men within them are no good?

"The truth," he continues, "is that if I had disobeyed the oracle of Apollo, by abandoning my philosophical calling out of the fear of facing a death sentence, you might have arraigned me for impiety with greater justification. For then I would indeed have been laying claim to godlike knowledge, fancying that I was wise in areas where I was not. The greatest of man's fears, the fear of death, is, after all, a pretense of wisdom. It cannot be real wisdom because it falsely lays claim to knowledge of the unknown. Nobody is even certain whether death, which the fearful assume to be life's greatest evil, may not, in fact, be our greatest good. This is the worst sort of ignorance, which I call *double* ignorance. For, ignorant of his own ignorance, man conceitedly takes himself to know what he does not know.

"Those who make an exhibition of themselves, begging teary-eyed for your mercy, behave as though they will suffer something dreadful upon dying. They act as though they could somehow be immortal if only you allowed them to continue living. In one key respect I consider myself to differ from, and perhaps to be wiser than, these and other men. Although I know very little about Hades, the world below, I do not *pretend* to know anything about it, nor do I expect to live forever. I do know, however, that injustice is an evil and that disobedience to one's better, whether god or man, is both foolish and dishonorable. *Never, therefore, will I fear what is possibly good more than I fear what is certainly evil.*

"Suppose you were to say to me, 'Socrates, we will turn a deaf ear to your accusers. You may go free, as long as you abandon philosophy, but if you are ever caught doing it again you shall be executed.' I would reply, 'Men of Athens, I honor you, and I love you, but I shall obey the god Apollo and not you. While I have life and strength I shall never cease from the practice of philosophy, and I shall continue to exhort anyone I meet to do the same.'" He turns toward the audience and glares at them, in his notorious fashion, from under his thick eyebrows. "'You are my friend,' I shall say, 'a citizen of the great city of Athens. Are you not ashamed of heaping up money and reputation, while caring so little about wisdom and the improvement of your soul?'

"If he replies that he *does* care, I will cross-examine him thoroughly. If I think he has no wisdom or virtue in him, but only says that he has, I will rebuke him both for undervaluing the most important things in life and for overvaluing less important things. I shall continue telling this to everyone I meet, young and old, Athenian or foreigner, but especially to the citizens, as they are my kinsmen. For I do nothing but go around persuading you all, old and young alike, not to worry about your reputation or your property but to make it your greatest concern to achieve the greatest improvements possible in your own character. Moral wisdom is not acquired through money. On the contrary, such wisdom is a *source* of true wealth and everything else that is good for man and for the city. I do this at the command of Apollo, and I am confident that no greater good has ever befallen Athens than my pursuit of philosophy, in his service.

"No man here can deny that this is my teaching. If you believe that this doctrine corrupts the youth, then you may perhaps conclude that I am a criminal. What puzzles me, however, is how you could believe that any man would deliberately *intend* to make his own city worse. In doing so he would, of course, harm not only others but also himself. Perhaps you might assume that I am so foolish that in attempting to teach wisdom and virtue, despite my best efforts, I accidentally achieve the opposite. Yet our law does not punish one for doing harm unintentionally, but only for doing so deliberately. Whether or not you find me guilty, and even if you sentence me to death, as my accusers desire, understand that I shall never turn my back on philosophy, even if you were able to execute me many times over."

Upon hearing these brazen words of defiance, the jury erupts. Hundreds of bodies, crowded into the court, press forward, yelling, arms flailing, while others try, with difficulty, to pacify or at least restrain the outraged mob. Socrates pauses briefly, amid cries of "Step down! Step down!" peppered with coarse insults. He stares directly into their eyes. Again, he asks the members of the jury to calm themselves and be patient. They had agreed to hear him until his time was up on the water clock, and a few minutes still remain. "Men of Athens, please do not interrupt me," he says. "I have one more thing to say, which may cause you to cry out loud, but I believe that to hear it will be good for you, so I beg you to listen.

"If you kill a man such as I am," he says, "you will injure yourselves far more than you injure me. Nothing you can do will ever injure me. My accusers, indeed, *cannot* harm me. For, as I shall explain, nature will never permit a bad man to injure one who is good. They may, of course, have me killed, or driven into exile, and even confiscate what little property is mine. They may imagine, as others will, that they are inflicting great harm on me by doing so. There we must disagree. For, in truth, the evil of wrongly taking a life, or inflicting any other form of unjust punishment, is far greater than the evil of suffering it."

Moments before, nothing could be heard in that court above the roar of the indignant mob. Now the room has become very still and quiet once again. The water clock is beginning to run out. Socrates ends the silence, turning to face his fellow Athenians. "Anytus and Meletus may kill me," he says, "but they cannot harm me."

THE PRACTICE OF DEATH CONTEMPLATION

HOW ARE WE TO REMEMBER who we really are when, throughout our lives, powerful and often eloquent voices seek to persuade us of something else? We can begin from the simple premise that what appears to be true may turn out to be false. Socrates developed a method to help us distinguish between *appearance* and *reality* and expose the conceit of wisdom in ourselves and others. Those who believed themselves most wise were typically the ones who left his company feeling most foolish. Some people believe that philosophy can be learned by reading books, memorizing the best parts, and repeating what they have read. Socrates believed that this leads not to real wisdom but to the illusion, or appearance, that you possess wisdom—opinions rather than knowledge.

Philosophy, for Socrates, was a practice and a way of life. The Socratic method begins with a *negative* revelation: the insight that we cannot acquire wisdom from books in the same way that we acquire onions from a greengrocer. Wisdom cannot be purchased, at any price, from the labor of other people. It can only come from our own efforts. The Socratic method is an active *process* of thinking. Its constant refrain is "Yes but . . . ," because it happily seeks out one exception after another to our definitions, assumptions, and other verbal rules. It forces us to think for ourselves by continually placing in question our most important assumptions and values, such as our goals for self-improvement.

Socrates did not think books were useless. In fact, he was an avid reader who enjoyed quoting other writers. He believed, though, that like the cryptic oracles of Apollo, we must question what we read and put it to the test by trying to identify exceptions, or situations where it no longer holds true. Even the pronouncement that no man was wiser than Socrates, and the imperative to know ourselves, need to be examined in this way to be properly understood. Wisdom cannot be taught, but, perhaps, it *can* be learned—especially if we make the effort to examine our own lives and the assumptions on which our actions are based.

You can start right now. Where should you begin? At the very end, of course. Imagine you are facing execution like Socrates, perhaps even having your life judged, and possibly condemned, by your peers. For the sake of argument, let's assume your fate is sealed, and there's no point trying to convince the jury to acquit you. Looking back on your life, what would matter to you the most? What, in other words, would you want your life to stand for?

Let's go further. Like Socrates, you're raising the cup of hemlock to your own lips, about to take the fatal sip that will close your eyes for eternity. Imagine that these are your last few moments. Pause and think of what *seemed* most important to you throughout life. If you're not sure how to answer, use this question to find a clue: What did you *spend most of your time* doing? Time is one of our greatest assets. In what did you actually *invest* your time, yesterday and the day before? How important do you think these activities really were, as you imagine looking back on them from the end of your life?

The pursuit of wealth is easy to examine from this perspective. As the saying goes, you can't take it with you. How much good would a million dollars be doing in your bank account as you are on the verge of passing away? Suppose it's too late to spend it, either wisely or foolishly. Once you know that your time is up, it's obvious that money itself is of no intrinsic value. What matters, if anything, is the use we choose to make of it. Many of the things that appear valuable throughout life are of this nature. We store them up, hoping to use them one day, when we get around to it, but they're of no real value unless they're used wisely.

Today we can quantify fame even more simply than we do wealth. Perhaps you have a million followers on social media. Imagine, on your deathbed, asking yourself: Did that alone make life worth living? Fame, like wealth, is at best a means to an end. It creates the opportunity to influence many people. If you never used your reputation for anything good, though, what was the point of spending time acquiring it? What if this is true of *most* of the things that appear valuable to the majority of people? What if we are born into a society that perpetually confuses the appearance of value with real value?

How about the pursuit of knowledge? That seems like a more noble goal to many people than acquiring wealth and fame. Is all knowledge equally valuable, though? Have anyone's final words ever been, "I only wish I'd finished watching all the *Friends* DVDs, so that I might know how the series ends!" What about knowing how to help people, through the study of science or medicine? Of what value is that, or any other knowledge, unless you put it into practice, and do so wisely? When confronted with our own mortality, it often appears obvious, in retrospect, that many of the things we imagined to be important were only of *potential* value. What matters is how we use them, *before* our time is up.

You don't need to face execution to find this out. Why? Because Socrates has already done it for you. His whole monologue above takes place under the shadow of death. Socrates, during his trial, presents himself as a man who was willing to live in relative poverty, and risk making powerful enemies, in order to pursue his philosophical mission. Even knowing that his life was about to end, he still considered wisdom to be immeasurably more important than things like wealth and reputation. We should ask ourselves, as he asked the jurymen, whether we have somehow been duped, throughout our lives, into "undervaluing the greater, and overvaluing the lesser."

Many people, perhaps most people, never consider this perspective until it's too late, but sometimes, if we're lucky, we get a second chance. In the Charles Dickens novel *A Christmas Carol* (1843), the miser, Ebeneezer Scrooge, has a moral epiphany and decides to share his wealth with the poor, after a dream in which the Ghost of Christmas Yet to Come shows him his own gravestone. In 1888, Alfred Nobel, the inventor of dynamite, got a similar shock when he read his own obituary, published by mistake, as he didn't like its depiction of him as a "merchant of death."[9] He decided to rewrite his will, using most of his personal fortune to set up the famous Nobel Prizes, which reward those individuals who have conferred the greatest benefit on humankind in different branches of the sciences and arts.

Philosophy for Socrates was, first and foremost, a process for improving ourselves by critically examining our deepest values. He believed that the purpose of life itself is to *converse daily about virtue*, or the improvement of our own character, because "the unexamined life is not worth living." After his trial, he reminded his friends to keep questioning themselves and others, including his own sons, in order to purge intellectual conceits, especially if they seemed to care more about wealth than about wisdom.

THE SENTENCE

THE OUTCOME OF THE TRIAL is well known. The jury deliberated while they voted, each man dropping one of two small bronze disks he had been given into an amphora, to indicate either acquittal or guilt. Once they had returned to their benches, the herald called out, "Who hasn't voted? Stand up!" Nobody stood up. So the urn was emptied out and the votes counted. The herald announced the jury's verdict: *Socrates was guilty*. Athenian law allowed the accused to propose an alternative to the death penalty. Socrates was expected, like most individuals in these circumstances, to throw himself on the mercy of the court, parading his tearful wife and children before the court, begging the jury to send him into exile as long as they spared his life. They would certainly have agreed to do so. None of them really wanted his death on their conscience.

Socrates, though, remained unapologetic. The absence of his family made it clear that he did not intend to make an emotional display. He was, as he put it, "a man, like other men, a creature of flesh and blood, and not of wood or stone," who loved his wife and children. However, "I had not the boldness or impudence or inclination to address you as you would have liked me to," he said, "weeping and wailing and lamenting, and saying and doing all the things that you have been accustomed to hear from others." Least of all, in the hour of his greatest danger, did he want to behave in a manner he considered beneath him. "Nor do I now repent of my defense," he said, "and I would rather die having spoken in my manner than speak in your manner and live."

Instead of exile, he proposed that the jury should "punish" him for his alleged impiety, and for corrupting the youth, with free meals for life at public expense. This was an honor typically granted to victorious athletes. After some discussion with his friends, Socrates told the court that he would be willing to accept a fine, amounting to thirty pieces of silver. It was too late. His "big talk," as one of his students later described it, offended the jurymen. An even larger number now voted against him than had originally found him guilty. They sentenced him to death.

This arrogant old man, who dared to question the things they held in highest regard, seemed too dangerous to let live. The jury were convinced, based on the impression they'd received from satire and gossip, that the philosopher before them was nothing more than an intellectual charlatan whose habit of questioning everything merely posed a threat to their society. In reality, they did not know Socrates at all.

2

THE FIRST PHILOSOPHER

AS A YOUNG MAN, SOCRATES worked in stone. His father, Sophroniscus, a master sculptor, hoped to teach his sons a valuable trade. They were put to work, toiling under clouds of dust, among his slaves.[1] Socrates had been given the job of roughing out a block of Parian marble for a frieze, which would later stand before the *Propylaea*, the grand entrance to the Athenian Acropolis.[2] Ropes and pulleys clattered as workmen positioned one heavy block after another to be chiseled and chiseled until they were ready to be smoothed and painted. The life of a craftsman in a busy stonemason's workshop was tedious, dusty, and deafening. Socrates must have struggled to hear himself think at times.

His mother, Phaenarete, claimed that as soon as he had learned to speak, Socrates had begun asking questions. He asked questions about the nature of the world around us. How did the sun come into being? From what was it made? Will it one day cease to appear above the horizon? He was also curious about *human* nature. Do we think with our blood, our breath, or the brain? What is knowledge—is it more like having an opinion or a memory? Of all the youths in Athens, Socrates was the one most troubled by such questions.[3]

The sculpture he was working on would depict three goddesses, called the Graces, or *Charites*.[4] They personified the virtues involved in graciously bestowing and receiving favors. One maiden offered a precious gift, another received it with gratitude, and a third repaid the giver. The three Graces symbolized this virtuous cycle by dancing together in a circle. As soon as Socrates was set to work on this piece, dedicating his entire day to its preparation, he found himself besieged by new questions. What *are* generosity and gratitude? What do they look like in their perfect form? Having pestered his father to no avail, he had approached the finest sculptors in Attica, the region in which Athens is located, searching for answers. He came away totally unsatisfied. They could point to examples of great men from history, but that wasn't enough. From early childhood, Socrates had been taught to admire the ability of craftsmen to render human virtues such as wisdom and courage beautifully in stone. It was the Greeks who had introduced and mastered the art of lifelike sculpture. As a young man, Socrates was now growing dismayed by their inability to put their vision of human perfection into words by answering one simple question: *What is virtue?*

Socrates could barely wait for his work to end so that he could meet his two best friends, Chaerephon of Sphettus and Crito of Alopece. He had known Crito since childhood, as they grew up in the same deme, or suburb, of Athens. Chaerephon, who came from across town, he got to know later. They would talk excitedly about the latest theories of the greatest Greek minds. They looked, particularly, toward Ionia, a narrow region on the western coast of Asia Minor composed of a string of prosperous colonies on the frontier between the Greek and Persian worlds. The Ionian cities had formerly been ruled by Persia but had in recent decades become allied with Athens, providing an influx of unfamiliar customs and ideas.

Chaerephon was an unconventional and outspoken fellow, particularly infatuated with an emerging movement that some people were calling "love of wisdom" or *philosophia*, known today, of course, as philosophy. He was something of a misfit. He grew his hair long, carried a cane, and, like Socrates, walked barefoot. His jaundiced complexion, lanky frame, and dark bushy eyebrows would later cause satirists to compare his appearance to that of a specter, raised from Hades by some form of necromancy. Chaerephon would become so animated when arguing about new ideas that his dark, loose-fitting cloak would flap around like the wings of a crazed bat. Following the monotony of the stonemason's workshop, located far outside the city walls, Socrates came alive when he was able to meet with his friends talk about philosophy. He would have given anything for the chance to learn more.

The first philosopher had arrived in Athens a few decades earlier, from the Ionian city of Clazomenae.[5] Anaxagoras lived in Athens as a foreign resident, or *metic*, where he was inevitably suspected by some of sympathizing with the Persians, the most powerful of Greece's "barbarian" enemies.[6] A polymath, he devoted his life to multiple fields of study, which later earned him the nickname *Nous*.[7] Although derived from a technical term employed in his philosophy, it was also akin to calling him "Brains" or "the Intellectual," and could perhaps be used to mean someone who thinks *too* much.[8] Everyone had heard of Anaxagoras, and he was often seen in Athens, though he remained aloof and seldom talked to strangers.

The philosopher had been brought to Athens to serve as the

teacher of a young nobleman called Pericles, who would later surround himself with some of the most influential thinkers of the age. Pericles colored his speeches with innovative philosophical doctrines learned from his new advisor. Natural philosophy attempted to explain the world through logic and careful observation. Combined with Pericles's innate talent for speaking and his training in formal rhetoric, this education turned him into the greatest political orator of his lifetime, described as wielding the "dread thunderbolt" of Zeus in his tongue.

Though born into a family of wealthy nobles, Anaxagoras had abandoned his estate in Clazomenae, allowing the land to lie fallow for sheep to graze upon. When his relatives berated him for neglecting his inheritance, he reputedly signed it over to them, shrugged, and said, "Why don't you look after it then?" At Athens, he lived modestly but could depend on the patronage of his famous student. He did not need to earn a living by delivering public lectures. Socrates and Chaerephon were young and neither wealthy nor prominent enough to be invited into the intellectual salons of Athens's foremost men. They could only dream of conversing one day with a thinker of Anaxagoras's stature.

In addition to his philosophy, Anaxagoras had brought several pieces of state-of-the-art technology to Athens. One was a map of the known world, with the Mediterranean Sea at the center, based on a diagram created years earlier by another Ionian philosopher.[9] Pericles and his friends would walk around this curious object, debating its accuracy. Sometimes, though, they would just stare down at it in rapt silence. The novel experience of gazing godlike upon an image of the world became a symbol for the lofty equanimity that seemed to be attained by students of natural philosophy. Anaxagoras embodied this "greatness of thought," and some saw it in Pericles too.

When the philosopher was criticized for having neglected the land of his birth, he would point up toward the sky and quip, "Oh but I am very much concerned with my fatherland!" When he spoke of the planets and other mysteries of nature, it sounded as though he viewed the whole cosmos as his homeland and had immersed his mind in a world immeasurably more vast than our own. Anaxagoras shunned public attention and kept his discussions of philosophy private, confining them to a close circle of friends. In the middle of his friendship with Pericles, though, a remarkable phenomenon occurred that would both turn him into a household name and expose him to great personal danger.

One night, far to the north of Athens, while Socrates was still a small child, boatmen gathering their nets had witnessed something brilliant and yet terrifying blazing its way toward earth from the heavens. It was seen near Aegospotami, the mouth of a small river that flowed into the Hellespont, a narrow strait that connects the Aegean with the Sea of Marmara, and separates Europe from Asia. The fishermen looked on wide-eyed as an enormous explosion threw clouds of dust into the air, and a huge wave crashed into their small boats, almost overturning them. A meteorite the size of a wagonload of rocks had landed at Aegospotami.[10]

Some claimed Anaxagoras had predicted the impact of the "falling stone," although others disputed this. In any case, it lent its considerable weight to his "naturalistic" theories about celestial bodies. It took a foreign intellectual to say the unsayable: that perhaps the planets were not the supernatural beings of legend but merely lumps of rock. They only sailed across our skies, he postulated, because the rotation of the heavens kept them in motion like pebbles flying around inside a spinning bowl. The uneducated were not prepared for such a dramatic challenge to their ancient superstitions. So Anaxagoras kept his doctrines relatively quiet.

Following the discovery of the meteorite, though, his philosophy had become the talk of Athens and famous throughout the Greek world.

While Socrates was still a child, the winds of controversy were gathering around natural philosophy. By the time he reached adulthood, they had swollen into a storm. Many Athenians, particularly the unread, assumed that phenomena such as the movement of stars, comets, and winds and the occurrence of thunder, lightning, and earthquakes were caused by the gods. Ionian philosophers, by contrast, tended to explain these in *natural* rather than supernatural terms, by attributing everything to physical causes. This, of course, made Anaxagoras a divisive figure.

He held that the cosmos began as a chaotic mass, infinite in size and undifferentiated in nature, composed of tiny particles, much smaller than the naked eye can see, that mingled together. At some point, somehow, these ingredients were shaped into the creatures, plants, and natural substances familiar to humankind. There remained, Anaxagoras speculated, "a portion of everything in everything." Things only *appeared* to be composed of whichever substance predominated in them, although every other substance was present, in smaller quantities. Of course, this means that *nothing is pure*. Everything is contaminated with everything else. This provided a metaphor for Athens's nascent democracy: perhaps, regardless of birth, virtue and vice mingle within everyone, nobles and commoners alike. Anaxagoras therefore believed that although our senses provide us with direct experience of nature, we're nevertheless prone to be deceived by *appearances*. A statue may seem to be carved from marble, for instance, if it is predominantly composed of marble particles, but it must contain traces of other substances as well.

This simple idea thrilled Socrates and his friends, firing their imaginations and compelling them to question the world around them more radically than previous generations had ever dared. The natural philosophy of Anaxagoras and other Ionian thinkers was an early precursor of today's natural sciences. For many young Athenians, it provided a radical method for questioning the ways of thinking taken for granted by older generations. Natural philosophy would even prove to be a decisive factor in Athens's military campaigns and her evolution into the dominant regional power.

During the Persian invasion led by the great king Xerxes decades earlier, the Greek city-states had been forced into a defensive alliance. Sparta, the city with the most military prowess, might have seemed to provide a natural leader. Defending Greece against future invasions would, however, require a strong maritime alliance. Having no taste for politics, or naval warfare, the Spartans withdrew, leaving a power vacuum. Athens, their greatest rival, stepped forward. The Greek cities attended a summit on the island of Delos, where they pledged allegiance to one another, forming what later historians would call the "Delian League." To finance this alliance, members paid taxes and tributes, which were to be secured in the treasury of the isle's famous temple of Apollo.

Before long Athens's wealth and power had grown considerably. The city began to dominate the rest of the league, which became known simply as "Athens and her allies." The other cities were offered a choice between contributing crewed ships to the league's navy or paying tribute. The majority chose tribute, being keen to avoid the dangers of military service. This effectively reduced the navies of other Greek cities while providing Athens with funds to build more ships of its own. Its navy came to rule the Aegean waves uncontested.

Socrates had witnessed Pericles's rise to power, with Anaxagoras by his side.[11] In theory, Athens had no ruler, except the *demos* or "people" themselves, or at least the adult male citizens entitled to vote in the Assembly. The most powerful citizens were the ten individuals elected by the Assembly to the office of *strategos*, or military general, each year, who doubled as Athens's most senior statesmen. Pericles's main political opponent was Cimon, a prominent *strategos*, allied with Athens's wealthy aristocrats. In 461, as Socrates was nearing the age of ten, Pericles used the law of *ostracism* to instigate a vote against Cimon, alleging that he hated the common people and sympathized too much with the aristocracy and Athens's rivals, the Spartans. Pericles succeeded in having his opponent banished for a decade, clearing the way for him to become the city's leading statesman. The following year, Pericles was elected *strategos* for the first time, and he would remain the foremost figure in the Assembly for about four decades, a feat that granted him exceptional personal authority.

Tensions that had long existed beneath the surface now caused Athenian politics to split into two opposing factions: the *Democrats* and *Oligarchs*. The Democrats, led by Pericles, believed power should be shared by all male citizens, which was still a progressive notion at the time. (Women, foreign residents, and slaves could not vote, however, and Athenian democracy was unlike modern democracy in several other regards.) The Oligarchs, a more conservative group, associated with Cimon, distrusted the rabble, and wanted power to return to the hands of a narrow elite, mainly the wealthy sons of Athens's ancient aristocratic families. The Spartans mistrusted foreign democracies, which they viewed as unpredictable, and would rather see Athens ruled by a handful of Oligarchs, drawn from the aristocrats friendly to them.

Pericles gained power in the Assembly by implementing populist measures while nevertheless remaining a moderate. One of his major achievements was to introduce pay for public office and jury service, which meant even the poorest Athenian citizens could potentially occupy these roles, thereby giving them a greater voice in Athens's affairs. During times of war, the poorer citizens served as rowers in triremes, or warships, meaning that the Democrat faction effectively controlled the Athenian navy.

While Socrates had still been in his teens, in 454, Pericles persuaded the Assembly to commit to a hazardous path from which there could be no turning back. The treasury of the Delian League was relocated to Athens, supposedly out of fear that Persia might loot the island of Delos. Now at its peak, the alliance consisted of approximately three hundred city-states. By taking control of the purse strings in this way, Athens, which had been imposing its will on other members of the alliance for years, made its preeminence undeniable. A few years later, with access to all this wealth, Pericles would begin the ambitious building program on the Acropolis, which transformed his city into the envy of the known world. By now, he commanded such authority that the satirists jokingly compared him to Zeus, king of the gods.

As the city's leading statesman and *strategos*, during its cultural golden age and the height of its military power, Pericles had become the *de facto* ruler of an Athenian Empire. He nevertheless remained committed to the Democrat cause. Pericles always portrayed himself as a servant of the people's Assembly, despite the awkward fact of his towering personal authority. To consolidate power over the rest of the league, Athens had for decades treated foreign cities harshly: a proud democracy at home but an imperialist aggressor abroad. The other Greek city-states, especially Sparta, observed the rapid evolution of the Athenian Empire with concern. Sparta was located deep within the Peloponnese, the large peninsula constituting the south of Greece. Whereas

Spartan hoplites, or heavy infantry, were superior in land battles, the Athenian fleet had control of the sea. Sparta and her allies dominated most of the Peloponnese, but Athens now ruled over many coastal cities and islands. Everyone could see that a great war was looming.

Later generations of philosophers liked to cite a famous incident to show how philosophy could be of practical importance, even during times of war. When Pericles was about to depart from Athens in command of a fleet, his crew became alarmed upon witnessing a solar eclipse. (This would happen much later, in 431, when Socrates was in middle age.) After noon, the sun, we're told, "took on the appearance of a crescent and some of the stars became visible before it returned to its normal shape."[12] It was not unusual for soldiers to retreat or sailors to refuse to set sail when they saw an omen that appeared to foretell disaster. Superstition determined the outcome of many battles, especially for more credulous people. The Spartans had notoriously refused, for religious reasons, to join the Battle of Marathon until the moon was full. The Athenians, however, had a secret weapon, which could be deployed against fear of the supernatural.

Pericles addressed the helmsman of his flagship, who was terrified and cowering at the sight of what he considered a grave warning sent by the gods. With the rest of the crew listening, the great statesman patiently explained that according to the teachings of his friend Anaxagoras, solar eclipses were a completely natural phenomenon. Although, based on its appearance, some early philosophers had claimed the sun was about the size of a human foot, Anaxagoras had taught that it was much larger. How big, he did not know, except that it must surely exceed even the Peloponnesian peninsula in size. The moon, he said, was nothing but a massive lump of earth, smaller than the sun, but closer to us, and therefore capable of passing before it and obscuring its light.[13] Pericles raised his cloak before the helmsman's eyes, thereby blocking his gaze, and asked if there was anything dreadful or portentous about it. "How then," he continued, turning and gesturing toward the sun, "is that phenomenon in the sky any different, except that an object much more distant, and larger than my cloak, obscures the sun?" Pericles commanded such authority that his men were freed from the tyranny of superstition, and the fleet set sail to war.

Pericles, under the influence of Anaxagoras, had shown the Athenians that philosophy was capable of replacing irrational superstition with belief in more down-to-earth naturalistic explanations. Today we might even point to this use of reason to question false beliefs and eliminate irrational fear, as a primitive example of cognitive psychotherapy. As the story shows, although philosophy could give Athens a military advantage over some of its enemies, this obviously came at a price. There were conservative religious factions within Athenian society who resented any threat to their traditional views.

One morning, as Socrates watched the cadets going through their exercises in the grounds of the Lyceum, at the foot of Mount Lycabettus, Chaerephon came running over, flapping his old cloak like the wings of a frightened bat. "Have you heard the news, Socrates?" he cried. "Anaxagoras is to stand trial in the Agora; he has been charged with *impiety*!"[14] Socrates was not surprised. After having been ostracized for a decade, Cimon had recently been allowed to return to Athens, emboldening the Oligarch faction. The case against Anaxagoras was brought by one of Cimon's relatives who sought to harm Pericles's reputation by destroying that of his mentor, and he even called for the philosopher to be put to death. The charges focused on Anaxagoras's most controversial claim, that the sun was a blazing rock, a lump of molten iron ore, from which the stone at Aegospotami had fallen to earth.

On the day of the trial, Socrates and Chaerephon joined thousands of other Athenian citizens, crowding around the courtroom in the Agora. The building became hushed as Anaxagoras entered. Natural philosophy helped him maintain his composure in many situations. He seldom changed his expression and had never been seen smiling, let alone laughing. Nevertheless, he was completely unprepared for what must have seemed to him a great injustice and public humiliation. He did not even have the courage to look his accusers in their eyes. The crowd gasped to witness the frail and heartbroken figure he had become. They were touched, though, to see the gentleness with which his friend Pericles supported him.

As a general, Pericles was renowned for his prudence and caution, never risking a battle for the sake of glory when doing so would place his soldiers' lives in unnecessary danger. The saying was always on his lips that, if only it lay within his power, he would wish to see every one of his fellow citizens live forever. Now Pericles was forced to stand by and watch as the people he had sworn to protect threatened to execute one of his closest friends.

Socrates and his companions expected to hear Anaxagoras speak in defense of philosophy. Instead, Pericles spoke on his behalf, addressing the court in his familiar manner. There was very little philosophy in his speech. Instead, as was customary, he pleaded for mercy on behalf of his friend and mentor. Despite his famous composure, his eyes grew moist as he lamented the philosopher's situation. First he attacked the integrity of the accusers, calling them out as enemies of the democracy, hypocrites, and religious fanatics, then he evoked the jurymen's sympathy for his humiliated friend, drawing their attention to the man's noble birth, humble means, poor health, and the deep sorrow and regret he exhibited.

Anaxagoras sat with his head in his hands, mute and impotent. Occasionally he glanced in the direction of the water clock, a device introduced to the Greek world, according to some, by previous generations of Ionian philosophers. He had always found its dependability reassuring, but now the mechanism seemed oppressive, as the time allotted for his defense slowly began running out. Pericles concluded, and the jurymen began their deliberations.

They voted and returned the majority verdict that the philosopher Anaxagoras was *guilty of impiety*. Pericles, who was unused to such defeat, was stunned. Even he could not undo the harm done to Anaxagoras's reputation by decades of gossip circulating the streets of Athens. His friend's ancestors were Persian, and many Athenians viewed foreign intellectuals with the utmost suspicion. Now the philosopher's accusers called for the death sentence. Pericles had staked his reputation on the defense of his teacher, and he knew this verdict would be used against him for as long as he remained in public office. He had already been advised to distance himself from his old friend. In one of the boldest moves of his political career, however, he did *precisely the opposite*.

Anaxagoras, barely able to stand because of his illness, appeared completely crushed by the verdict. The small group of students, seated with the philosopher, became uncharacteristically emotional, some beating their chests in grief. Pericles, with a thunderous voice, demanded to know if there was any man present in court who could find a single thing to say against his own conduct. The room fell silent for what seemed like an age as Pericles, pausing, glared into the eyes of the foremost men on the jury. Nobody said anything. Finally, in a raised voice, he boomed, "Well, I am this man's student!" The jurymen were aghast. "Do not allow yourselves to be carried away by slander into putting him to death," he added, lowering his voice, "but listen to me and release him immediately." It was a test of his authority. Pericles was daring the Athenian people to condemn him along with his friend. They did not, however, want to lose their greatest statesman, so they agreed to compromise. Anaxagoras was fined five talents of silver, more than a craftsman like Socrates might earn in a lifetime, and sent into exile.

Anaxagoras was banished to the Ionian city of Lampsacus, on the eastern shore of the Hellespont, where he would spend the remainder of his days gazing out across the water at Aegospotami, the very spot where his famous falling stone had landed. Ashamed to have been brought down by the charges against him, the philosopher concluded that he should have mentally prepared himself for such events well in advance. Later, his students would report that he taught them to set before their imagination, frequently, whatever misfortunes one might conceivably encounter in life, including exile and death. If any of these setbacks should befall them, he reasoned, they would be more prepared than he was, and the blows of fate would not injure them as deeply, having been foreseen.

Anaxagoras, nevertheless, took his exile badly. Over time, Pericles reputedly became so preoccupied with affairs of state that he forgot about his aging mentor. Many years later, the philosopher's friends found him lying on his couch, in despair, his head covered by his cloak, in the process of starving himself to death. When this news reached Pericles, he rushed to his former mentor's side. Pericles pleaded with Anaxagoras to live, saying that he still had much need of his wisdom and guidance. Anaxagoras uncovered his head and said to him, "Pericles, even those who need a lamp pour oil therein."

While exiled in Lampsacus, Anaxagoras received two devastating pieces of news at once, more than most men could bear. The Athenians had tried him a second time, this time *in absentia*, without a court even hearing his defense. After decades of whispering, the charge of *Medism*, or collusion with the Persians, was finally added to that of impiety. The jury sentenced him, by default, to death—the method of execution to be forced suicide by drinking hemlock.[15] He was also informed that his sons had died.

Philosophy did console Anaxagoras in the face of death and loss, as he had followed his own advice to prepare for future catastrophes well in advance. When news of his sentence reached him, the frail old philosopher calmly replied that nature had long ago condemned him to die anyway, and likewise the Athenians. It was also said that when Anaxagoras was informed that his sons were dead, he merely replied that he had always known they were mortal. "Yes," someone said, "but are you not perturbed to be dying in a foreign land?" The philosopher, unfazed, simply replied that the road to Hades is much the same from wherever you depart.

Natural philosophy permitted Anaxagoras to view death with a degree of studied indifference. He taught that the Greeks were wrong "to accept coming to be and perishing" as anything more than an appearance, "for no thing comes to be, nor does it perish." The tiny particles from which things are composed are merely reorganized, like wax being molded to resemble a human form, and then melted down again and used to make something else. Appearances, in this regard, are deceptive. Strictly speaking, nothing is ever created or destroyed, and nobody is ever born or dies. We must face the *appearance* of death, but recognizing it as a natural process can, to some at least, be a consolation.

A Greek author, writing centuries later, composed the following epitaph, summing up Anaxagoras's life in a few lines of verse:

The sun is a molten mass,
Claimed Anaxagoras;
This is his crime, with his life he must pay the price.
Pericles from that fate
Rescued his friend too late;
His spirit crushed, by his own hand he dies.[16]

Pericles had saved his friend from execution, but it was too late to save his reputation. Indeed, according to some accounts, the first philosopher to teach at Athens never recovered from the humiliation of his trial. Many years hence, shortly after Pericles's demise, a broken man, having been exiled and sentenced to death, Anaxagoras would finally take his own life.

Following the trial that led to the philosopher's exile, Socrates and Chaerephon walked quietly together from the Agora, still pondering the tragedy they had witnessed.[17] Suddenly, they heard a familiar voice calling their names. Their friend Crito had another man by the hand and was leading him briskly in their direction. "This is my fellow demesman," said Crito, smiling and gesturing toward Socrates. He introduced Archelaus, whom they recognized as one of the students seated beside Anaxagoras in the courtroom, although unlike his teacher, he was an Athenian citizen.[18] "You're the sculptor who asks all the questions," said Archelaus.[19] Socrates nodded.[20] "Come with me," he said, "I have something important to show you." At first, Chaerephon feared that they would get themselves into trouble being seen among philosophers so soon after the trial, but Socrates did not hesitate.

Archelaus led them out of the city gates to a large house in the northern deme of Cholargos. There they met a small group of Anaxagoras's friends who were gathering in private to discuss the trial. Among them were several notable Athenians, including a young poet, Euripides. Many years later, he would compose a tragedy called *Phaethon*, reflecting on the trial of Anaxagoras. It tells the story of a mortal son of Helios, the sun-god, who is identified with Apollo. Phaethon, "the radiant one," wants nothing more than to scale the heavens, his rightful home, and learn their secrets. He foolishly tries to master the chariot of Helios, carrying the sun, which he describes, in the language of natural philosophy, as merely a golden clod of earth. However, this turns out to be much more dangerous than he anticipates. He completely loses control of the horses, flying too close to the earth and scorching its surface with the fire of the sun. For the sake of humankind, therefore, Zeus is eventually forced to intervene and destroy Phaethon with a thunderbolt, which sends him blazing like a falling star, or meteorite, crashing to earth by the banks of a mighty river. The Athenian people likewise saw Anaxagoras's desire to learn the secrets of the heavens as dangerous *hubris* and an affront to the gods, for which they made sure he was destroyed.

Archelaus produced a scroll from another room, which he began to read.[21] "These are the teachings of our master," he said, causing the room to fall silent. The others looked nervous, but Socrates was captivated and eagerly pressed forward to listen. Anaxagoras was thought to have been the first philosopher ever to compose such a book, consisting of Greek prose and even diagrams. It set forth an account of the world in unusually sober, rational, and objective language.[22]

At first, the study of natural philosophy had been confined largely to the wealthy elite. In the years that followed Anaxagoras's exile, his students, who included many young Democrats and friends of Pericles, circulated his book widely, making countless cheap copies that could be purchased in the marketplace. The doctrines of natural philosophy would become the object of popular satires, attended even by the illiterate. The teachings of Athens's first philosopher would eventually be familiar, even if sometimes in a mangled form, to rich and poor alike.[23] The attempt by Cimon and his faction to silence Anaxagoras by condemning his teachings had, therefore, spectacularly *backfired* by placing his philosophy in the hands of the masses.

Socrates had mostly heard secondhand discussion of ideas from natural philosophy and gossip about its ill-fated representative at Athens. Now, for the first time, he was able to study the teachings of Anaxagoras directly, in the philosopher's own words. According to legend, Zeus and the other gods ruled the world, but they did not create it. Previous thinkers had assumed that nature was shaped either by random events or through some strict law of causal necessity. As Socrates listened to Archelaus reading, for the first time, he heard him say instead that *Nous* was the cause that organized everything. Anaxagoras claimed, it seemed, that a vast Cosmic Intellect, or Consciousness, was responsible for imposing order on the original chaos of the universe. Nous, his book said, is the finest of all substances, and it alone remains pure, whereas everything else mingles together. Nous acts with absolute freedom, permeating, moving, and organizing the whole cosmos. Perhaps surprisingly, Anaxagoras did not equate this Nous with Zeus, or indeed any of the gods of Greek mythology—he seemed to think of it as having a more abstract and impersonal nature.

Socrates at first assumed that Anaxagoras must have meant

that *Nous*, a perfect Intellect, organized everything in accord with perfect *reason*. For a philosopher to study nature would therefore mean studying what reason deems *best* for each thing and, presumably, what is best for human beings. Moreover, a flawless Intellect must itself surely be perfectly *wise*. Socrates therefore anticipated that this philosophy would entail the study of *ethical* concepts, such as the nature of wisdom and folly, good and evil, virtue and vice. "These hopes," he later said, "I would not have sold for a large sum of money, and I seized the books and read them as fast as I could in my eagerness to learn what reason considers good and bad."[24]

Socrates's hopes were soon dashed, however. He discovered that the natural philosophy of Anaxagoras had little more to say about Nous and almost nothing to say about virtue. The book continued to explain almost everything in terms of physical causes. "It is as though Anaxagoras accepts that his actions are caused by his own mind," muttered Socrates, "yet prefers to explain how he ended up in exile using purely mechanical terms." Natural philosophy would have us describe how the muscles of Anaxagoras's legs contracted in order to move the bones and thereby carry his body off into exile. The defense speech that Pericles delivered in court would be explained in terms of the air from his lungs being channeled through his vocal chords in a particular way, to create certain syllables. This sort of philosophy was absurd, thought Socrates, and of no help to anyone.

There was, he believed, a much better and more obvious way to explain the Ionian philosopher's plight. "Surely," thought Socrates, "Anaxagoras's natural philosophy is guilty of a strange error, which consists in confusing *reasons* and *causes*." It was certainly true that *without* bones and muscles, Anaxagoras could not walk from the court and sail to Lampsacus. It was not, however, a very helpful way of putting things to say that his bones and muscles were the *reason* for his going into exile. Anaxagoras's obsession with explaining events solely in terms of their physical causes left him groping around in the dark when it came to understanding human behavior. The Athenian people thought it best to condemn Anaxagoras to death; Anaxagoras, by contrast, thought it best to have his friends plead for mercy on his behalf and what appeared to him a lighter sentence. Those were obviously the reasons for their actions. Socrates would therefore become increasingly preoccupied with questions regarding our values, such as what men consider best in life and how it relates to what is ethically good or bad.

THE PRACTICE OF VALUES CLARIFICATION

MOST PEOPLE ASSUME, AND IT is often stated, that Socrates wrote nothing. However, that is not entirely true. According to Plato's *Phaedo*, while Socrates was awaiting execution, he tried his hand at writing poetry for the first time. (There were also persistent rumors he'd previously helped his friend Euripides compose some of his tragedies.) In prison, he wrote a paean, or hymn of praise, to the god Apollo, the Lord of the Muses, who was, in a sense, also the patron god of philosophy. A later source claims it opened with the lines:

All hail, Apollo, Delos' lord!

Socrates was an admirer of Aesop's *Fables*, and he also tried to turn one of these into verse. Our source claims that it opened with the following words:

"Judge not, ye men of Corinth," Aesop cried,
"Of virtue as the jury-courts decide."[25]

"Virtue" is the conventional translation for the Greek word *arete*. Modern academics tend to prefer "excellence," as *arete* refers to those qualities that make something exceptionally good. A good table, for instance, is one that is sturdy and even, a good horse is one that is strong or fast—but what makes a good human? The quote seems to make the point that it would be foolish, as when consulting a jury, to take the opinions held by the majority of people as a guide to what is best in life. Today we call that error the *argumentum ad populum*, the fallacy of appealing to an idea's *popularity* as though that proves that it is correct. It would certainly be in keeping with Socrates's character to open his poem by reminding us to think for ourselves.

The question "What is best in life?" is far too important to be entrusted to other people. We each have a duty to answer it for ourselves, by using our own reason. Socrates grew frustrated with the natural philosophers because he believed they were too focused on physical causes and not concerned enough about ethics, which poses the most important questions of human life. Although, the word *philosophy* literally means the *love of wisdom*, Anaxagoras had very little to say about the nature of wisdom or about moral goodness and virtue. He was preoccupied with the "how" of life, whereas Socrates wanted to know the "why"—for what goal or purpose do we live?

The first step we'll take, therefore, consists in focusing squarely on the question of what is *best* for a human being: What does it mean to live well and flourish? The Greek word used to denote this concept is *eudaimonia*. It's an unusual word and difficult to properly translate, but *eudaimonia* basically refers to the condition of someone who is living a good life, or rather the best possible life. It has traditionally been translated by the word *happiness*, but this derives from an outdated English usage. "Happy" once meant *blessed* or *fortunate*. There's still a trace of this earlier meaning in its antonym *hapless*, which means wretched or *unfortunate*. Happiness, in its original sense, is the opposite of being hapless. Happiness is more than just a feeling, in other words; it's a state of being.

A good therapist will tell you that there's a big difference between merely "feeling better" and actually "getting better." Ancient philosophers show us that there's a big difference between "feeling good" and "being good," or even between "feeling happy" and "being happy." It's an example of our tendency to confuse appearance and reality—feeling good *seems* good to us. An addict, for instance, might be *happy* in the sense of feeling good but be utterly *hapless* in the sense of living badly. The word *eudaimonia*, by contrast, means having a happy life in the sense of being fortunate or *flourishing*.

We no longer even have a satisfactory word in English to describe this concept, whereas the ancient Greek philosophers took it to be the most important thing in life. Maybe that's a sign that over the intervening centuries we've grown more complacent, more dependent on the opinions of others, and so lazy that we neglect to reason for ourselves about the fundamental goal of life.

Over time, Socrates began engaging in discussions with his friends every day, examining their own lives and debating the meaning of *eudaimonia*. Several of his students wrote *dialogues* supposedly based upon these conversations, and it was mainly through these "Socratics" that his philosophy became known to subsequent generations. We're told the foremost of Socrates's students were Plato, Xenophon, and Antisthenes. Aeschines, Phaedo, Euclides, and Aristippus also wrote Socrates dialogues and attracted their own followers. Although most of these works are now lost, as noted earlier, those of Plato and Xenophon survive. These dialogues typically focus on the task of defining an important concept, often an ethical virtue. For example, Plato's magnum opus, the *Republic*, is mainly concerned with the definition of *justice*.

Although Socrates himself did not leave behind any dialogues, the poems mentioned above may not be the only writing he did. Many centuries later, the Stoic philosopher Epictetus would tell his students that Socrates wrote as much or more than any other philosopher. How could this be, as he left behind nothing? Epictetus claimed that Socrates kept copious private notes—perhaps like an ancient version of a self-improvement journal. In these writings, he used to examine and reevaluate his own deepest assumptions. Because he could not always have interlocutors with whom to debate, Socrates "used to argue with and examine himself," we're told, by means of written notes. At any given time, he was always using his private notes to apply his philosophical method to at least one practical question. "These," says Epictetus, "are the things which a philosopher writes."[26]

Socrates began his poem about Aesop by referring to the concept of *virtue*; his private notes quite possibly had a similar focus. Indeed, Epictetus claims that Socrates wrote only for his own benefit and the care of his own soul. He left the writing of philosophical essays and dialogues, we're told, to his followers, who were more concerned than him with public recognition. In other words, Socrates kept some sort of *self-improvement* journal, but it was never intended for publication. Even if these private notes existed, we have no idea what they may have looked like. Except, perhaps we do. As it happens, we possess a short dialogue, written by Xenophon, in which Socrates is portrayed teaching a young philosopher how to clarify his values, by means of a *formal written exercise*.

In the previous chapter, we looked at questions designed to help us critically reevaluate our existing goals and desires in life. Now we're going to turn our attention from the destructive or negative use of questioning to its constructive or positive use. Socrates was asked, many years later, by a young man concerned with self-improvement, where the best place was to begin applying philosophy. He replied that our philosophical journey should begin with understanding the concepts of good and bad, specifically in relation to leading a virtuous life. Socrates then demonstrated how to apply his philosophical method to such concepts, using an exercise remarkably similar to the "two-column technique" found in modern cognitive therapy.[27] We're going to begin with a simplified version, which I call the "one-column" technique.

Take a piece of paper, or use a computer, and brainstorm a list of things that you believe contribute to *eudaimonia* or the good life. In other words, what constitutes *flourishing*? Another way of approaching this would be to ask yourself to define what is *good* by listing all the most important things in life. Try to think for yourself and, as Socrates advised, question your assumptions about what is good or contributes to flourishing. For example, at first you might say that flourishing requires physical health, but can you think of any examples of individuals who seem to have flourished despite poor health or disability?

You'll almost certainly need to repeat this exercise several times. It may even feel as though your list is constantly evolving. That's normal. Each time you review your answers, try to push yourself to go further than before, creating a definition that's more accurate and complete. Here are some questions, derived from one of the Socratic dialogues, that you may find helpful:

- What is happiness or flourishing (*eudaimonia*), in your opinion?
- What sort of person can be said to be flourishing?
- What sort of qualities or possessions might contribute to "flourishing"?
- How may we define what we mean by a "flourishing" person?
- How shall we describe flourishing?

This is akin to asking ourselves what it means to live the best possible life. That's what ancient philosophers were getting at when they asked the fundamental question: "What is the good life?" or "What is *eudaimonia*?" It's similar to asking "What is the fundamental goal or purpose (*telos*) of life?" Greek philosophers generally assumed that *eudaimonia* denoted the supreme goal of life, although they disagreed about how to define it further. In a way, asking these sorts of questions was the ancient equivalent of asking "What is the meaning of life?" For virtually all Greek philosophers, the good life seemed to consist, at least in part, in certain virtues, most notably *wisdom*.

One of the biggest innovations in the field of modern psychotherapy over the past few decades has been the shift toward greater emphasis on personal values. For example, it used to be believed that in order to treat clinical depression, we would have to help clients identify pleasurable activities and introduce more of them into their daily routine. Now we realize that depression is more about a lack of *meaning* than a lack of pleasure. Modern evidence-based psychotherapy for depression, such as what's known as "behavioral activation," focuses on clarifying one's authentic *values*, particularly those related to character strengths, and engaging in more activities that are consistent with them.[28] People often become depressed when their lives feel empty or meaningless, because they've strayed too far from their core values and the type of people they truly want to be. We can all benefit, though, from clarifying our values, and learning to live more consistently in accordance with them.

SOCRATES LEAVES THE WORKSHOP

QUESTIONS OF A DEEPER KIND about natural philosophy continued to bother Socrates, as he toiled in the din of his father's workshop. He ran his fingers over the smooth Parian marble of the *Three Charites*, by now nearing completion. When asked what his life's purpose was, Anaxagoras had turned his gaze skyward, answering wistfully that he was born "to study sun and moon and heavens." That passion for knowledge had infected his students and gradually spread to the youth of Athens. Anaxagoras was called both a *philosopher*, or "lover of wisdom," and a "wise man." He had expertise in many different fields. Whatever wisdom he possessed, though, had been of little avail during his trial. A broken man, he had cowered in shame before the jury, throwing himself on their mercy. What was the point of knowing whether the sun is a blazing rock if you had no wisdom that could help you stand your ground in court, facing injustice as bravely as a soldier faces the enemy in battle rather than fleeing into exile and living in fear for your life? When he found himself looking death in the eye, Anaxagoras blinked, but Socrates would not.

Anaxagoras had convinced his followers that the goal of life was contemplative philosophy and the study of nature, which can free us from superstition. Socrates, though, would become convinced that it was, in fact, the study of man. The Ionian philosopher assumed that we become wise by contemplating the heavens and learning many things about nature, but what if he was wrong? How can we be sure unless we first answer the question: *What is wisdom?* To do so we would need to examine not the heavens but our own lives. Philosophy, decided Socrates, cannot promise man anything external. For whereas stone is the material in which the stonemason works, each individual's own life is the only proper material for those who would practice the art of living.

Socrates turned to his friends in despair. "I am putting down my tools," he said sullenly. "How can I continue?" Some of them were shocked and warned him that if he didn't return to work, he risked provoking his father's notoriously violent temper. Chaerephon and Crito understood, though, because they were troubled by precisely the same questions. Chaerephon even became quite worried for his friend. What would Socrates's family have to say about him abandoning his father's profession? How would he support himself? Then something happened that would change Socrates's life forever.

Crito smiled and gestured toward the *Three Charites*. "Socrates, my friend, suppose that the gods were to hand you a boon this very day," he asked. "Should you accept it *graciously* or with *ingratitude*?" "With gratitude, of course," replied Socrates. "If only I knew what you meant but, by the dog, I should try to be gracious anyway!" "As everyone knows," said Crito, "I was fortunate enough to inherit what many consider to be a great asset, in the form of lands left to me by my father, which I have turned to profit admirably, I think you will agree." Socrates, bemused, nodded. "Our little circle of friends has come to love nothing more than to discuss philosophy," he continued, "but, in truth, without your skill at questioning, our conversations would be of little value." "What do you mean?" asked Socrates. "You have a unique talent, my friend, for posing the most crucial questions, ones routinely ignored by everyone else. Though I often depart from your presence feeling confused, and we never seem to arrive at the answers we're seeking, nevertheless, over time I've grown to believe that this journey, spurred by your skillful questioning, has been of more value to me than any lecture I have ever attended, or any book that I have read." "It's very generous of you to say so . . ." Socrates was amused that for once his questioning nature had pleased rather than irritated someone.

"You shall no longer require your tools," said Crito, "for you shall never return to your father's workshop." Socrates was taken aback and tried to speak again, but Crito hushed him. "I wish to make a gift to you of just enough land for you to build a small home, and enough besides for you to rent out, making a living thereby from your property while helping others to profit from their labor." Socrates tried to refuse but Crito continued, "If you wish to exemplify gratitude, as you said, you will accept my gift graciously, and repay me in the following way." "I will repay you in whatever way I can, my friend," said Socrates, "but without the labor of my hands, how can I hope to do so?" "Through the labor of your mind," said Crito with a laugh, "and I expect you to exercise it to the utmost by attending the lectures of wise men, whenever possible, and spending your newfound leisure time discussing their ideas with us, your friends, for it seems to me that is what benefits all of us the most." Chaerephon could contain himself no longer and pounced on Crito and Socrates, cackling with delight.

Socrates came to realize that the philosophy with which he had grown up was not the one he needed. We're told that "Crito removed him from his workshop and educated him, being struck by his beauty of soul." He was free to spend his days discussing moral philosophy with friends and strangers alike, among the shops and colonnades of the Agora. Anaxagoras and the other natural philosophers had assumed that *philosophy*, the love of wisdom, meant acquiring as much knowledge as possible. For Socrates, though, some forms of knowledge were immeasurably more important than others. Philosophy required examining the nature of wisdom and ideas such as goodness, virtue, and justice. Instead of working in stone, crafting likenesses of the gods, Socrates would therefore begin roughing out his own character. He would sculpt himself, chiseling away the debris of false beliefs, in the hope of revealing the true nature of his own soul. On this day, therefore, Socrates was removed from his father's workshop by Crito, his friend, and his entire life henceforth was committed to discovering a new form of philosophy.

3

THE FEMALE SOCRATES

HAVING LEFT BEHIND THE STONEMASON'S workshop, Socrates immersed himself in the study of philosophy. He had a talent for spotting contradictions, which his new circle of friends found exhausting. Socrates, they said, couldn't consider a statement without immediately coming up with some exception or contrary observation. His old friends Crito and Chaerephon, however, found his questioning exhilarating, and gradually others started taking note of Socrates's talent for rational debate, or what the Greeks called *dialectic*.

Anaxagoras, for instance, had claimed that the sun was a huge lump of red-hot iron ore, like the metal smelted in a forge. At first this seemed plausible to Socrates; even today, many people still think of the sun as a big ball of fire. Soon, however, he began to notice subtle problems with this hypothesis. "Blacksmiths look all day upon the metal being worked in their forges, and anyone can look upon even the largest of fires," he said, "but nobody can gaze into the sun for long without being blinded."

For once, Chaerephon was lost for words, as were his fellow philosophers. "Our skin becomes tanned following exposure to sunlight," Socrates added, "but how does it respond to fire?" Chaerephon agreed that proximity to fire can burn our skin but never causes it to tan. "Anything else?" he sighed. "Yes, actually," replied Socrates, "sunlight nurtures plants, but fire kills them."[i] In short, the sun looks like fire but does not behave like fire.[2]

As Socrates saw it, the explanations of natural philosophy, while *plausible*, were often merely speculative. As more doubts of this kind arose in his mind, he began to view the supposed "wisdom" of Anaxagoras as presumptuous, even ridiculous, such as his claim to know that men lived in habitations on the moon. Socrates was also disappointed by the conservative attitude of the natural philosophers toward ethical questions. If they spoke about virtue at all, it was typically, like traditional moralists, to hand down maxims or examples of great men, derived from the works of Homer and other famous poets. Socrates was still searching for a philosophical method that would allow him to critically evaluate these claims about the good of man, in order to examine the very goal of life itself.

Phaenarete, Socrates's mother, was said to be a formidable and intelligent woman.[3] Described by her son as a "noble and burly" matron, she was looked up to as a *maia*, a wise older woman who both advised fathers on matchmaking for their daughters and subsequently attended expectant mothers as a midwife.[4] She was adept at identifying the virtues of young men and bringing them to the attention of young women and their families. Her name, rather appropriately, means "She who brings virtue to light."

It had not escaped Phaenarete's notice that her relentlessly inquisitive son was outgrowing the natural philosophers. So whenever Socrates was within earshot, she began mentioning another foreign teacher who had arrived in Athens and found favor with Pericles, not long before Anaxagoras went into exile. She was one of the most remarkable and controversial women in Greek history—her name was *Aspasia of Miletus.*

Phaenarete had gone to the home of Aspasia several times to hear her speak about her favorite topic, the *art of love.*[5] She had been pleasantly surprised to discover herself in the presence of a female intellectual, albeit one with a questionable reputation about town. When the opportunity arose, she naturally brought this woman's qualities to her son's attention. "Have you heard of Pericles's guest, the lady from Miletus?" she asked. "The Ionian who wears fine Koan silks?" said Socrates, shrugging. "In the Agora they call her a prostitute and a procurer of other women for the wealthy."

There was a moment of uncomfortable silence. Socrates had narrowly avoided a scolding—matrons like his mother, who introduced young women to potential suitors, were careful to avoid being accused of procuring. "It would be more accurate to describe her as a female philosopher and an *expert* matchmaker," said Phaenarete patiently. "What do you mean?" asked Socrates, suddenly intrigued.

"What do you suppose," asked Phaenarete, "are the duties of a good matchmaker?"[6] "Not unlike those of a good *pimp* or *madam*," said Socrates, "and perhaps there's the confusion." Phaenarete frowned but was used to her son's candor. Socrates thought for a moment and then added: "To present their client in the most appealing way possible." "How so?" asked Phaenarete. He replied that it involved arranging their hair and clothing nicely, as he'd seen his mother do. "Of course," said Phaenarete, "but is it nevertheless possible for someone with fine clothing, a pretty face and attractive eyes to give hostile looks?" Socrates agreed. "And that even a person with a voice that sounds very sweet and charming might nevertheless use it to say quite unpleasant things?" Her son nodded. "Some ways of talking make friends, whereas others make enemies," he mused. "So you see," explained Phaenarete, "a good matchmaker must also train her client to speak and act in a manner more appealing to others." Socrates admitted he'd often heard about his mother doing just this with the eligible young women, upon whom she'd been called to visit.

"Who, moreover," said Phaenarete, "would be the better match-maker, she who could make her client appealing to one person or to many?" Socrates supposed the answer must be *many*, although it didn't escape his notice that this description of his mother's art, influenced no doubt by Aspasia, was indeed beginning to sound more like that of a *madam* than a matchmaker. Phaenarete, noticing his puzzled look, nevertheless continued: "And would the greatest matchmaker of all not be the one who can make her clients appealing in this way to the entire city?" Socrates nodded in agreement. An expert matchmaker who can describe her client in ways that make them appealing could even become an ambassador for Athens and help the city to befriend and form alliances with other cities, he noted, although in Greek society such a role had never been given to a woman.

Socrates was captivated by the sense that his mother was talking not only about matchmaking but also about training in virtue. "What else have you heard this Aspasia teach concerning the art of love?" asked Socrates. "The goddess Aphrodite, as you well know, has two different types of shrines," replied Phaenarete. "Some are dedicated to the Common and some to the Heavenly Aphrodite." *Aphrodite Pandemos* and *Aphrodite Ourania* were their Greek names. "The Common Aphrodite, a child of Zeus, is mainly responsible for physical love. The Heavenly Aphrodite, though, was created from Ouranos, an older and wiser god, and she is concerned with loving others for their character." Phaenarete paused because she knew she was approaching a point that would be of supreme interest to her philosopher-son. "People often pray to the Common Aphrodite to lend her charm to their words and actions," she said, "but this prayer can only be fulfilled by her Heavenly counterpart, who teaches us to love the mind more than the body."

Phaenarete observed that, in her experience, those who fall in love with others only because of their good looks often become frustrated with their beloved's character, especially if the lover's affections are not reciprocated. They often end up loving and hating the same person. Even if we fall in love with someone's physical beauty and don't end up frustrated with their behavior, we must recognize that looks fade as we grow older. "If your affection for someone is purely physical, it's bound to wane over time," she said, "whereas, if you have fallen in love with their character, your love may become deeper as they become wiser with age." Moreover, she explained, physical attraction can become gradually dulled simply through too much familiarity, much as our appetite for food and drink becomes sated if we have too much. Love of someone's character, though, if they are truly good, is only enriched by familiarity, as we learn to further appreciate their virtues. Moreover, if the beloved progresses toward wisdom and virtue, they become even more deserving of our love.

"It is more natural for love of the mind to be reciprocated than love of the body," added Phaenarete. "First, how could you hate someone whom you know sees you as being a truly good person? You're not guaranteed to love them in return, but you're more likely to do so if they're interested in your personality and not merely your looks. Second, how could you hate someone if you know they are more concerned with what is good for you than what is sexually gratifying for themselves?" Socrates agreed. The love of another can influence our moral character. Someone who believes that he is loved mainly for his physical appearance will cultivate his looks, even to the neglect of his soul. One who knows that he is loved for his soul will cultivate *that* above all else, and he will become a better person.

"However," Phaenarete continued, "in addition to improving his beloved, a lover of goodness also improves himself, and that is the greatest benefit he can obtain from love." "How so?" asked Socrates. Phaenarete explained that if the lover has any sense, he will realize he cannot make his beloved good unless he becomes good himself. "Suppose, moreover, that you love two individuals," she asked, "one for his body alone, his good looks, and the other for the goodness and wisdom of his mind." Socrates listened intently. "Which one would you trust to look after and improve your property?" asked Phaenarete. "Which to raise and improve your children?" Socrates did not need to answer. "Then to which of these two," asked his mother, "should you be willing to entrust your entire life, your soul, and your own improvement?"

Socrates appeared lost in thought for a moment. "How then," he finally asked, "can one entice someone good to fall in love with him?" "In order to charm the beloved," replied Phaenarete, smiling, "the goddess Aphrodite teaches her followers how to cast spells and spin magic wheels." Socrates looked puzzled confused. "Come now," Phaenarete said smiling, "answer me this: What should you do if you want a friend to invite you to dinner?" "Well, of course," said Socrates, "I would invite him to my own home first." "And if you want a foreigner to show you hospitality when you visit his country," she asked, "what should you do?" Socrates said he presumed one should first show the visitor hospitality when he is in Athens.

"So you already know how to weave the spells that can charm others," said Phaenarete. "You must behave as you wish others to behave. If I wished to simplify the incantation even further, I would say: *those who wish to be loved, must first learn how to love others*."

Socrates was astounded. He had never dreamed that he might learn more about virtue by asking his mother about her expertise in matchmaking than by scouring the writings of the greatest living philosophers. "Where can I study this art?" asked Socrates. Phaenarete was gratified by her son's eagerness. She explained that Aspasia resembled a priestess of the Heavenly Aphrodite, as she taught those who came to see her how to improve themselves and others, through love of the mind's virtues. "How is it possible," muttered Socrates, "that I have been studying philosophy all these years without learning of these mysteries?" Phaenarete smiled, and waited for him to answer his own question. "Because up until this very moment," he murmured, in bewilderment, "it had only occurred to me to ask men."

THE DIALOGUE WITH ASPASIA

ASPASIA WAS ALMOST THE SAME age as Socrates and although she came from a different class and a different culture, they were kindred spirits. She was an intelligent woman with an inquiring mind and a fascination with language. She hailed from the birthplace of the Ionian school of philosophy, whose teachings Socrates had been studying. Phaenarete, an expert matchmaker, saw it as her duty to introduce Socrates to Aspasia. The two quickly became friends.[7]

During one of their first encounters, Socrates suggested that love was among the highest goods, by which he meant it was one of the most important things in life.[8] Aspasia had spent her life pondering these mysteries. Her raised eyebrow made it clear that she found his views too naive and simplistic. "Tell me," she asked him, "is love of *something* or is it of *nothing*?"

"You mean, does love always have an object?" Socrates replied helpfully. He continued, "Surely it does, since all love is directed toward what is loved; indeed, we often refer to its object as 'the beloved.'" "How might we define love's object more precisely?" asked Aspasia. Socrates replied that, in his view, the true object of love is what we call "beauty" or "goodness," which he said may even amount to the same thing. "Love then is a *desire*," continued Aspasia, "to have whatever is beloved, such as the beautiful or the good?" Socrates nodded slowly in agreement.

"Can the lover already possess what he desires?" asked Aspasia. Uncertainty crept into his voice as Socrates answered that, no, we typically *lack* whatever we desire. "But wait," he stammered, "surely the rich, for instance, sometimes speak of their love for whatever wealth they already have?" Aspasia had anticipated this objection, one often given by novice students. When such individuals say that they love something they already possess, what they really mean, she told him, is that they desire to *continue having it*. Even if they now have silver or any other precious thing, they do not have it permanently, as the future is uncertain. Whatever we can desire, therefore, we do not yet fully possess. "Love," whispered Aspasia mysteriously, "is a desire for something we are not, and do not have."

Socrates felt his head spin, as if perhaps he were falling in love himself. He muttered hesitantly: "If the true object of love is the beautiful, then—" He paused, lost in thought, so Aspasia concluded on his behalf: "Then love *wants* but does not *have* beauty." Socrates gazed at her awkwardly for a moment in silence. Her large brown eyes gave her a look of innocence but her wit and intelligence were undeniable, and she spoke with remarkable eloquence and self-assurance. She was one of the most beautiful and enigmatic women he had ever seen. Reluctantly, he conceded that, based on this logic, love itself cannot be beautiful, for its very nature is a want of beauty, which it desires to find in those we love. Worse, as Socrates had sought to equate goodness and beauty, this meant that love cannot even be called something good—love always looks outside of itself for goodness.

These arguments are troubling enough in terms of their meaning for human relationships. Socrates and Aspasia were both conscious, moreover, that love was personified by the god *Eros*. Her argument therefore seemed to be toying with impiety, by implying that Eros is not good. Socrates blushed and began to fidget nervously. Aspasia, an undisputed expert on the art of love, had forced him to concede that love was neither good nor beautiful. Perhaps the Athenians were even mistaken to consider love, or Eros, to be a god.

Although Socrates had come to hear Aspasia speak on the topic of love, something else about their conversation had captured his attention. The way this young noblewoman had questioned him was like nothing he had ever experienced before. She had brought philosophy down from the heavens and applied it to human affairs by examining his assumptions about the nature of *love*, something only poets usually talked about. His thoughts returned to a favorite quotation from Homer. It comes when Odysseus learns *what evil and what good has been wrought in thy halls, while thou hast been gone on thy long and grievous way.*[9] After being lost on his philosophical journey for almost a decade, Socrates had been shown a method that brought him back to earth with questions about human life and relationships. Aspasia was using philosophy to investigate matters far more important and much closer to home than those with which the stargazer Anaxagoras had wrestled.

"If love is neither beautiful nor good," continued Socrates, "does that mean that it is something ugly and bad?" Aspasia smiled again. "Hush now, my dear Socrates, you should know better than to assume that what is not beautiful must necessarily be ugly." He felt chastised and listened in silence as Aspasia continued: "Does everyone who lacks wisdom exhibit foolishness, or is there a third alternative that lies between these two opposites?" Socrates asked Aspasia to illustrate her point. "Someone who holds a correct opinion," she said, "is not exactly ignorant, but neither is he wise, unless he is able to justify it rationally." "I see," said Socrates confidently, "the foolish man is like someone lost in the woods, the wise man like someone who knows exactly how to find the path he needs. The man who holds a correct opinion, without knowing the reasoning behind it, however, is like someone who happens by *chance* to be walking along the right path. He wouldn't know how to find it again if he got lost."

"Yet," said Socrates, "it is agreed by everyone in Athens that love, or Eros, is among the greatest of the gods." Aspasia laughed. "Do you mean that it is agreed by everyone who is *wise* or everyone who is foolish?" "By all of them in unison, I think," said Socrates awkwardly. He noticed she was not at all swayed, though, by this appeal to popular opinion. "Come now," replied Aspasia, "how is that possible when some do not even consider him to be a god?" "Who do you mean?" asked Socrates. "Well, you for one, and I for another," she replied. Aspasia went on to explain that the gods are assumed by Athenians to be completely happy and fulfilled (*eudaimon*). Being fulfilled means having whatever is good in life, but if Eros lacks what is good, he cannot be truly fulfilled, and so he is no god. She concluded that Eros is neither a mortal nor a god but a *daemon*, a supernatural being that exists *between* mortals and gods.

Aspasia went on to say that Eros did not have the appearance typically attributed to him—that of a beautiful winged youth crowned with roses. Instead, she described him as a paradoxical figure. On the one hand, he looked completely impoverished, tough and dirty, and went around shoeless and homeless, sleeping in doorways, like a vagrant. On the other hand, he appeared as someone extremely intelligent, resourceful, and skilled at hunting down the beautiful and the good. He was like a cunning sorcerer, always searching for wisdom in the company of strangers, all the while enchanting them with his words. In short, Eros resembled a *philosopher*, and Aspasia made him sound very much like Socrates himself.

None of the gods philosophize, said Aspasia, because they are already wise. Nor do mortals who are so foolish that they do not care about wisdom. Philosophy, or the *love of wisdom*, is an intermediate condition, providing a bridge between folly and wisdom. Aspasia said that Eros was therefore not a god but a philosopher. Socrates, she proposed, had mistakenly assumed that love was beautiful because we tend to confuse the qualities of love with those of the beloved. Anaxagoras, the first philosopher at Athens, and those like him, professed to have knowledge of many things, which they considered to make them wise. People came to these philosophers for *answers* about the nature of the universe. Aspasia seemed to hold a radically different notion of philosophy, which placed less emphasis on purveying answers and more on asking the right questions, a talent for which Socrates was developing a reputation.

"All right," said Socrates, looking her in the eye, "but if what you say is true, and love itself is not good, then of what possible use can it be to humankind?" "Let me show you," replied Aspasia, "by asking another question: Given that love somehow desires what is beautiful, what is it that it desires *from* the beautiful?" Socrates replied that love desires to *have* what is beautiful. "But more specifically," said Aspasia, "how will someone benefit by getting what is beautiful?" Socrates could not answer, so Aspasia asked the same question another way: "What will he have, who desires what is truly *good*, and gets it?" This answer came more readily to the Greek mind because everyone agreed that, by definition, someone who gets what is truly good will live a good life and will experience fulfillment or *eudaimonia*. He will, in short, have achieved the goal of life.

Most of the things we desire in life are really just a means to some other end. The most obvious example would be money, which consists of coins or bits of paper, of no intrinsic value, but can be useful as a means of getting *other* things. Fulfillment, explained Aspasia, is an end in itself. There is no need to ask what fulfillment is "good for" because it means already having whatever is good. There is no deeper goal—this is the meaning of life! Love, properly understood, would therefore be the desire to achieve *eudaimonia* and to become fulfilled by possessing what is truly good.

"The only additional thing we desire from possession of our supreme good," said Aspasia, "is for it to be *lasting*. Love is a desire for the good to be *always* one's own. What then," she asked, "should those who earnestly love and desire the good do?" "If I knew," said Socrates, smiling, "I would not have come here, seeking to learn the answer to precisely this question."

Aspasia proceeded to explain that true love, in practice, seeks to create something from beauty, both physically and psychologically. "Love, strictly speaking, does not simply desire to *have* the beautiful," she said, "but rather to give birth to something by means of the beautiful. Why should love wish to procreate?" she asked. "Because, as we've agreed, love wishes to have the good forever, which would require immortality, but for mortals the closest we can get to immortality is to continually create something new."

"The closest that the physical body can get to immortality is to create offspring, thereby leaving behind young to replace the old. Bear in mind," she continued, "that although you are said to be the same person from the day you are born until the day you die, from childhood to old age, nevertheless you are constantly changing. Your hair and nails, flesh and blood, are constantly dying and regenerating. Moreover, your mind is ever changing, from day to day, with different habits, character traits, opinions, fears, and desires coming and going. Even stranger, our knowledge is constantly evolving in the same way, as every day we forget old things and learn new ones.

"In this way, mortal beings are preserved, not by being forever the same, like a god, but by continually replacing the old with the new. For this reason, every mortal being loves its own offspring and creations, as these can make it feel a step closer to immortality, and thereby give it a glimpse of the eternal good." Socrates was amazed by this notion. "Priestess," he stuttered, "is this really true?" "Look how much your fellow Athenians love glory," she said. "Why is it so important to them? It seems incomprehensible unless you understand that it is for the sake of *immortality* that they are willing to risk everything, including their own lives, and even the lives of their children." She added, quietly, "Do you suppose that Achilles would have risked his life and died at Troy unless he believed that his courage would be honored by countless generations?"

"Now some wish to procreate physically," she added, "and they find sexual partners, have children, and in this way approach immortality, or so they believe, by continuing their family line. Some, however, grow pregnant in terms of their minds, conceiving and giving birth to what most befits human nature—namely, wisdom and the other virtues. The greatest and most beautiful of all these virtues is *justice*," she said, "which consists in arranging the affairs of households, communities, and even cities. Through justice, we apply wisdom to our relationships, and share our wisdom with other humans.

"The lover of wisdom, or philosopher, will go about in search of the beautiful and good with whom he might create wisdom and conceive of justice. When he finds someone in whom he detects the potential for learning, the two friends will naturally find themselves discussing the nature of virtue. Lovers of wisdom maintain a closer friendship than those who have children together because their creations—the thoughts they share—are more beautiful and closer to being immortal. For instance, none of us envy Homer, Hesiod, and the other great poets because of their children, whom nobody can name, but because of the magnificent literary creations they left behind. We envy them precisely because their offspring, their poetry, is closer to being immortal than human children."

Socrates was enthralled and perplexed by Aspasia's speech. She paused, for what seemed like an eternity, and looked directly into his eyes, as if searching for the potential within him. Socrates had been so captivated by her that, to his shame, he only now realized that Aspasia had been playing the part of the lover, and he of the beloved, in their conversation. "Were her questions really designed to impregnate me," he wondered, "and cause me to give birth, somehow, to wisdom?" Suddenly she stood and turned away, saying that although Phaenarete's son may have been initiated into the *lesser* mysteries of love, she was unsure whether he would be ready for the more advanced revelations that constitute the *greater* mysteries.

Socrates looked dismayed at the thought of their conversation ending. Aspasia offered to proceed, therefore, if he would try his best to follow. She explained that when learning the art of love, a typical young man begins by contemplating beautiful bodies, finally settling upon the one whose physical form he most admires. He should eventually come to realize, though, that the beauty he so admires in one body exists also in others. Indeed, throughout the centuries, poets have employed the *same* words and phrases to praise the physical appearance of countless *different* lovers. "Unless you are quite foolish," she said, smiling, "you should realize that all examples of physical beauty are ultimately one and the same." What we love most in one individual's appearance, such as pretty brown eyes, cannot be unique—that physical quality must be found in countless other individuals. Our attachment to the beloved individual's body naturally lessens due to this realization, which transforms us, according to Aspasia, into lovers of the human form in general.

"With time," she added, "you should achieve a deeper revelation: that a beautiful mind is more praiseworthy than a beautiful body and, indeed, that the beauty of the body is relatively trivial." Socrates recognized this as the doctrine of Heavenly Aphrodite, to which his mother had previously introduced him. Aspasia likewise claimed that anyone who grasps this will find himself drawn more to those who have good character, even if their physical looks are modest. "The lover, wishing to enjoy this form of beauty," she said, "will seek to improve his beloved, by guiding the person toward greater knowledge and virtue. In time, he will no longer confine himself to just one beloved but will head out upon the vast open sea of the beautiful, where he will give birth, through the tireless practice of philosophy, to magnificent conversations and insights, with countless friends and lovers. Finally, he will be able to discern a special philosophical art, which aims to contemplate the eternal idea of beauty, the good itself.

"This is the true art of love," she said in conclusion, "which proceeds as though climbing the steps of a ladder. It begins with an appreciation of the physical beauty of another, then of many, then of *everybody*. It moves from beautiful bodies to beautiful actions and finally to beautiful thoughts, until it reaches the thought of pure beauty itself. When you have ascended in this way to the contemplation of beauty," said Aspasia, "life becomes worth living, and you will possess genuine fulfillment or *eudaimonia*. You will give birth to true wisdom and virtue for the first time, from this contemplation, and your creations will bring you as close as any human could ever get to attaining the immortality of the gods."

Philosophy was not, therefore, about amassing knowledge, as Anaxagoras had mistakenly assumed, but rather a sort of love that, humbly recognizing its own impoverished nature, seeks to glimpse the ideal of perfect wisdom and goodness in conversation with like-minded friends. Philosophy is, indeed, an *activity* of reason rather than merely a set of doctrines that could be committed to memory.

THE PRACTICE OF THE GOLDEN RULE

ASPASIA'S POINT WAS THAT BY learning to appreciate the potential for wisdom and goodness exhibited by others, we pave the way to a broader understanding of our own highest good. Socrates was constantly talking with his friends about virtue because he found that their efforts helped him to perceive it more clearly. We come to know ourselves best, he believed, *in conversation with others* about the most important things in life. There are several reasons for this, but the one we'll focus on in this chapter has to do with the fact that we typically apply a different moral standard to other people than to ourselves.

Socrates employs many different strategies to expose the contradictory nature of our beliefs. One of his simplest and most important methods is often overlooked. In the dialogues of both Plato and Xenophon, he uses a version of what modern cognitive therapists call the "double standards" strategy. This entails drawing your attention to the fact that you are applying a different standard to someone else than to yourself—whether to their character, beliefs, or actions.

One day a young man called Critobulus, the son of Crito, his lifelong friend, came to Socrates for his advice on making friends.[10] "Aspasia," said Socrates, "once advised me that good matchmakers are successful in making marriages only when the good reports they carry to and fro are true." She warned against giving *false* reports by praising individuals too highly, because those deceived in such a manner end up resenting not only one another but the matchmaker as well.

Socrates therefore began by asking Critobulus what sort of person a good friend is. They agreed on the following examples:

- He is no slave to eating and drinking, lust, sleep, or idleness, because otherwise he would be unable to do what is right for either himself or his friends.
- He is no spendthrift, always begging his companions for help, borrowing from them without paying them back or growing resentful if they refuse to lend him anything.
- He is not a greedy businessman, trying to make money by exploiting his acquaintances, without doing anything for them in return.
- He is not so obsessed with succeeding in his own career that he has no time for leisure and his friends.
- He is not a quarrelsome type who is always looking for a fight, thereby burdening his friends with many new enemies.

Even if he is free from all such faults, they agreed that if he accepts goodwill without reciprocating it, he is not a true friend. I call this Socrates's strategy of "negative definition." The Greek term *apophasis*, which means "denial" or "negation," can be used to describe this approach. We may find it easier to state what something is *not* before we attempt to explain what it *is*. In mystical theology, for instance, the concept of God is sometimes expressed by saying only what he is *not*.

It would normally go without saying that someone who financially exploits his acquaintances is *not* a good friend. It is only a short step to infer, as Socrates does, that a good friend exhibits the *opposite* of these traits. "We shall look," he said, "for someone who is in control of his physical appetites, who is trustworthy and honest, fair in his dealings with us, and wants to help his friends as much as they help him." This is an extremely useful technique when it comes to clarifying our values. For some reason, many people find it more natural to say what they *hate* about the behavior of others than to say what they admire. Vices can be easier to identify than virtues, but once you know the bad you should, by figuring out its opposite, be able to define the good.

Critobulus asked Socrates how he could "hunt down" a good friend of this sort. Socrates replied that unlike capturing an animal by using deception, chasing it down, or using force, such tactics tend to backfire when used on potential friends and risk turning them into our enemies. Rather, there are spells and potions, he said, that those in the know use to charm others and win their love and friendship. He was speaking about the charms of Aphrodite, mentioned earlier, which were thought to make others fall in love with the caster. Socrates said that Pericles did this through his words, which entranced the Assembly like a magic spell.

"I think you mean," said Critobulus astutely, "that if we are to win a good man's friendship, we ourselves must be good in word and deed alike?" Critobulus said that he had assumed at first that bad men could use the art of persuasion to win good friends. Now, however, he realized that this only worked on foolish people. As Socrates pointed out, the wise do not succumb so easily to persuasion—and they are the sort of friends who are most worth having. So if you want to win them over, you will need more than honeyed words—you must show them you *deserve* to be their friend.

Critobulus wanted Socrates to introduce him to good people, telling them that he had all the virtues of an ideal friend. Socrates, however, refused, saying that this would benefit *nobody*. "It appears," huffed Critobulus, "that you would only help me if I am deserving to make good friends: but if not, you won't make up a story to help me." "How can I help you best?" replied Socrates.

"By false praise or by urging you to become a good man? No, Critobulus, if you want to be thought good at anything, you must try to be so; that is the quickest, the surest, and the best way." This became a famous maxim of Socrates: *We should be as we wish to appear.*[11]

Sometimes people complain that philosophy gives no practical guidance when it comes to everyday morality. They feel it is too complicated and too obscure. Yet throughout the centuries, countless individuals have made use of a simple and well-known ethical guideline, which can be found in several different religious and philosophical traditions. Christians call it the "Golden Rule," and its most famous instances are found in the New Testament.

> All things therefore whatsoever you would that men should do unto you, even so do you also unto them.[12]

To do the opposite would be moral hypocrisy. The advice to treat others as we would wish to be treated by them is not, however, a *complete* ethic: it must assume that we make certain allowances for differing tastes and needs. I might want others to feed me apples, and they might prefer to be fed oranges; nevertheless, we both wish to eat something when we're hungry.

We find similar advice in the writings of the Stoics. Predating them, though, we find it attributed to Socrates, four centuries before Christianity, in the dialogues of both Plato and Xenophon. Socrates's use of the double standards strategy constantly implies something akin to the Golden Rule, although it is not as clearly stated by him because he prefers to teach by question and answer rather than by stating moral precepts. Critobulus is led to the conclusion, for instance, that to win good friends he should first become a good friend himself. He should, in other words, treat his prospective friends as he wishes to be treated by them. The qualities he admires in a friend are ones he should seek to cultivate in his own character.

One of the leading clinicians in the field of CBT, Judith Beck, has described how the double standards strategy is used with psychotherapy clients. The therapist first asks whether it would be reasonable for another person to adopt the same attitudes and behavior that the client exhibits.

> When patients consider *other* people's beliefs, they often get psychological distance from their own dysfunctional beliefs. They begin to see an inconsistency between what they believe is true or right for themselves and what they more objectively believe is true about other people.[13]

We are better able to judge other people's behavior than our own, particularly when it comes to our values. Moreover, simply highlighting the contradiction between what we expect from others and what we expect from ourselves can, sometimes, be enough to motivate us to change.

Take a sheet of paper and draw a line down the middle to create two equal columns. Write the word *admired* at the top of the first column and the word *desired* at the top of the second. In the first column, list three to five qualities you admire the most in others or look for in an ideal friend.

Now imagine moving each of those items from the "admired" column to the "desired" one. Note down what the *consequences* would be if you were to desire to cultivate those qualities in your own character. What would it be like, in other words, if you were to become more like the people you admire? How might that benefit your life?

Example Diagram: Admired versus Desired

ADMIRED	DESIRED
What qualities do I most admire in others?	*What would be the consequences if I desired to embody these qualities myself?*
Self-control with regard to food and drink, and sleep.	Physical and mental health would improve, and would be more able to help friends and family.
Good management of finances.	Would feel less financial stress and be more able to support family, and help friends.
Value friends for their personal qualities rather than for what we can get from them.	People would appreciate me more for who I am in return, rather than what they can get from me.
Devote more time to friends and family and less to work.	Life would have more balance and be more fulfilling.
Good at resolving arguments and not getting into quarrels.	I would experience less stress, save time and energy, and improve the lives of others around me.

Socrates didn't draw a diagram like this, but I think doing so can help us to understand the approach he exhibits in dialogues such as the one with Critobulus. As we'll see, he did employ another sort of two-column exercise with students wishing to learn his philosophical method.

THE BIRTH OF THE
SOCRATIC METHOD

AS A YOUNG MAN, SOCRATES was profoundly influenced by Aspasia, who introduced him to the art of love. During this formative period, he was still honing his distinctive philosophical method. Aspasia helped him to realize that philosophy should be understood as a dynamic process of inquiry rather than as a set of fixed doctrines, such as those propounded in the book of Anaxagoras. Socrates also experienced for the first time how the dialectical method could come alive in conversation with another person, a kindred spirit, such as Aspasia herself. By applying philosophy to questions concerning love and the nature of beauty and goodness, the process had acquired a new vitality.

Socrates quickly discerned, however, that Aspasia had a personal motive for directing his passion toward philosophical truths and away from attachment to any individual man or woman. Aspasia could plainly see that Socrates was falling in love with her. Already envisioning a future for herself with Pericles, Athens's leading man, she took steps to temper Socrates's affection for her. By teaching him about a higher form of love, stripped of possessiveness, she was equipping him to cope with the emotional pain of unrequited love.

While Socrates was still coming to terms with having lost Aspasia to Pericles and wrestling with the nature of love, an unforeseen event would plunge him into an even deeper crisis. It would force him to reconsider his concept of philosophy and to commit himself, with renewed vigor, to the love of wisdom.

4

THE ORACLE OF APOLLO

"WHY DON'T WE ASK THE god who is wise?" shrieked Chaerephon, as he waved his arms, gesturing in the direction of Delphi. More than fifteen years had passed since the trial of Anaxagoras, but his exile still cast a shadow over the practice of philosophy. Athens, because of its democratic ideals, was the city most tolerant of free speech—but only up to a point. The man they nicknamed "Nous," the great intellect, had been dragged into court and publicly vilified. Those who condemned him felt his newfangled wisdom crossed a line by questioning the nature of the gods. Pericles had praised the Ionian philosopher for his wisdom, whereas the Athenian jury had found him guilty of impiety. "Can the wise be called *impious*," chirped Chaerephon, "or the impious *wise?*"

The youths of Athens were now confronted by a question that had long troubled Socrates: *What is wisdom?* The most prominent young men wanted the best teachers. Associate yourself with the wrong teacher, and you might risk your reputation, or worse. Opinion in Athens was divided between those who saw philosophers like Anaxagoras as wise men and those who accused them of being dangerous charlatans. One way of resolving the problem would be to approach the Oracle of Apollo, the god of prophecy and Lord of the Muses, whose broad remit encompassed philosophy, and ask him who should be considered wise. The natural philosophers, for the most part, had no time for divination. Socrates, however, kept an open mind on theological matters because it seemed to him that natural explanations were quite compatible with belief in the gods. Even if thunder was the result of a physical cause, he said, such as the friction of clouds against one another, the behavior of the clouds could still express the will of Zeus.

Despite attempts to destroy Anaxagoras's reputation and suppress his teachings, following his exile, philosophy only became more popular at Athens. A new wave of teachers appeared who claimed that they were wise and could teach virtue to others. These teachers of wisdom charged handsomely for delivering elaborate lectures containing clever slogans and maxims. Socrates was uncertain, however, whether wisdom and other virtues could be learned, as they claimed, simply by listening to and repeating their words. He also couldn't afford to pay their fees. This left him and his friends with a problem: Where should one go to seek wisdom?

Chaerephon had come up with a solution: they would ask the Delphic Oracle to confirm the identity of the wisest man alive.[1] "How are we to know whether a teacher is as wise as he claims," said Chaerephon, "and worth the money he charges?" Socrates, for some reason, was reluctant to leave Athens. The temple of Apollo, which housed the Oracle, was about one hundred miles away on the slopes of Mount Parnassus. However, he was persuaded by the opportunity to study the ancient inscriptions there and to ask the priests what they meant.[2]

Socrates and his friends, including the two brothers Chaerephon and Chaerecrates, left Athens late in the summer of 434, making their way toward Delphi.³ It would take them about five days. They walked past scattered farms in the picturesque Attic country-side north of Athens, traversed wooded mountain paths, on their guard against wolves—the most arduous part of the journey. Then came a long trek across the fertile plains of Boeotia before they joined the Sacred Way, which would ascend the slopes of Mount Parnassus and take them straight to Delphi and the magnificent temple of Apollo.

THE DIALOGUE WITH CHAERECRATES

ON THE APPROACH TO DELPHI, in the foothills of the moun-tain, an argument broke out between Chaerephon and his younger brother, Chaerecrates, about the way their family inheritance had been divided.⁴ Noticing that they were no longer speaking to each other, Socrates brought it up with Chaerecrates. "Surely you're not the sort of fellow," he said, "who believes that some property is of more value to him than his brother?" Chaerecrates was, at first, taken aback. "Material objects are incapable of reason, whereas your brother has a mind," said Socrates, "the most valuable thing imaginable. You have many possessions, all of which require pro-tection," he added. "You have only one brother, but in exchange for benefiting from your protection, he offers you protection in re-turn." Chaerecrates could hardly deny that people are more valu-able than objects. However, he grumbled that wealth could attract friends, or be used to buy slaves, who might be far less irritating than his brother.

Socrates furrowed his brow and said, "It puzzles me that some individuals will go out of their way to make new acquaintances, as though they feel the need for more helpers or companions. Yet they will show no interest in their own brother. Why do they place more value on the friendship of strangers than upon their closest kin?" He thought that being born of the same parents and raised together should give us good reason to maintain friendship with our siblings, as we have so much in common with them. "You know, even many animals," he said, "feel a natural attachment to their own siblings. Humans in close-knit families," he added, "just like animals in a pack, are not only treated with respect but also less likely to be preyed upon by others."

Chaerecrates had a great deal of respect for Socrates, but he was still furious with his brother and would not be so easily persuaded. "No doubt," he said, "having a brother is a great benefit in life, just as you say, Socrates, but only if he behaves himself." Socrates nodded. "One should never turn one's back on siblings for petty reasons," continued Chaerecrates, "but if the disagreement is serious enough, their company may become quite unbearable." Socrates was about to speak, but Chaerecrates wasn't finished: "So why should I attempt the impossible, if my brother is useless in every regard," he added through gritted teeth, "and the exact *opposite* of what he should be?" Socrates paused for a moment, then smiled gently. He knew his friend Chaerephon wasn't the monster his brother was making him out to be. "Tell me, Chaerecrates," he said, "does everyone find your brother *equally* unbearable, or are there some who get along with him quite well?" Socrates was leading Chaerecrates toward the therapeutic insight that his anger was caused not by Chaerephon but rather by his own way of thinking. It was not his older brother who upset him, in other words, but rather his opinions about him.

Chaerecrates would have none of it. "That's precisely what I can't stand about him, Socrates," he said, his lip curling with un-concealed contempt. "He can get along with other people when he wants to, but whenever I have to deal with him, he's nothing but a liability." "Well," said Socrates, "much as a horse becomes a nuisance to its owners if they don't know how to look after it, perhaps a brother also becomes a problem when we don't know how to deal with him." "How can you possibly say that I don't know how to behave toward my own brother?" snapped Chaere-crates. "I know perfectly well how to be civil toward those who are civil to me." Socrates listened. "But when a man does his level best to annoy me," Chaerecrates snorted, "nobody can expect me to treat him well—*and I'm certainly not going to try!*"

"That's an odd thing to say," remarked Socrates, with a shrug. Chaerecrates, taken aback, stared at him blankly for a moment. "Imagine a man," said Socrates, "who owns a dog that is friendly with everyone else but becomes aggressive only when he comes near it himself. Such a man," he said, "if he has good sense, would realize that the dog's aggression may be curable, simply because it does not always behave in this way. There appears to be no reason why it can't learn to be as friendly with him as it is with others. You said that your brother would be a great asset to you if he treated you properly," added Socrates, "and you admitted that you know how to treat with him civility, yet you don't attempt to do so, because he does not appear civil to you." "Yes, I'm afraid that I must not know the art required," sneered Chaerecrates, "to make my brother behave properly toward me!"

Socrates looked pleased at this, which surprised Chaerecrates. "Oh, I can assure you," he replied, "you won't need to use any subtle or original techniques on him—I think you could win high regard from your brother by using a method you already know quite well." "Oh really?" said Chaerecrates, raising an eyebrow. "If you honestly believe that I'm in possession of some magic formula for winning people over, you better speak up, Socrates, because I still have no idea what you're talking about!"

Socrates smiled again, taking this as an invitation to impart some of the practical advice he'd learned from his mother and Aspasia. "If you wanted someone to invite you to a dinner party, what would you do?" he asked. "Obviously, I should invite him to my house as a guest first," replied Chaerecrates. "What if you wanted to persuade one of your friends to look after your property," continued Socrates, "while you're away from home?" Chaerecrates replied that, likewise, he should offer first to do the same thing for the friend. "What if you wanted a foreigner to show you hospitality," asked Socrates, "when you're visiting his city?" Chaerecrates replied that he would, of course, go first by offering to play host to the other man whenever he came to Athens.

"So you can recite all the magic charms that influence human behavior but have been keeping your knowledge a secret until now," exclaimed the philosopher in mock surprise. "Why not begin using them?" he asked. "You appear to be saying, my friend, that we should consider behaving toward others as we wish them to behave toward us, and I have no doubt that you are correct." In this way, Socrates gradually helped Chaerecrates to cure his anger and resolve the feud with his brother.

Socrates added that whereas the friendship of worthless individuals can be bought with material gifts, the friendship of good men was more often earned by displaying *courtesy* toward them—and he included the two brothers in the latter category. "What if I take the first step but he continues to mistreat me?" asked Chaerecrates hesitatingly. "Well," said Socrates, "it will have cost you nothing, and you will at least have conclusive evidence that you are a good brother and that he is a bad one, undeserving of your kindness." Putting his arm around Chaerecrates's shoulder, he added, "Knowing you both as I do, though, I doubt that will be the case."

This incident had a profound effect upon young Chaerecrates, who soon began to display greater tolerance and courtesy as Socrates had advised. It also impressed Chaerephon, his older brother, who thanked Socrates effusively for mending the rift between them. Despite Socrates's tendency to ask provocative questions, he was earning a reputation as someone adept at ending quarrels and restoring friendships.[5] Perhaps it was the influence of his new mentor, Aspasia, with all her talk about the art of love.

The questions Socrates liked to ask his companions seemed peculiar, even trivial, at first. Over time, however, they proved to be of more practical benefit than the teachings of any other philosophers. For the first time, therefore, it dawned on Chaerephon that Socrates was no longer doing philosophy in the manner to which they were accustomed. Socrates, true to his word, was applying philosophy to the question of virtue at home, among his friends, even counseling them regarding their family and other relationships. Philosophy, in his hands, began to resemble a sort of medicine, applied to the mind rather than the body.

As the friends approached the main temple, the pleasant fragrance of the wind blowing through pine and olive trees was slowly replaced by the odor of pungent fumes, which wafted up from a crack in the rocks beneath Apollo's shrine. The place was once known as *Pytho*, meaning putrid, because according to legend, the corpse of the great serpent killed by Apollo lay there and rotted in the sun. At the commencement of the Pythian Games, which were second in importance only to the Olympic Games, this mythic battle was reenacted in a public ceremony.

Religion, philosophy, music, poetry, and athletics blended in one great festival honoring the god.

Apollo's priestess, also known as the Pythia, sat upon a sacred tripod, or three-legged stool, within the main temple. As she inhaled the fumes, she would reputedly enter a trance in which she was possessed by the god who spoke through her. Faith in the accuracy of these oracles was almost universal, although they were often ambiguous and open to interpretation. For example, when the Athenians consulted the Oracle following the second Persian invasion in 480, Apollo proclaimed through his priestess: "Though all else shall be taken, Zeus, the all-seeing, grants that the wooden wall only shall not fail." Athens did not have wooden walls. Themistocles, the founder of the Athenian navy, persuaded the Assembly that the god must be referring to the defensive capability of wooden triremes, or warships. It was therefore said that Apollo, the Lord of Delphi, neither concealed nor revealed his meaning but rather gave a sign, like a riddle that must be correctly interpreted.

Socrates and his companions solemnly climbed the hillside, following the Sacred Way alongside others visiting the temple. When they reached the narrow ravine containing the Castalian Spring, they washed their hair in its sacred waters. After purifying themselves by this ritual, they were allowed to pass through the gates into the sanctuary of Apollo. They followed the steep, winding road past dozens of memorial sculptures and several small, ornate buildings where Athens and other Greek cities had deposited votive offerings dedicated to the god. The friends paused to admire the Athenian treasury, on whose base was inscribed the following: "The Athenians dedicated this to Apollo as first fruits from the Persians at the Battle of Marathon." Chaerephon, the eldest of the group, had been nominated by his friends to present their question to the Oracle. He made a donation to the priests, sacrificed a goat, poured libations to the gods, and recited the prescribed prayers.

Socrates and the others waited among the crowds outside Apollo's temple. As Chaerephon was about to walk between the pillars, he looked back at them and smiled. He had a mischievous look in his eyes. Despite his eccentricities, he was regarded by his fellow citizens as a man of both intelligence and honor. A moment later, Chaerephon was gone, having been ushered inside by the priests. While his friend was presenting their question to the Pythia, Socrates ran his fingers across the famous inscription he had been looking forward to seeing. The words *Know thyself* were engraved on one of the pillars at the temple's entrance, just as he had been told. "What do you think it means?" asked Chaerecrates. "I suspect it has several meanings," replied Socrates.

THE PRACTICE OF THE SOCRATIC METHOD

SOCRATES USED A WRITTEN EXERCISE to teach his philosophical method, as we have seen. Xenophon clearly describes it in his *Memorabilia Socratis*.[6] The dialogue in which he does so is set many years *after* the events of this chapter, but it provides one of the best introductions to the Socratic method. Socrates is shown explaining his way of philosophizing to a new student, using a diagram to help train him in the basic skills required. It's *the* definitive exercise in how to think like Socrates.

Socrates arrives at a saddlery shop, just outside the Athenian Agora, where he meets a young man named Euthydemus, known for his good looks and intelligence. Euthydemus prides himself on his personal library, which includes, among many other things, a complete edition of Homer. He has also amassed, and continues to collect, the writings of various wise men, which he is carefully studying in order to improve himself—if he was alive today, we'd call him a typical "self-help junkie." As far as Socrates is concerned, anyone who immerses himself in books and has attended lectures on self-improvement deserves praise for his desire to learn. Yet Euthydemus would potentially be wasting his own time and money unless he also learns how to think for himself about the "wise" things he has read and heard. Much like learning to play the flute, or any similar skill, this requires daily practice.

"I've been told that you admire the treasures stored up for us by the wise men of previous generations," says Socrates. Euthydemus smiles. "By Zeus, I do, more than any amount of gold and silver!" "Then I admire this, by Hera," exclaims Socrates, "and it shows you're the sort of fellow who knows that, whereas gold and silver cannot make men better, the maxims of the wise enrich their possessors with virtue." Socrates mentions that some people are described as being the slaves of their own ignorance. He asks Euthydemus what sort of ignorance could possibly enslave a man in this way. Surely not lacking knowledge of trades such as those of the cobbler or blacksmith or carpenter? They agree, rather, that those who are ignorant of the beautiful or good or just are the ones most constrained by ignorance, as they lack knowledge about the most important things in life. Each one of us should therefore, claims Socrates, make it our utmost priority to escape such a wretched condition.

Socrates asks Euthydemus what his main goal is in life. He is relieved to hear that the young man aspires to become a great leader, like Pericles, and that he takes it for granted that this requires first becoming a *good person*. "Have you achieved this?"

asks Socrates. Euthydemus is somewhat taken aback. He had assumed that all the effort he was putting into self-improvement must somehow be improving his character. Socrates muses that, in the same way carpenters and other craftsmen can display their work, a person who has spent many hours studying self-improvement should be able to provide tangible evidence of progress. "I can assure you, Socrates," says a slightly indignant Euthydemus, "that I can give you an account of moral virtue and of moral vice—of the latter there are plenty of examples to be heard and seen every day!"

Example of Two-Column Exercise: Injustice

JUSTICE	INJUSTICE
	Telling lies and other forms of deceit.
	Stealing from others.
	Mistreating others and doing them harm.
	Selling others into slavery.

Socrates offers to put this to the test by means of a simple *two-column diagram*, which he has drawn, presumably, on a wax tablet. He writes down the initial letters of the words *Justice* and *Injustice* as the headings of the two columns.[7] He then proceeds to ask for examples of *injustice*, as Euthydemus said these are particularly easy to identify. Socrates asks whether things like telling lies and stealing are morally wrong and should be noted down under that heading. Euthydemus agrees. So far, this resembles the one-column technique and process of "negative definition" discussed in a previous chapter. Listing examples can be a good way of clarifying our initial definition of a concept. Listing *negative* qualities, of which we disapprove, is often easier than starting by listing positive ones—perhaps because people love to complain!

The Socratic method proper really begins with the next step. Socrates now uses *creative thinking* to come up with situations where these examples might be moved across to the other column.[8] "What if an elected military general tells lies to the enemy or otherwise deceives them during a war?" he asks. Euthydemus thinks that this is an exception and that it should be listed under *justice* rather than injustice. "What if he captured the enemy and seized their weapons and armor?" asks Socrates. Euthydemus had said earlier that all theft was unjust, but he thinks that in warfare this is potentially acceptable, so it would also go under the heading of *justice*.

Example of Two-Column Exercise: Justice

JUSTICE	INJUSTICE
Lying to or otherwise deceiving the enemy during a war.	Telling lies and other forms of deceit.
Plundering enemy camps and hostile cities during a war, and confiscating enemy weapons.	Stealing from others.

Euthydemus believed that he was acquiring wisdom and becoming a better person, by memorizing sayings about morality
from the books of famous wise men. By their very nature, though,
these were *generalizations*, which don't always hold true. Genuine
wisdom would consist in the ability to spot exceptions to these
rules and adapt them accordingly. Socrates and Euthydemus
agree to revise their initial definition of justice to say that it is
always unjust to steal from or lie to one's *friends*, but it may be
just to do so to one's *enemies*. They have in mind an ancient Greek
saying that justice consists of helping one's friends and harming
one's enemies.

The Socratic method is relentless, though. Socrates now proceeds to think up exceptions to the revised definition. "What if a
general sees that his troops are in danger of losing heart," he asks,
"and lies to them about help being on its way in order to restore
their morale?" He also gives the example of a father concealing
medicine in the food of a small child who refuses to swallow it otherwise. What if one of your friends is depressed and suicidal, moreover, so you hide his sword from him out of concern for his safety?
Euthydemus concedes that in cases such as these it could be considered just to mislead or even lie to a friend. Socrates was particularly
good at coming up with examples that contradict any given assertion. We're told he practiced these skills every day of his life.

Euthydemus had begun confidently but soon finds himself
unsure and changing his answers. "Upon my word, Socrates,"
exclaims the youth, "I felt quite certain until today that my studies in philosophy had been providing me with the best education
available, teaching me everything needed to improve myself and
become a good person." Socrates smiles warmly. "Despite all my
efforts," continues Euthydemus, "I appear incapable of answering
even the most basic questions about some of the most important

things in life—such as the meaning of justice! In truth," he adds, lowering his head, "I feel utterly disheartened."

"Have you ever been to Delphi?" asks Socrates, to the young man's surprise. Euthydemus says he has indeed been, twice. "Did you notice the words *Know thyself* inscribed before the temple of Apollo there?" asks Socrates. The bemused Euthydemus says that he had noticed the inscription but paid little attention to it because he took it for granted that he already knew himself very well. Socrates explains that people often behave as if they know *about* something just because they know its name. To genuinely know and understand the thing itself, though, usually requires more effort. Euthydemus felt certain that he knew what justice meant, having read many books about it, but Socrates all too easily demonstrated that this was nothing more than opinion rather than *real* knowledge. Verbal definitions and maxims tend to lead to sweeping generalizations, which can be easily refuted by pointing to a single exception. Any fool can remember some words and repeat them, without understanding them. We must therefore be on our guard against confusing opinion, the mere *appearance* of knowledge, with *real* knowledge.

Socrates explains that to really know ourselves we must know what qualities a good man possesses, and how he differs from a bad one. If we wanted to buy a horse, we'd carefully examine its hooves, teeth, and body. We'd test it to find out if it is docile or stubborn, strong or weak, fast or slow, and so on. We would examine it in terms of the qualities most important for a horse. To know someone, we must examine the person in terms of the qualities of most value in a human being. To know ourselves, that is, we must know how we are doing when measured against human virtues such as wisdom and justice. We must clarify our thinking about our values and expose the sort of conceit that consists in believing we know what virtue is when we do not.

"Through self-knowledge," says Socrates, looking out from under his bushy eyebrows, "men come to much good in life, and through self-deceit, they come to much harm." Euthydemus thinks that this should be obvious to us. By knowing our strengths and weaknesses, we avoid making many mistakes. However, our most important weakness would be ignorance about the most important questions in life, such as what is good, wise, just, and so on. Someone who realizes that he is ignorant about the most important things in life will naturally seek to learn from someone he considers wiser than himself, according to Socrates. The real danger consists in believing that we know what is good for us when, in reality, we do not know anything of the sort. Knowing what we do and do not know is the most important form of self-knowledge. Socrates also believed that self-knowledge better enables us to know other people and to manage our relationships with them wisely. Realizing how his own beliefs affected his emotions and behavior may have helped him understand how his friends, such as Chaerecrates and Euthydemus, could be misled by *their* assumptions. That explains how he was able to help them.

Euthydemus was a clever student. "You can rest assured," he tells Socrates, "that I appreciate the importance of knowing myself in this way, but where exactly should the process of self-examination begin?" "Well," replies Socrates, "do you know which things in life are *good* and which are *bad*?" "Of course," says Euthydemus, taken aback once more, "for if I didn't even know the difference between good and evil, I really *would* be enslaved by ignorance!" It was precisely his overconfidence regarding this knowledge, though, that blinded him to his biggest opportunity for self-improvement.

When asked for an example of what is good for us, Euthydemus says the most obvious one must surely be health, as everyone agrees that illness is bad. Health is *usually* a practical advantage in life, and preferable to sickness. However, the good health of a serial killer or evil dictator might simply give that individual more opportunity to do foolish and vicious things. Even if we use our good health as an opportunity to pursue wise and virtuous goals, if we're unlucky, the outcome may be the opposite of what we desired. As Socrates points out, having good health and being able-bodied could be the reason that someone gets enlisted for an ill-fated military expedition, perhaps leading to their death or enslavement. From that perspective, it would have been better for that person to have been too sick to be recruited into the army.

Socrates goes on to list beauty, strength, wealth, and glory as typical examples of things people consider good. Euthydemus agrees and thinks these are obviously part of *eudaimonia* or the good life, exclaiming, "How can anyone possibly flourish without them?" Socrates advises him to examine his assumptions more carefully, though, as these are *questionable* examples of human goods. "To add them to our list of goods," he says, "would be to include the sources of much trouble to humankind." Euthydemus is puzzled, so Socrates gives some examples.

"Many individuals are ruined by admirers whose heads are turned by their *beauty*," he explains. "Many men of great *strength* become cocky, end up attempting tasks that are too dangerous for them, and suffer destruction as a result. Many individuals are corrupted by money or fall victim to those who envy their *wealth*. And many through glory and public acclaim," he adds, "have also suffered great evils."

"If such things are sometimes beneficial and sometimes harmful," observes Socrates, "why should we say that they are any more good than bad?" Whether we say they're good or bad depends entirely on the *consequences* of having them, which can vary unexpectedly, especially over the longer term. What seems at first like an advantage in life can often turn out to be a disadvantage, and vice versa.

Euthydemus agrees but feels that wisdom must be, unquestionably, a good thing. Socrates replies that it depends what we mean by wisdom. Many men who are considered wise because of their technical expertise, such as sculptors and engineers, have been captured and enslaved for that reason. The king of Persia had the most educated men in his kingdom seized and brought to his palace as slaves. (He could have added that the supposed wisdom of Anaxagoras ended him up in court and was of little benefit to him as a means of coping with the perceived injustice of his trial.) Euthydemus says, with a laugh, "Well, it seems I was mistaken even to praise these things. So I no longer know what one should ask for in one's prayers!"

Socrates had noticed Euthydemus's initial overconfidence. He took it to be a sign that despite all his reading, he had probably never questioned his assumptions in this way. Although the young man at first felt quite humbled by this exercise, and a little confused, he kept coming back to Socrates to discuss similar matters with him, and eventually he became one of his most devoted students.

The Socratic method is a complex and subtle philosophical procedure. Nevertheless, Socrates believed that the basic cognitive skills required could be taught in this way, using a simple two-column exercise. Anyone can memorize a definition of wisdom or justice from a book. Self-help books are full of sweeping generalizations about the good life. Folk wisdom likewise contains notoriously contradictory sayings. From "Fools rush in where angels fear to tread" to "He who hesitates is lost," we have many proverbs that offer conflicting advice. The truth, of course, is that *sometimes* it is good to rush in; *other times* it is better to pause for thought. We must learn to adapt to circumstances. Wisdom requires being able to identify when a rule no longer holds true, and good advice becomes bad advice. We should also revise our assumptions accordingly, such as our definition of the goal of life.

Nearly five centuries after Socrates lived, a Roman poet named Persius wrote a satire about the lectures attended, in his day, by students of Stoic philosophy.[9] "Has philosophy taught you to live a good, upstanding life?" asks Persius. You must, he adds, be able to tell what is true from false appearances, "alert for the false chink of copper beneath the gold." As we have seen, distinguishing appearance from reality was a central concern for ancient philosophers. He follows this by saying something that echoes the Socratic dialogue we've just discussed:

> *Have you settled what to aim for and also what to avoid,*
> *marking the former list with chalk and the other with charcoal?*

He's referring to examining the goal of life, by *drawing* two lists or columns, with the goods to aim for on one side and the evils to be avoided on the other. Perhaps, like Socrates, the Stoic teacher would then ask his students whether some of the items they had listed potentially belonged in the other column.

Two-column techniques are widely used in cognitive-behavioral therapy, as a way of facilitating Socratic questioning. It is striking to find Socrates describing a similar technique nearly two and a half thousand years *before* CBT was even invented. For instance, a depressed client who thinks "Nobody likes me" might be asked to list pieces of evidence for and against that belief on a table with two columns, headed "evidence for" and "evidence against."

At first it might seem that the goal of this exercise is simply to disprove a mistaken assumption. It can benefit us in more subtle ways, though. What if we view it as being more about the *process* of challenging our beliefs than the outcome? What if we get into the habit, as Socrates advises, of challenging our assumptions about the most important things in life every day?

Socrates, it seems to me, has what psychologists call *cognitive flexibility*. He is adept at generating multiple *alternative* ways of viewing a situation or concept. This prevents him from becoming too fused with a particular assumption. If you tell Socrates that you believe having good looks is an advantage, he'll think of one situation after another where it appears to be a disadvantage. Tell him the sun appears to be a ball of fire, and he'll list several ways in which it doesn't behave like one. Everything is a hypothesis, waiting to be refuted. That type of cognitive flexibility may be inherently therapeutic. In contrast, rigid thinking, which can only consider a limited number of perspectives, has been found to be associated with a variety of psychological problems, including *pathological worrying*.[10]

There's a fascinating body of modern research that I believe holds the key to understanding another of the main benefits of the Socratic method. Definitions of our values, such as the goal of life itself or specific virtues, can be understood as *verbal rules*. Studies carried out by behavioral psychologists have shown that although verbal rules can be useful, they also tend to cause a problem, best described as *insensitivity* to change in our environment. For example, when participants in an experiment are told to "push this button rapidly to earn points," (a verbal rule) they are less likely to stop pushing when the points are no longer being awarded than another group of participants who have instead discovered how the button works through trial and error.[11] This research finding has profound implications for psychotherapy because many of the psychological problems that therapy clients experience involve rigid persistence in following certain rules, or using certain coping strategies, despite the fact that they're clearly not working. We can easily get stuck in a rut, doing what we believe we should do, again and again, even when it's hurting us.

Someone who has learned, for instance, that "lying is *wrong*" from their parents or from a book or a lecture may stubbornly refuse to tell even a "white lie," which would benefit their loved ones. Or as William Blake wrote, "A truth that's told with bad intent beats all the lies you can invent." To adapt the example used by Socrates above, if you *rigidly* define lying as wrong, you might think that when a suicidal friend asks where his gun is, you should answer him truthfully rather than lying to save him from harm. Socrates is more *flexible* than that in his thinking. He trained himself and his students to constantly examine their verbal rules, especially moral definitions and maxims, by creatively thinking of *exceptions* to them. Perhaps lying is unjust in some contexts but not others; perhaps standing your ground is courageous in some situations but not others; perhaps knowledge is good for us sometimes but not always.

Whereas the earlier philosophers taught moral maxims, or rules, Socrates encouraged his students to question them. It seems to me he realized that true moral wisdom requires some degree of openness, flexibility, and adaptability in our thinking. In a word, it's healthier in the long run for us to learn to think for ourselves than to depend too much on memorizing the sayings of wise men.

In the dialogue above, Socrates asked Euthydemus if he'd ever been to Delphi and read the famous inscription there: *Know thyself.* He explained that although most people naively assume that they know themselves, they are, in an important sense, mistaken, and therefore intellectually conceited. Genuine self-knowledge means knowing what we do and do not know. In other words, it means grasping the limits of our knowledge, especially concerning some of the most fundamental things in life. The two-column exercise uses a simplified version of the Socratic method to test our knowledge of the good life, or *eudaimonia*, and our definition of virtues such as wisdom and justice. Through constant practice, with methods such as this, we come to realize that what appears certain to us is often easily contradicted and must be subject to revision. Knowing ourselves means knowing that we don't know everything about the goal of life.

THE PRONOUNCEMENT OF APOLLO

WHEN CHAEREPHON FINALLY EMERGED FROM the temple, his face was even paler than usual. "Don't keep us waiting, my friend," said Socrates.[12] "What did the god say? Who is the wisest man alive?" Chaerephon looked around sheepishly at his friends. "Well, that wasn't exactly how I phrased my question," he croaked. "What do you mean?" said Socrates, his eyes widening. "Don't you realize how important it is to word a question correctly, especially when you only have one chance of hearing the answer?" Chaerephon said nothing. "Well, what question did you ask?" said Socrates. There was a long pause before Chaerephon, with uncharacteristic hesitation, replied: *Is any man wiser than Socrates?* That, indeed, was the question he asked the god of Delphi, and, speaking through the Pythia, his priestess, Apollo answered: *Of all men, Socrates is the most wise.*

Socrates, for once, was dumbstruck. "That was not the question you were supposed to ask," he finally stammered. "The priests confirmed the answer," replied Chaerephon awkwardly.

Socrates scolded him for wasting his opportunity to question the god. "Don't you realize that your question has an assumption?" said Socrates. "Whenever you ask a question that makes an assumption, you're putting words in the other person's mouth," he exclaimed, "and in this case it was the mouth of a god!" "What assumption?" asked Chaerephon, slightly indignant. "That Socrates *is* wise!" said Socrates, scowling. "I said no such thing," shrugged Chaerephon. Socrates thought for a moment. "Perhaps you're right," he said. "What, then, can Apollo mean?" he muttered to himself, furrowing his brow in concentration as if trying to solve a riddle. "I have no wisdom," he said, looking up at his friends, "either great or small." Socrates had been convinced of this by Aspasia, who had taught him, paradoxically, that one cannot both be a philosopher and wise. "The god cannot lie," said Chaerephon, smiling. "To do so would be against his very nature." Everyone agreed.

If the god's baffling pronouncement were true, it would suggest that those who called themselves wise, and even those who were called wise by others, were no wiser than Socrates. After considering this at length, he arrived at a decision. Socrates would seek out a man wiser than himself and report back to Delphi. As though he were cross-examining a witness in court, he would present the priests with contrary evidence, and they would be forced to clarify or revise the Pythia's testimony. He would question anyone who seemed to have wisdom and try to refute their beliefs, to establish whether they were really wise or merely *appeared* wise. Where should he go first? To speak, of course, with the wisest man alive.

5

THE WISEST MAN ALIVE

ONE SPRING MORNING, ON HIS way to the Agora, Socrates, now in his thirties, noticed a group of boys playing knucklebones in a narrow alleyway.[1] Suddenly, the youngest leaped up and yelled "rotten cheat!" at one of his playmates. After a brief quarrel, they resumed play. Just as the lad who had shouted was about to take his turn, a cart pulled by two oxen rounded the corner, rumbling toward the boys. They scattered, all except this youngster, who was so determined to win the game that he refused to budge. He raised his hand for the cart to stop but the driver paid no heed. Scowling, the boy threw himself in front of the advancing bulls' hooves. The driver yelled out in anger but was forced to halt his cart abruptly.

Anyone could see this boy was fearless, to the point of foolhardiness. He possessed what the Greeks called *philotimia*—a passion for victory, honor, and fame. Such a child was destined either for greatness or catastrophe. Socrates quietly asked one of his young playmates, "Who is this child, and what is the name of his father?" "His father was killed in the war," came the answer, "and now he's being raised in the house of Pericles; they call him Alcibiades."

About a decade earlier, Aspasia, along with her father and their extended family, had sailed from her home in Ionia. Shortly after their arrival, her niece, who lived in Athens, gave birth to a boy. He was named Alcibiades after his grandfather, Aspasia's brother-in-law, an Athenian noble, who had been living in exile. The family lost Alcibiades the Elder, though. Next, his son, Cleinias while still in his thirties, was slain in battle at Coronea, fighting against the Boeotians. At the age of four, therefore, the now fatherless child was taken into the household of his father's best friend, Pericles, who became his legal guardian. Pericles later divorced his first wife, and Aspasia moved in with him, becoming his consort, and eventually his second wife. Pericles and Aspasia would go on to raise her great-nephew, the young Alcibiades, as if he were their own son.[2]

In the years to come, Socrates would watch as the whole of Athens became entranced by the son of Cleinias. Aspasia, the boy's great-aunt, was like a stepmother to him, and inevitably took an interest in his education. As the boy reached adolescence, Socrates began to notice him in the company of prominent Athenian intellectuals.

Alcibiades retained his youthful good looks as an adult, for which he became famous throughout Greece. Later in life, just like other nobles, he would keep his hair long—a symbol of status because the poor found it more practical to cut theirs short. He spoke with a lisp, which made him pronounce the letter *rho* as if it were *lambda*—so that instead of "Socrates" he would say *Soklates*. His speech impediment was thought of as charming precisely because, in the eyes of many, it seemed to be his only imperfection. Socrates did not approach the boy, although they were often in the same company. The two had seldom exchanged words. Instead, the philosopher listened with interest as Alcibiades argued with his friends and even his teachers. The rest of Athens treated Alcibiades like a celebrity. They flocked around him and gossiped about him. They loved him, indulged him, and heaped praise upon him. He could be reckless and arrogant, but he was also charismatic, intelligent, courageous—and a born leader.

The names of Alcibiades's illustrious ancestors were on the lips of everyone he met. His father's side of the family were nobles, of the Salaminioi clan, who traced their ancestry back to the legendary hero Ajax. The Alcmaeonids, his mother's clan, were one of the wealthiest and most powerful dynasties of ancient Greece. Through them, Alcibiades claimed descent from Nestor, the legendary king of Pylos, who, like Ajax, was immortalized in Homer's *Iliad* and *Odyssey*.[3] In the sixth century, some of the Alcmaeonids played a crucial role in overthrowing the last tyrant to have ruled Athens. (By "tyrant" the Greeks meant a sole ruler who stands above the law, like a dictator or absolute monarch.) Cleisthenes, one of the Alcmaeonids, established Athenian democracy, for which the city had since become famous. Despite their noble blood and great wealth, therefore, Pericles and other Alcmaeonids remained leading figures in the *Democrat* faction, which sought to keep power in the hands of the people. Alcibiades, who was born into the same noble clan and had since become the ward of Pericles, was expected to follow in his footsteps.

Pericles was an early populist, whose exceptional power came, ironically, from his claim to give the common people more control over the governance of their city. The Athenian citizens loved him and looked up to him as their leader. Whereas political tyrants impose obedience with threats of violence, Pericles exercised almost as much authority because the citizens freely offered him their support. He was also a master of international diplomacy. Throughout their growing empire, he was respected for saying that Athens made allies not by receiving benefits but by bestowing them on others. His motions had to be put to the vote, like anyone else's, but he almost always got his way. The greatest political orator of his era, he held the Assembly in the palm of his hand.

Whereas Pericles had built his authority over decades, Alcibiades, desperate to outdo his guardian, courted controversy as a shortcut to fame. While learning to wrestle, he once sank his teeth into an opponent who was getting the better of him. The boy yelled at him: "You bite like a girl!" Alcibiades, stood tall, and retorted shamelessly: "No, like a lion!" This piece of theater became legendary.[4] In the years that followed, Alcibiades would often be compared to a lion. If Pericles was effectively the ruler of a great empire, then his young ward resembled an imperial princeling. All of Athens wanted Alcibiades to be the next Pericles, or even greater than Pericles.

When he reached his late teens and entered military cadet training, Alcibiades began looking for a mentor who could prepare him to become Athens's next great leader. It was no job for the fainthearted. A few years earlier, he had asked one teacher to give him a book of Homer's works. When the man stammered that he had none to hand, he received a punch in the face—and other prospective tutors were no match for the teen either. Like many Athenian youths, Alcibiades idolized Achilles, the tragic Homeric hero, whose father had implored him "always to be best and to surpass all others."[5] Achilles, according to legend, had been tutored by Chiron, the wisest of the centaurs. Alcibiades wanted to be tutored only by the wisest of the Greeks.

Since Anaxagoras's exile, two decades earlier, the celebrated orator Protagoras of Abdera had become Pericles's most trusted political advisor and envoy. Protagoras was the first person to adopt the title of *Sophist*, meaning expert or wise man. He had avoided Anaxagoras's mistake of making claims about the celestial bodies, and being charged with impiety, by insisting that such things were unknowable. Instead, he specialized in teaching oratory, virtue, and general improvement of one's character. The English word *sophistication* derives from the Sophists, and that is what they offered to impart to the ambitious young sons of wealthy Greek families, along with the ability to speak persuasively in the courts and before the Assembly. For a course of lectures, Protagoras charged one hundred minae, more than a craftsman such as Socrates might earn in his lifetime. Despite such exorbitant fees, he had become a celebrity and attracted many devoted followers, including apprentices, seeking to become Sophists themselves.

Having come back from Delphi, still vexed by the Oracle's pronouncement, Socrates went in search of a wise man. There could be no better candidate than Protagoras, whose followers claimed that he was *the wisest man alive*. For many years, the great Sophist had been away on political service in Magna Graecia (southern Italy). When Socrates heard of his return, he set out immediately for the house of Callias, a famous patron of intellectuals, with whom Protagoras was staying.[6]

Socrates's friends had always admired his philosophical acumen, although he remained unknown, for the most part, beyond this small circle. Now, as news of the Oracle's pronouncement spread, despite his relatively humble origins, his name began to reach the ears of Athens's most celebrated intellectuals and their elite students. Nevertheless, when he arrived at the villa of Callias, the doorman didn't recognize him and refused at first to let this nobody in. He only changed his mind when Socrates implied that he had a friend who was interested in paying for Protagoras's services as a tutor.

Socrates entered, eventually, to find the great orator, dressed in crimson robes, pacing up and down Callias's lavish courtyard. Some foreign Sophists-in-training and a group of prominent young

Athenians walked behind Protagoras, hanging on his every word. Among them were the sons of Pericles, Paralus and Xanthippus, nicknamed the "cabbage suckers" by those who considered them slow-witted. As Socrates observed Protagoras being followed around by his students, he was reminded of having seen a beautifully choreographed dance in which the devotees of Orpheus were portrayed falling under the spell of his voice. To crown it all, Alcibiades arrived, accompanied by a wealthy nobleman named Critias, about ten years his senior, who had invited him, for the first time, to hear Protagoras speak and perhaps become his student.

Socrates was most intrigued by the claim that an orator could *teach* wisdom and virtue. Protagoras encouraged his followers to use reason as their guide to living wisely. His most famous slogan was "Man is the measure of all things, of those that are that they are, of those that are not that they are not." Despite its oracular nature, it earned him the reputation of being the first ever humanist. Later, he wrote a book, *On the Gods*, that opened with the following words:

> About the gods I am able to know neither that they exist nor that they do not exist nor of what kind they are in form: for many things prevent me from knowing this, its obscurity and the brevity of man's life.[7]

According to some, it would eventually lead to Protagoras's exile from Athens on charges of "impiety," like Anaxagoras before him.[8] Whereas the natural philosophers were perceived as atheists, however, Protagoras thought it was safer to position himself as an *agnostic*.

Socrates approached Protagoras and told him of a young man he knew who was looking for the best teacher available. The

Sophist replied that he was old enough to be the father of anyone present and had pursued this profession for many years. He added that he must be cautious, though, as he traveled between cities persuading the finest young men to leave their previous teachers and follow him instead. "My wisdom can arouse jealousy," he said.

Sophistry was an ancient art, according to Protagoras. The writings of great poets, especially Homer and Hesiod, taught virtue, as did the mystery religions, such as the cult of Orpheus. Many athletic coaches and musicians, he claimed, secretly taught virtue. Their most prominent students were young noblemen from wealthy and powerful families, who sought to acquire the qualities of a future leader. Fearing persecution by their political enemies, these tutors practiced Sophistry under various guises but thereby risked being accused of dishonesty, if they were discovered. Protagoras, to avoid this charge, became the first to *openly* assume the title. He therefore wished to answer Socrates's questions before a larger audience, because it gave him a chance to turn the conversation into a public performance, demonstrate his expertise, and defend his art. Callias and Alcibiades quickly gathered the others.

Socrates repeated before the assembled crowd that his young friend, who was looking for a teacher, wished to know what Protagoras actually taught. Protagoras smiled and with a voice as sweet as honey, addressed his pitch to the room: "From the very first day that he becomes my student, he will go home a better person, and the same will happen every day thereafter." The Sophist was pleased with his answer, as it earned a round of applause. Socrates, unimpressed, responded with a shrug. The same would be true, he argued, whatever is learned, as all education improves us in some regard. Protagoras had spoken too vaguely about *how* his teaching was meant to improve his students. Physicians teach medicine, and musicians teach music, but what exactly, asked Socrates, does a professional wise man teach?

Protagoras replied that although some of the younger Sophists taught everything from astronomy to poetry, he focused on teaching the ability to have good judgment and give good advice. His students learned how to manage their own private lives, and their estates, well. They would also study the art of politics and excel in public life, in both their words and actions. This piqued Alcibiades's interest. Protagoras seemed to be implying that he could teach one how to emulate his friend Pericles's greatness as a political orator and statesman.

"If I understand correctly," said Socrates, "you are, in effect, promising to teach the art of good *citizenship*, which surely amounts to the same thing as teaching virtue or how to become a good person." Protagoras nodded in assent. Although Socrates had received an answer, everyone could see from the expression on his face that questions still troubled him about Protagoras's response. A few moments of silence followed. Then Socrates said something so bold that it caused a few gasps. "The truth is, Protagoras, that I have never believed that this could be taught by *anyone*. Although, if you say you can teach it, I assume you are sincere." All eyes were on Socrates as he began to elaborate.

He told them that he had two key reasons for calling Protagoras's statement into question. The first was that the Athenian Assembly did not appear to believe that virtue could be taught. When it was making decisions about matters such as building triremes or fortifications, the Assembly only consulted experts, who had knowledge of the relevant technical arts. Yet Pericles had seen to it that every male citizen had a right to speak on general questions of governance and justice. None of these men were expected to have specialist training in the art of good citizenship. This, said Socrates, implied that the Assembly thought the virtues relevant to public life were common property rather than being the product of education.

The same goes for private life, which Socrates introduced as his *second* point. If virtue could be taught, as Protagoras claimed, why did the *greatest* Athenians not teach it to their own children? "Look at these two young men," he exclaimed, gesturing toward Paralus and Xanthippus. "Pericles, their father, has provided the best education for them in everything that can be taught, yet with regard to virtue," said Socrates, furrowing his brows, "they are left to browse like stray cattle, picking up nourishment wherever they may find it . . . and the less said of their relative, young Alcibiades, the better." Nobody made a sound. Though most in the room were aghast at his candor, Socrates continued.

"There are many men who, despite being good themselves, have never made their own children, or anyone else, good," observed Socrates casually. Nobody, except perhaps Alcibiades, wanted to hear any more controversial examples, so out of respect for Protagoras, Socrates concluded. "When I consider the matter in this way," he said, turning to the Sophist, "I doubt that virtue can be taught." "However," he added, "I may be mistaken in this, as I know you are a man of great learning with much experience in education, so please explain how it is possible to teach men wisdom or any other virtue."

Protagoras smiled for a moment. His followers, unsure what to make of this eccentric former sculptor, exchanged glances; a few had taken offense. Protagoras was growing slightly irritated with Socrates but attempted to conceal the fact. "I would welcome the opportunity to explain my views to you," he said in a voice so charming that the whole audience appeared to fall back under its spell. "Rather than developing an argument, though, I think it would be most pleasing if I simply told you a story." Socrates was about to object to what seemed like a diversion, but everyone else applauded Protagoras, begging him to speak. What followed was one of the most remarkable speeches in the history of philosophy. It would come to be known simply as The Great Speech of Protagoras.[9]

THE GREAT SPEECH OF PROTAGORAS

THERE WERE GODS, IN THE BEGINNING, said Protagoras, but no mortal creatures. When the time came, Zeus, the king of the gods, fashioned countless species of animals by mixing the elements of earth and fire. He then commanded two of the titans, Prometheus and his brother Epimetheus, whose names mean *Foresight* and *Hindsight*, to assign different abilities to each living creature.

Hindsight begged for the right to assign the abilities all by himself. Foresight agreed, and said that he would inspect his brother's work when it was done. Some creatures were slow moving and so to make up for this, Hindsight gave them great strength. Others were weak, so to these he granted speed. Some creatures he armed, while others were given various forms of protection. Small creatures were granted winged flight or the ability to conceal their dwellings underground for safety. Large beasts had their size for protection. He took care to grant all creatures some means for their own preservation.

Having equipped all living beings to survive among each other in this way, without fearing that one species should eliminate another, the titan next granted them protection against their environment and the harshness of the seasons. He covered some animals with skin tough enough to endure the heat of summer and others with thick pelts, to ward off the cold through winter months. Some he shod with strong hooves and others with padded feet, to walk upon the rough earth. Every creature was assigned its own source of food. Some pastured on the earth, others ate fruits hanging from trees or dug up roots from the ground. Still others were hunters who fed on the weaker animals. To these predatory creatures he assigned limited offspring, whereas their prey were so numerous that there would always be enough of them to serve as food.

Hindsight lacked wisdom, however, and having assigned to each species its own special capabilities, he realized he had nothing left to give humans. When Foresight inspected his brother's work, he found that man alone was born naked and had been left unshod, unarmed, and with no bed in which to lay his head and rest safely. Not knowing what else to do, he stole the technical expertise of the goddess Athena and gave it to humankind, along with the fire of Hephaestus, the blacksmith god. Together, these gifts allowed humankind to survive in the wild, though they were as yet unable to found cities.

Once human beings were granted these divine gifts, they sensed their kinship to the gods and began praying and building altars to them. They invented clothing, bedding, dwellings, agriculture, and even the use of language to express their thoughts and acquire learning. Men lived apart at first, in scattered isolation, but finding themselves beset continually and harassed by wild beasts, they sought to build cities for their mutual protection.

However, no sooner than humans had gathered to save themselves, being still lawless, they began to wrong one another and fighting broke out among them. The wisdom that governs our relations with other people, the art of politics, belonged to Zeus alone, king of the gods and patron of friendship and families. Without the art of *war*, which is part of *politics*, men did not know how to conquer their enemies, build alliances, or secure peace. Scattering once again from their failed cities, they continued to perish in the wild.

Looking down on this chaotic scene with dismay, Zeus feared for the destruction of the human race. He therefore sent Hermes, his messenger, to teach mortals about justice and to instill in them a sense of shame concerning wrongdoing, as a deterrent against injustice. By this means, Zeus now granted humankind the capacity to unite themselves in cities, maintaining order through the bonds of friendship and fostering their sense of community.

Hermes asked Zeus whether he should distribute the virtue of justice and other social and political arts among men *selectively*, in the same way as knowledge concerning the technical crafts. One man who possessed the knowledge of medicine, he said, was enough to benefit many men, one architect was enough to build many houses, and so on.

However, Zeus decreed that every human being must be granted at least some knowledge of justice and a sense of shame regarding their own wrongdoing. Finally, he set it down that if a criminal was found incapable of respecting the rule of law, he should be exiled or put to death as a plague on the city.

With this, Protagoras concluded his story, and the audience broke into applause, led by Alcibiades. Their hearts swelled because the great speech seemed to glorify the democratic ideals of Athens by means of its allegory. Pericles, like Zeus in the story, had said that the welfare of the city depended on the ability of every Athenian citizen to have his say regarding matters of justice, whether sitting in the courts or participating in the Assembly, a right granted to them by his ancestors. The Sophist waited for the cheers and adulation to die down, and then began the concluding part of his argument.

Before Protagoras had given his crowd-pleasing speech, Socrates had told the audience that he doubted whether virtue could be taught. His first objection noted that *any* male citizen was permitted to speak in the Assembly, without expert training, on questions of a general nature, such as what is just or unjust. Protagoras, having finished declaiming, now answered Socrates's criticism by explaining that this is because anyone who claims to be ignorant of justice risks being expelled from society or even put to death. Indeed, if someone does not display the virtues of a good citizen, the people think he deserves to be punished, precisely because they think he *should have learned* such virtues.

No intelligent and civilized man, Protagoras explained, punishes a wrongdoer simply because he has done wrong. To do so would not be justice but merely the mindless violence of a wild beast. The wise consider it unjust to punish past wrongs as a form of revenge. They realize that we cannot undo what has been done. Instead, their intention is to deter both the wrongdoer and whoever witnesses his punishment from committing similar crimes in the future. This attitude toward punishment presupposes not that virtue is innate but rather that most human beings *learn* virtue because Athens, and its laws, compel them to avoid vice.

"So, while I agree with you that the Athenians are right to consult only builders or shipwrights when it comes to making fortifications or ships," said Protagoras, "nevertheless, every citizen is expected to have some knowledge of civic virtue precisely because it can be taught and it is considered a disgrace for anyone not to have learned it."

Socrates's second objection had been that great men, such as Pericles, often raise children who are no wiser or more virtuous than anyone else. The answer to this, said Protagoras, lies in the same observation. "Is it conceivable," he explains, "that the greatest men of Athens have taught their sons every art *except* good citizenship, the one which might save them from being punished by the state, with exile, death, or even the ruin of their whole family? As soon as a child can talk, his parents, nurses, and tutors strive to make him as good as possible, pointing to every action, saying, 'This is just,' 'This is unjust,' 'This is wise,' 'This is foolish,' and so on. If he is unwilling to learn, they punish him, with threats and blows, until they straighten him out like a crooked piece of wood. "Given that so much effort is put into the teaching of virtue," said Protagoras, "would it not be surprising if it were unteachable? Nobody can afford to be a layman in the art of virtue," he adds, "if he wants to be part of a city.

"As everyone is being taught to be a good citizen, the children of the leading citizens face stiff competition. Suppose a law required every citizen to learn the flute or risk punishment by death or exile. The sons of the best flute players would face so many rivals that they would be unlikely to stand out as much as their fathers. Nevertheless, everyone would play better than if they had received no training. Likewise, even the most unjust person reared in a city, having learned its laws, excels in justice compared with barbarians who have grown up in the wild. Almost everyone in Athens is a teacher of virtue, although you pretend you are unable to see even one. You may as well claim, Socrates, to see no teachers of Greek, although that is learned from the speech of everyone around us."

Protagoras insisted that virtue was more widespread than it seemed. Socrates raised an eyebrow at this, as the Sophist had enriched himself by claiming to turn good citizens into great leaders, offering to train them until they excelled in virtues such as wisdom and justice. "If any man is the least bit more advanced in virtue," explained Protagoras, "he should therefore be prized for his wisdom, and I consider myself to be such a person." The great Sophist was confident that he was worth the fees he charged. Indeed, he says, a student need only pay the full price if he wishes; otherwise, he may go into a temple, swear under oath how much he thinks the lessons are worth, and pay that amount.

"And it is no wonder," said Protagoras in conclusion, "if Paralus and Xanthippus" (he waved his hand in their direction) "have not yet attained the reputation of Pericles, their father, when lads their age, who are the sons of artisans, such as great sculptors, have yet to surpass their own fathers in the arts for which they are known." Socrates smiled awkwardly. "It was not fair of you to accuse these two of lacking wisdom and virtue," Protagoras said diplomatically, "for they are still young, and there is yet hope they will become great men like their father."

The two sons of Pericles smiled when they heard Protagoras's compliment. The room erupted in cheering and applause. Except for two individuals: Socrates, who was still looking intently at Protagoras, and young Alcibiades, whose gaze was now fixed on Socrates, as if he wanted to study every word of his reply.

THE DIALOGUE WITH PROTAGORAS

ONCE HE SAW THAT PROTAGORAS had nothing more to add, Socrates rose to his feet. "I used to believe," he said, "that there was no method by which a man could become good, but now Protagoras has all but persuaded me, except for one small obstacle, which I am sure he will deal with quite easily."

First, though, Socrates pointed out that fine speeches like this could be heard from Pericles and other orators, who emulated

Protagoras and had memorized his words. If you asked them to explain some point, however, they would be as unable to answer your questions as the inanimate pages of a book. Indeed, such men make it difficult to question anything because what answers they do give turn into prepared speeches, which, like the ringing of a bronze bowl, sound like they could go on forever. In other words, Protagoras, as the originator of these teachings, was the only one able to explain the reasoning behind them, and Socrates, finally, had a chance to pin him down.

"I only require you to answer one simple question," said Socrates. Protagoras nodded in assent. "You said that virtue is teachable, and I have heard you mention justice, temperance, and other such things. Could you be more precise? Are justice, temperance, and so on, distinct *parts* of virtue or are these all just different *names* for the same thing?"

"That's easy to answer," replied Protagoras, smiling as though it were a familiar question. "Virtue," he said, "is one thing, which has several parts. Think of the way in which a person's face is made up of parts such as the mouth, nose, and eyes. What we refer to as virtue can be divided up, in the same way, into qualities such as justice, temperance, and so on." "In that case," said Socrates, "can someone have one part of virtue without having the others?" "Of course," replied Protagoras, "for whereas some men exhibit courage but also injustice, others may exhibit justice but lack wisdom, and so on." "So wisdom and courage are also parts of virtue?" said Socrates. "Indeed," said Protagoras, "and of all the parts of virtue, wisdom, in fact, stands above the others." "But they are *different* from one another?" asked Socrates, who was beginning to frown, as he often did, when puzzled by some paradox that, as yet, everyone else had failed to notice.

"Well then," asked Socrates, "suppose someone asked us whether piety is just or justice is pious?" Protagoras hesitated, saying that it was a difficult question. He did not think the virtues were identical but reluctantly agreed that they are similar, although he insisted the resemblance was trivial. Socrates exclaimed in mock surprise, "Are you saying that the relationship between justice and piety is only very slight?" Protagoras scowled in irritation, so Socrates changed tack. "Let us examine these similarities," he said, "in order to decide how important they are."

Socrates adopted a more serious expression: "Do you believe, for instance, that those who act *unjustly*, in so doing, judge the consequences of their actions *wisely*?" Protagoras launched into another beautiful speech, which won applause but failed to answer the question. "My apologies," said Socrates, "but I happen to be a very *forgetful* person." Protagoras raised an eyebrow. "You will have to cut your answers short," Socrates insisted, "if you want me to follow you." Protagoras knew this was a ruse meant to force him into playing the "question and answer" game, at which the philosopher excelled. "Socrates," he exclaimed with a sigh of frustration, "I have taken part in debates with many men over the years, and I have earned a reputation for wisdom throughout Greece, but if I were to agree to answer these sorts of questions, I fear that I would never be deemed superior to anyone again."

At this point Callias intervened. He was keen to hear Socrates's questions answered, he said, but didn't want to offend his guest of honor. An argument ensued about whether Socrates, who was about to leave, should be allowed to question Protagoras more rigorously. Suddenly, Alcibiades leaped from his seat, exclaiming, "You're talking *nonsense*, Callias! Protagoras must allow his reasoning to be put to the test in a debate with Socrates, and not spin out long speeches to fend off difficult questions, going on and on until everyone has forgotten where he started!" Critias laughed. "Alcibiades, as usual, wants to be on the winning side." Protagoras, shifting awkwardly, agreed to continue and, after some further digression, submitted himself again to Socrates's interrogation.

Socrates insisted that he merely wanted to clear up some questions that still troubled him about the idea of teaching virtue. As usual, that seemed like it could be true but not the whole story. His thinking was obviously a step ahead of Protagoras, although it was unclear exactly where he was taking the conversation. "The question I asked was this," said Socrates. "Are wisdom, justice, courage, temperance, and piety all names for one thing, called virtue? You had said that, on the contrary, they are distinct aspects of virtue, like the different parts of a face." Socrates asked whether the Sophist had changed his mind. Protagoras twisted his lips into a smile, barely concealing his unease. He said he believed that the other parts of virtue were somewhat alike but *courage* was something quite distinct from the rest. "This is proven," he said, "by the fact that we find many people are extremely unwise, unjust, intemperate, and impious, and yet exceptionally courageous."

Socrates leaned forward. "Would you describe courageous men as being *confident*?" "Yes," replied Protagoras, "insofar as they are ready to act where most men would be afraid." After some discussion, however, they agree that even the insane and those consumed by rage may exhibit a sort of rash confidence. This stems from ignorance, Socrates noted, and should not be confused with the virtue of courage, which requires knowledge about what one is doing. The courage and self-confidence in battle of a well-trained hoplite, for example, would be completely different from the rash and foolish self-confidence of a madman who, in a rage, grabs a weapon without understanding how to wield it or the dangers of doing so wrongly.

"Most people believe that our minds are ruled by the desire for pleasure and avoidance of pain," mused Socrates, "and that men are dragged around and enslaved by their passions in this way." He asserted, however, that genuine wisdom is more powerful than pain or pleasure, and Protagoras agreed. "Few will be convinced, though," said Socrates, "because it seems the passions can easily usurp one's reason." People say, for instance, that they are overcome by cravings for food or drink or sex, which they indulge in ways that are bad for them, despite knowing that they will later regret their actions. They see the better path but follow the worse.

"Most people will tell you," explained Socrates, "that though certain forms of indulgence feel pleasant, they may have unpleasant consequences, such as poverty, illness, and suffering, and deprive us of other pleasures. Likewise," he added, "they think of athletic exercise, military training, and medical surgery as good things. Despite often being unpleasant or painful, these sort of activities may bring about good health, which is ultimately pleasant. So," he concluded, "they regard pleasure as good and pain as bad in themselves, and in terms of their consequences. Indeed, the majority consider some action good if the overall pleasure it causes outweighs the pain. It is judged bad, however, if it brings about more pain than pleasure."[10]

"When someone claims he is seduced by a desire he knows to be wrong," said Socrates, "what he often means is that he has sacrificed a greater pleasure in the future to enjoy a lesser one now. Likewise," he added, "when he says he has been overcome by fear, he means that he has fled from a lesser pain now, at the cost of suffering greater pain in the future." Protagoras nodded.

"Everyone knows that appearances are deceptive," continued Socrates. "Things nearby look larger than when seen from a distance, a noise sounds louder when closer than when farther away, and so on. Most people recognize that their well-being requires both having sufficient temperance or self-control to abstain from small pleasures in order to obtain larger ones and having the courage to endure small pains if it helps to avoid larger ones."

"Those who lack self-control," added Protagoras, nodding, "often feel they have sacrificed the better course of action in order to take the worse." "Their ruin," said Socrates, "evidently lies in the misleading power of appearances. So why don't they realize that their salvation requires a sort of wisdom, a method of *measuring* their pleasures and pains rationally, as if weighing them against one another in a set of scales?" Protagoras listened without saying a word, as though he was beginning to glimpse where Socrates's questions might be leading.

"Appearances have us wandering all over the place in confusion," said Socrates, "because they constantly deceive us about what is greater or lesser, when it comes to pain and pleasure, in ways that lead us to regret our choices. The art of measuring these things rationally would, by contrast, ground our decisions in reality rather than appearance, leading us to peace of mind." Protagoras agreed that such an art would promise to deliver us from our irrational fears and desires, and that this was obviously a type of knowledge, which would allow us to distinguish appearance from reality when it comes to the consequences of our actions. "Precisely what this knowledge consists in," said Socrates, "does not matter for now. What matters is the realization that it is in knowledge, of some kind, that our salvation lies."

"Those who believe that their good intentions are easily overcome by the desire for pleasure or fear of pain," said Socrates, "would have found it ridiculous, at first, if they heard us say that what overcomes them is a type of *ignorance*. Many of them would now be surprised, I think, to find themselves conceding that their lack of temperance and courage is due to a lack of *knowledge*, regarding the measurement of pleasure and pain. Yet it follows from everything we have so far agreed." Most people, in other words, greatly underestimate the role of cognition, or thinking, in shaping their desires and emotions.

"It is moral ignorance that the teachers of virtue, educated men such as Protagoras and his friends, claim to be able to cure," added Socrates. "Many people nevertheless place more value on their money than upon the knowledge in which their salvation, and that of their children, might lie, so they refrain from paying Sophists for their wisdom." Socrates asked Protagoras and his fellow Sophists in the audience if they agreed, and they did, wholeheartedly.

"What then is fear?" asked Socrates. "I put it to you," he said, "that fear is an expectation of something bad." Everyone agreed. It is against human nature, he added, for any man to approach what he believes to be bad, or painful, rather than what is good. "Would anyone, then, based on what we've been saying," asked Socrates, "be willing to go toward what he fears when he can avoid doing so?" Protagoras nodded uneasily in agreement.

"Well then," said Socrates, "when a courageous man and a cowardly one both face something they believe to be as bad as can be, does one approach it and the other flee to safety?" The Sophists agreed. "How is that possible," asked Socrates, "as we have just agreed that no man, whether courageous or cowardly, willingly approaches what he considers bad, *except* to avoid a greater evil?" With this, the mood of the audience shifted slightly, as the conversation was becoming more serious. Alcibiades, the youth famed for his courage, had been laughing and enjoying the debate with his friends, but something about this remark struck a chord within him. His gaze was now completely fixed on Socrates, as if he had forgotten about everyone else for the time being.

"Come on, Socrates," scoffed Protagoras, "what the courageous and the cowardly go toward are two opposite things—one goes to war while the other flees to safety!" "The courageous go to war because they consider it honorable to defend their country, do they not?" asked Socrates. Everyone agreed. "And because they believe honor to be the greatest thing in life," added Socrates. "So are you suggesting that the cowardly refuse to go toward what they know for certain to be more honorable, better, and more pleasant?" he asked. Protagoras admitted that this would contradict what they had agreed earlier.

"Therefore," said Socrates, "the fears of the courageous man are neither foolish nor disgraceful, but the fears of the coward are both foolish and disgraceful." Protagoras was forced to agree that men are cowards because of their ignorance concerning what it is or is not appropriate to fear. "Would the opposite of this ignorance, Protagoras, not be wisdom concerning what is and is not to be feared?" asked Socrates. The Sophist nodded silently, although clearly displeased at having to agree. "So, to sum up, is not *courage* simply *wisdom* about what is and is not to be *feared*," asked Socrates, "and is not cowardice, the *opposite* of this, a form of *ignorance*?" Protagoras refused even to nod in agreement now and said nothing. "Will you not say yes or no to my question?" insisted Socrates. "Answer it yourself," said Protagoras with a sigh.

"As you wish," replied Socrates, smiling, "but first I have one more question to ask. Do you still think, as you did at the beginning, that a man can lack wisdom and yet still be courageous?" Protagoras reluctantly conceded that it seemed impossible, based on their discussion, for a man lacking wisdom to have the virtue of courage. Socrates explained that his only reason for asking was that getting to the truth about these matters would allow them to answer the original question with which they were both concerned—namely, whether virtue can be taught.

What impressed many observers was that Socrates showed no sign of taking pride in winning the argument. Though he had approached Protagoras saying that he believed virtue could *not* be taught, their positions had reversed during the discussion. "Now, I find myself arguing," said Socrates with a shrug, "that justice, temperance, and courage are all types of wisdom, or knowledge, in which case virtue would appear to be the sort of thing that can be learned." "Protagoras," he said, "you wanted to say that the virtue of courage was something other than wisdom, in which case it would appear *not* to be teachable." Although Protagoras claimed to be wise, Socrates's questions showed the Sophist to be confused about the nature of virtue, the very thing in which he claimed to be an expert. How could he teach others what he did not understand himself?

Though Socrates had argued for its teachability, he was in fact still not entirely clear what virtue was and *how* it could be taught. He wanted to review the main points of their discussion, but the Sophist declined. "Socrates," he said, "I respect your enthusiasm for debate and the way you navigate through an argument." He heaved a sigh. "I am not the sort of man to take offense. Indeed, I have told many people here today that I admire you more than anyone I have met, at least among your generation. I would not be surprised if you gain a high reputation for wisdom. I would be happy to examine these questions later, whenever you wish, although for now, I think, it is time to turn our attention elsewhere." With their conversation over, they parted company.

THE PRACTICE OF
COST-BENEFIT ANALYSIS

DURING HIS DIALOGUE WITH PROTAGORAS, Socrates outlined a rational therapy of the passions or, in modern parlance, a form of cognitive psychotherapy. We could also describe it as a *philosophical* therapy, which aims to replace irrational fears and desires with rational ones.

Fear, he says, is due to the belief that something bad or painful will happen, a belief that can easily be mistaken due to false appearances. Conversely, desire can be seen as the belief that something good or pleasurable will happen, which can also be mistaken. We are especially prone to being misled by appearances when we focus too much on the present and fail to take account of the consequences of our actions. For instance, drinking a bottle of whiskey might appear pleasant at the time, but it can give us a painful hangover the next day. Socrates anticipated modern psychotherapy by suggesting that both the *causes* and the *cures* of our emotional problems may be *cognitive* in nature. That's quite remarkable, as these ideas only became established in modern psychotherapy with the so-called cognitive revolution during the 1950s and 1960s.

Socrates described a method of "rational measurement" that compared the longer-term consequences of our actions, in terms of the pleasure or pain they are likely to cause, to help decision-making. This weighing of pros and cons is very similar to what cognitive-behavioral therapists call cost-benefit analysis, which is an integral part of a more comprehensive method called "problem-solving therapy" (PST).[11] In some form or another, evaluating the consequences of a course of action plays a key role in almost all forms of CBT. For example, individuals who suffer from phobias and similar forms of anxiety usually *avoid* facing their fears. One of the first tasks in therapy is to show that the long-term benefits of confronting feared situations outweighs the short-term discomfort doing so inevitably causes. To someone with a dog phobia, the prospect of reaching out and stroking a dog appears worse, or as they usually say, *feels* worse, than that of simply avoiding doing so. Avoidance is everyone's favorite coping strategy because, at first, it invariably *seems* like the easiest option.

Often a therapist will help clients to reevaluate their coping by asking them to consider the pros and cons of alternative ways of behaving. For instance, here are some typical pros and cons of exposure therapy, which would require a dog phobic to endure being near a dog for a prolonged period.

1. **Cons.** You're going to feel uncomfortable and highly anxious during the prolonged period of exposure (perhaps twenty minutes or more).

2. **Pros.** By doing this repeatedly, you're likely to significantly reduce, and even eliminate, your phobic anxiety. Your self-confidence and general ability to cope with anxiety will probably also improve as a result. You will be able to do things you couldn't do before, like walk in the public park with your children, which could even improve your quality of life and relationships.

Sometimes cognitive therapists teach clients simply to ask themselves, regarding a particular course of action, "What do I have to *gain*?" and "What do I have to *lose*?" I think Socrates would have recognized this weighing of pros and cons as an application of the "art of measurement" that he discussed with Protagoras.

The same method can be applied, of course, to any number of different situations, including problems related to our *desires* and addictions as well as our fears. Suppose I crave cigarettes. I might compare the short-term pleasure and other seeming benefits to the longer-term problems that smoking can cause. Of course, most people will object that knowledge alone is seldom enough to overcome our most powerful fears and desires. We all know the better course of action but follow the worse. Socrates acknowledged that people would laugh at him, at first, for claiming that *knowledge* can overcome pain or pleasure. As he put it, people believe their problem is one of being overcome by fear and desire, or pain and pleasure, not one of being overcome by ignorance.

Nevertheless, as he explained, this is only because the pains and pleasures we experience in the present moment seem more intense than distant ones, which we anticipate in our future. He's describing a *cognitive bias*, which psychologists today call "temporal discounting." We react more easily to what is more immediate and *salient* than to what we know to be real, if it is less apparent or more distant in time. A cold beer that is in front of us seems more appealing than the prospect of receiving several cold beers tomorrow. Understanding the effect these cognitive biases have on us is, of course, a form of self-knowledge. You could even say that wisdom consists in knowing our own biases and attempting to compensate for them, in order to think about our lives more rationally.

Here are some specific techniques that can help to make the long-term consequences of a behavior more salient and therefore more effective in shaping our actions.

1. Spend more time than normal considering the long-term consequences of a course of action (e.g., by describing

them aloud or, even better, in writing) as if they were happening in the present moment. For instance, with smoking, you might write down the potential damage to your health, in detail, then read it aloud and revise it to add more details.

2. Elaborate on them by considering their pros and cons across different domains (e.g., your physical and mental health; your work life, studies, or hobbies; your relationships; your daily routine; and so on). For instance, to continue the same example, you might consider the long-term financial cost of smoking, how it may affect your confidence and self-esteem, any potential negative influence on your children and other relationships, inconvenience caused and time wasted, and so on.

3. Visualize them, in your imagination or by drawing pictures or diagrams, as if they're happening now. For instance, you might imagine seeing your face in twenty or thirty years, as a smoker, and then contrast that with how you might look in the future if you changed your behavior and quit smoking today.

4. Remind yourself of these consequences regularly—for instance, by writing them on a note and reading it several times each day, while using some of the techniques above.

To give another example, if you wanted to overcome a fear of public speaking, it might be helpful to write down a list of the long-term benefits of doing so. Consider how it would improve your confidence in several areas of life, and try to picture that regularly, as if it were happening right now.

THE YOUTHS OF ATHENS

AFTER SOCRATES LEFT CALLIAS'S HOME, the other Sophists talked late into the evening about the conversation they had
witnessed—apart from one youth, who left shortly after Socrates,
lost in his own thoughts. Alcibiades knew he had much to learn
before he could ever claim to be as wise as his guardian, Pericles.
His desire for greatness, which seemed to burn brighter than that
of anyone in Greece, had brought him into the company of the
great Sophist, but he did not become his disciple.

Alcibiades was struck by the questions Socrates asked. The
young noble already realized that self-confidence is all too often
confused with courage. No person who is ignorant of the danger
they face can justifiably be called courageous. In wrestling and
other combative sports, as well as in real fighting during warfare,
the overly confident are easily defeated. The courageous judge the
danger they face accurately but place less value than most on the
pain they may suffer and more on the glory of victory. Alcibiades
wanted more than anything to prove his courage, win great victories, and achieve lasting fame. Whenever he behaved more fearlessly than the other youths, it was, he realized, because he had
convinced himself that the benefits of doing so outweighed the
costs. Because Alcibiades desired glory more than he feared any
pain or loss, he was willing to risk far more for it than any of his
contemporaries. He must have felt as if Socrates had been speaking directly to him when he said that, in a sense, courageous men
overcome pain by calculating the consequences of their actions.

As Socrates's fame and influence grew, he would find that some
men were averse to his method of questioning, whereas others,
like Alcibiades, found it exhilarating and strangely addictive. At

the time of this conversation with Protagoras, the Sophist was aged nearly sixty, while Alcibiades was still in his late teens. Socrates noticed that older men with a reputation for wisdom had more at stake in such debates and were therefore reluctant to submit themselves to his questions. The pain of losing an argument and being temporarily made to look foolish seemed far worse to self-proclaimed wise men than any beneficial consequences they could imagine. The Sophists, in particular, had become very wealthy by professing to be wise and were afraid of damaging that reputation. Over time, Socrates would come to realize that he could learn more by questioning the youth of Athens, precisely because nobody considered them to be wise.

6

THE LION OF ATHENS

THE GREEK CITIES WERE DEFENDED by citizen armies, traditionally based on the middle class, to which Socrates belonged. These men could afford to provide themselves with a panoply of high-quality weapons and armor. They formed the phalanxes of hoplites, or heavy infantry, men armed primarily with eight-foot spears, but also carrying swords for close-quarters combat, who were the backbone of the army. In the case of Athens, they were supported by a large navy, crewed mainly by lightly armed poorer citizens and foreign residents.

Socrates, like all male Athenians, would have spent much of his youth in the gymnasia, training in wrestling and other sports, to prepare him for the military service that was every citizen's duty. At eighteen, he took the sacred oath, swearing to protect Athens, respect the laws and constitution, and honor the religion of his fathers, in order to become an *ephebe*, or military cadet. He would have completed two years of basic training before becoming a full-fledged hoplite. Now in his late thirties, he had probably already seen active service, perhaps in the Battle of Coronea, where Alcibiades's father was slain.

Philosophy, religion, athletics, the arts, and military training were not as distinct in ancient Athens as they are today. All these activities took place in the gymnasia, where philosophers and orators mingled with poets and wrestling coaches, providing the education that would help create the next generation of Athens's citizen-soldiers. Upsetting this traditional system of education, by questioning the wisdom and values of established teachers, could be seen as subversive, and a threat to the whole state. If Socrates was able to ask more radical questions than foreign intellectuals like Anaxagoras or Protagoras, it was, in part, because he had already earned the respect of his fellow citizens for displaying exceptional self-discipline during his military service. He had yet to earn acclaim for exceptional bravery.

Since the Persian invasion had been defeated, at the Battle of Plataea, by a combined force under the leadership of Sparta and Athens, most of the Greek cities enjoyed relative peace. Now this period of truce, known as the Pentecontaetia or Fifty Years, was about to come to an end. In 433 BCE, the city of Corinth, Sparta's most powerful ally, sent a fleet to attack the island of Corcyra (modern-day Corfu). The Corcyrians, a former Corinthian colony, had initially refused to ally themselves with either side in the conflict but now begged Athens for help. The Corcyrian fleet was the third largest in Greece next to those of Athens and Corinth, which meant that whoever joined forces with the Corcyrians would dominate the seas.

The terms of their truce, known as the Thirty Years' Peace, prohibited Athens from instigating an attack against a member of Sparta's Peloponnesian League. To avoid a war with Sparta, therefore, Pericles said he was merely sending a small squadron of ships, ten initially, to help defend a neutral state. Today we might call Pericles' strategy one of minimal deterrence. At first the Corcyrans seemed to be winning the sea battle, but eventually they were routed by the huge fleet of 150 ships sent by Corinth. However, the presence of the Athenians stopped them from pressing their victory and invading Corcyra, as they feared the political ramifications of breaking the peace treaty. The furious Corinthians immediately dispatched envoys to Sparta to complain about Athens's interference in the battle. As the Spartans patiently listened to their allies, knowing that the Athenian navy now dominated the seas, it became obvious to them that a great war was looming.

Since his return from Delphi, in an effort to understand Apollo's pronouncement, Socrates had gone around Athens questioning one learned man after another, but, starting with Protagoras, he had only succeeded in exposing their ignorance.[1] The most arrogant of them grew to hate him, as did their friends and associates. As the speeches of politicians and Sophists were peppered with quotes from the poets, Socrates turned to this group next. He found that some poets became conceited because of their mastery of language, and assumed themselves also to have great wisdom concerning matters such as justice and the good life. Socrates was disappointed to find, however, that they were no better at interpreting the significance of their poems than anyone else.

Art, he concluded, was created not through reason but through some kind of inspiration. Much like the Pythia and other oracles, the poets uttered apparently wise sayings, which they did not fully understand, and hence they often contradicted themselves. Nevertheless, certain sayings, such as "Know thyself" or "Nothing in excess" or even the pronouncement "No man is wiser than Socrates," provide launching points that can lead us toward wisdom if we think for ourselves and critically examine their meaning.

Finally, Socrates returned to his own former class, the artisans. They could certainly be called wiser than him in areas where he lacked expertise, such as making shoes or building ships. Success in their field led some, like the poets, to lay claim also to great moral wisdom. When he questioned them, however, it became evident that this was nothing more than conceit on their part. Although Socrates's questioning continued to provoke the anger of many, he felt he had no choice but to continue. It was the only method by which he could hope to discover the meaning of Apollo's oracle.

Having questioned the acclaimed intellectuals, politicians, and artists, Socrates noticed more glimmers of wisdom in the answers given by those *without* a reputation for great learning. When asked the right questions, such as how to define the qualities they most valued in life, and given a chance to reflect on any errors or contradictions in their own reasoning, even a lowly slave or prostitute might provide more insightful answers than an acclaimed intellectual, such as Protagoras. Perhaps there was an obvious explanation for this. Those without a reputation to defend incur less disgrace when they are refuted. In particular, older men who made a good living as teachers often exhibited less willingness to be questioned, and less capacity for learning, than their young students. Could our desire to *appear* wise be one of the greatest obstacles to acquiring real wisdom?

Socrates referred to these adventures, wandering around Athens from one philosophical dialogue to another, as his own "Herculean labors." He never managed to refute the oracle of Apollo by finding anyone who possessed genuine wisdom. Nevertheless, by questioning others and examining their beliefs, he acquired self-knowledge and perhaps a different *sort* of wisdom. "To concern myself with knowing that which is none of my business while still ignorant of my own self," he said, "would be ridiculous." Instead, his philosophy focused on ethics and increasingly resembled psychological therapy. "Am I inflamed with passion, a complex beast, like the Python," he began to wonder, "or am I a gentler, and more straightforward, creature?" The great dragon, Python, slain by Apollo at Delphi, could symbolize unbridled, irrational passions, such as fear and anger. Socrates wanted to ascertain if there was any vestige of this monster lurking within his own pscyhe.

By contrast, Apollo, who symbolized reason, sanity, and moderation, would become a kind of patron god of Socratic philosophy. Apollo was also the god of youth. Socrates realized that he could not do this alone. The great men he questioned were of little help. They were more concerned with appearing wise than actually being wise, and thus feared disgrace more than they loved wisdom. Socrates, therefore, turned his attention to a youth who seemed less fearful of disgrace than anyone else in Athens.

THE FIRST DIALOGUE
WITH ALCIBIADES

ONCE HE REALIZED THAT THE Sophists were reluctant to submit themselves to his method, Socrates decided to try questioning Alcibiades, one of the most gifted youths he'd seen in their presence. So he approached the young noble, and sat down beside him on a bench in the Lyceum. This took some courage. Alcibiades was much sought after and did not suffer fools—he had a habit of using his fists against those he considered pests. Although it seemed an unlikely match to most observers, Socrates glimpsed something of himself in Alcibiades, and the young man's fearless nature might make him honest in the answers he gave. So, armed with the knowledge that Alcibiades detested flatterers, Socrates approached him with the intention to do the opposite by criticizing his flaws.[2]

"Son of Cleinias," he said, "you must have wondered why, as others pestered you all these years, I remained silent." Rather than dismiss the philosopher with a sarcastic comment, Alcibiades looked intrigued. Socrates explained that his "divine sign" (*daimonion*) had kept him from approaching, but something had changed, and it no longer restrained him. The philosopher rarely spoke of this mysterious inner voice, except to say that it would occasionally warn him against certain courses of action and that he had always found listening to it worthwhile. The conversation they were about to have must therefore have felt to Socrates like an important step in response to his calling, the mission given to him by Apollo. His sign appeared to be telling him that something special was about to happen.

"Many men have approached you who had a high opinion of themselves, but you have turned every one of them away," said Socrates, "because you have an even higher opinion of your own worth." Despite having lost his father at an early age, Alcibiades's life was blessed. He was tall and handsome. He had powerful friends and relatives in Athens, the greatest city of Greece. He came from an influential family, both on his mother's and father's sides. He was the ward of Pericles, the greatest statesman in living memory. "You are also extremely wealthy," added Socrates, "although you seem to take pride least of all in this. I have often overheard you boast, in fact, that you have no need for anyone or anything." "All of that is true," said Alcibiades curtly, "so I wish you would tell me what you want."

Socrates looked at him searchingly. "If I thought that you were content with these advantages, I would have kept my silence," the philosopher said. "However, I believe you have greater ambitions."

"What on earth do you mean?" exclaimed Alcibiades. "Allow me to explain," replied Socrates. "It appears to me that if some god were to ask whether you wished to go on living as you are now and never possess anything greater, or to die that instant, you would prefer to die." Alcibiades looked startled. "That is true," he said hesitantly, "but you speak of something I have never dared to admit in public." Socrates had looked inside this young man's heart and glimpsed a love of glory, or *philotimia*, which burned stronger than anyone else suspected—Alcibiades had aspirations that extended far beyond the boundaries of the Athenian Empire.

"Your desire, unless I am mistaken," continued Socrates, "is shortly to present yourself as an advisor before the Assembly, which you hope will come to honor you even more than it does Pericles." Alcibiades raised an eyebrow, but he did not deny the claim. "You picture yourself becoming, in due course, an elected general and imagine leading a united Greece, in which Athenians and Spartans, once again, fight side by side. Not only that but you also hope to rule over barbarian races, beginning with the Thracians, to the north of us. More than anything, however, I think you dream of crossing into Persia at the head of a Greek army, which is why you love to talk so much about the great kings of Persia, Xerxes and Cyrus." Alcibiades was by now quite captivated. "You seem to know me better than anyone, Socrates," he said, "but why should my ambitions be any of your concern?" Socrates smiled warmly as he spoke, although their conversation was becoming more serious. "Because," he answered, "it will be impossible for you to achieve all the things you have in mind without my help."

He knew that Alcibiades had the potential to become Athens's leading statesman. It would take more than just fine words and the appearance of wisdom, however, to achieve such ambitious goals. He would need real knowledge and strength of character.

The Sophists could train political orators to be skilled at persuading others, but they did not know how to create great leaders who exhibited genuine wisdom and justice.

"It is my belief," continued Socrates, "that the god did not allow me to speak to you until I could demonstrate that neither Pericles nor any of his friends and advisers can help you achieve your true goal—only Socrates can." "You seem far stranger to me now," replied the young noble, "than you did when you kept your silence. Tell me what makes you so sure of all you say? I am willing to listen if you have prepared a speech," offered Alcibiades, gesturing for Socrates to take the floor. "That is not my way," replied Socrates. "Rather, as I think you know, I can better demonstrate my point if you are willing to answer some questions." "Ask away," said Alcibiades, smiling in amusement at the unconventional nature of the request. Whereas Protagoras was reluctant to be systematically questioned by Socrates, Alcibiades appeared quite intrigued by the process.

"Suppose," continued Socrates, "that you are mounting the speaker's platform at the Pnyx to address your maiden speech to the Assembly. What if I were to take you aside first and ask whether you believe you understand the matter in hand better than they do?" Alcibiades said that he would, of course, only rise to speak if he knew enough about the subject and if his advice would benefit the people.

"Would you agree," asked Socrates, "that you either learned whatever you know of your own accord, or were taught it by someone else?" "That goes without saying," said Alcibiades with a shrug. "And you would never have learned anything of value unless you wanted to do so, and made an effort to learn it?" "That, too, seems obvious," replied Alcibiades, looking puzzled. Socrates smiled. "There must, therefore," he said, "have been a time when you believed that you lacked the knowledge that you later attempted to learn." Alcibiades thought for a moment, then nodded.

Socrates listed all of Alcibiades's teachers—renowned experts on grammar, music, athletics, and so on. "Do you hope," he asked, "to advise the Athenians about any of these subjects?" "Of course not," said Alcibiades. Indeed, his teachers would have made better advisors when it came to their areas of expertise. "What do you wish to advise the Assembly about then?" asked Socrates. "Such things as when to go to war and when to negotiate peace," replied Alcibiades. "What do we call it when such decisions are made well?" asked Socrates. Alcibiades looked away for a moment, thinking carefully, then turned to Socrates and replied, "I suppose what you mean is that good political decisions are the ones most men would describe as being *just*."

"That's right," said Socrates. "So do you recall a time," he asked, "when you believed that you were ignorant of justice and sought a teacher from whom you might learn its nature?" "You're making fun of me," exclaimed Alcibiades. "Come now," said Socrates, "was there ever a time when you believed yourself to lack knowledge of what was just or unjust?" Alcibiades looked unsure. Socrates continued, "When you were a mere child, I witnessed you with the other children, and even with your teachers, behaving like you were sure of yourself in this regard. Indeed, I have often overheard you asserting in a bold voice that some scoundrel was acting unjustly, is that not so?" Alcibiades laughed. "What else would you have had me do when they were cheating or up to no good?" "Then even as a young boy," said Socrates, "you must have believed that you knew right from wrong, is that not so?" Alcibiades agreed. "How then," asked Socrates, "did you acquire this knowledge concerning justice?" "By Zeus," said Alcibiades, looking puzzled, "I cannot answer that question." For a moment neither man spoke. Then Socrates broke the silence: "And yet you said a moment ago that in order to have learned something there must have been a time when you realized you were ignorant of it, and *wanted* to learn it."

Alcibiades frowned and shifted uneasily while reviewing the conversation in his mind. Suddenly, he looked up, exclaiming, "Perhaps I was confused by your questions, Socrates. I believe I *did* learn the nature of justice, not from a teacher of the sort you mentioned but from everyone—from the people!" "How so?" asked Socrates. "Can we consider the people to be good teachers of subjects in which they squabble over even the most basic points?" "Clearly not," said Alcibiades. "And yet," Socrates continued, "the people agree with one another least of all when it comes to what is just or unjust. They fight," he added, "for what they consider just, and they blame one another for what they consider unjust." Alcibiades nodded emphatically. Socrates looked him dead in the eye: "And the Battle of Coronea, in which your own father died . . ." Alcibiades turned his gaze down as he completed the sentence, "was also fought over a disagreement about what was just."

"Would it be reasonable then for us to claim that the people understand justice," asked Socrates, "when they disagree so violently about it?" Alcibiades frowned and gestured no.[3] "If these are your only teachers," said Socrates, "is it likely you've learned the *true* nature of justice?" Alcibiades took a deep breath and lowered his head. "So are you saying," asked Socrates, "that Alcibiades the beautiful, the son of Cleinias, does not know what is just or unjust, but assumed he does, and was about to go to the Assembly to advise the Athenians on matters he knows nothing about?"

"By the gods, Socrates!" Alcibiades cried out, alarmed at his own confusion. "I don't know *what* I'm saying anymore. Your questions have already led me one way, then another, until it feels as if I'm losing my mind." Socrates calmly asked, "Don't you recognize this condition?" Alcibiades appeared shaken, and instead of answering clutched his head between his knees. "Well," said Socrates patiently, "if someone asked you whether you have four hands or three eyes, would you keep changing your mind about whether to answer yes or no?" Alcibiades looked up and gestured to indicate that he would not. "That's because you are certain of the answer," explained Socrates, "but if you kept changing your mind it would suggest you were *uncertain.*" "I suppose so," replied Alcibiades. "But when someone is ignorant of something, does he give conflicting answers about it?" "I imagine so," said Alcibiades. "Well, let's see," replied Socrates, "do you know how to fly up high in the sky?" "Clearly not," scoffed Alcibiades. "There you are," said Socrates, "despite your ignorance, you're *not* confused about how to answer that question—but why is that?" Alcibiades, blushing with shame, admitted he had no idea.

"Let me explain," said Socrates. "So long as you *know* that you *do not* know something, you're not confused. It's only when we think we know something that, in fact, we do not know, that we become confused." Alcibiades listened carefully. "When we falsely believe that we know something, our actions are guided by ignorance, and we make mistakes. If we recognize our ignorance, however, and we are reasonable men, we will seek counsel from experts. If you know that you know nothing about medicine, for example, you will obtain the guidance of a physician. Someone who falsely assumes that he is a medical expert, though, will behave in a confused manner due to his intellectual conceit. He will contradict himself and may even make dangerous mistakes. If such conceit leads him to advise others, whether in private life or in the Assembly, his ignorance will endanger not only himself but his friends, and perhaps even the entire state." Alcibiades stared down at his hands, deeply concerned by this remark.

"Someone who believes he knows what he does not know will therefore become confused and make errors," said Socrates, "and those who are confused about the most important things in life will make the most serious errors of all." Alcibiades agreed but he was worried where this was leading. "Can you name anything more important than *justice*?" asked Socrates. Alcibiades lowered his gaze again. "That was precisely what you were confused about, a few moments ago," added Socrates gently. "You wouldn't be alone, however, in rushing into the affairs of the city without first learning what is just and unjust. Indeed, very few lack this conceit," said Socrates.

"Why, then, should I be concerned," said Alcibiades suddenly, "if the majority of those who compete to win the ear of the Athenian people are uneducated when it comes to justice? I am no worse off than my rivals in that regard, and my natural ability will allow me to surpass them." "If only they were your main concern," said Socrates. "What do you mean?" retorted Alcibiades. "With whom else am I in competition?" "You should look to Sparta and Persia," replied Socrates, "and study those enemies with whom Athens has most frequently been at war. If your ambition is to unite many cities, then you need to understand that Spartan and Persian kings are your rivals and *not* your fellow Athenians."

Socrates patiently detailed the superior wealth and military discipline of Athens's traditional enemies. To cap it all, he brought up the famous hero of the Democrat faction, whose achievements he knew Alcibiades envied. "A generation before you were born," he said, "Themistocles managed to give Athens a navy and defeat the Persians, despite lacking wealth, noble birth, and all the other advantages you possess." Alcibiades was about to speak but paused, as he noticed his hands were slightly trembling. "He achieved all this," continued Socrates, "because he was a man of great knowledge who had studied the enemy, despite which the Athenians eventually turned against him." What the philosopher meant was that great leadership and popularity do not always go hand in hand.

Then something extraordinary happened, which took even Socrates by surprise. Alcibiades, who longed to surpass the achievements of Themistocles and Pericles, suddenly realized how unprepared he was to lead Athens. Tears began to roll down the young man's cheeks. He leaned against Socrates, who stroked his head. Alcibiades was weeping with shame.

"You're barely twenty years old," whispered Socrates gently, "and by your own admission completely uneducated with regard to the most important matters." He had never seen anyone respond like this to his questions, with such painful remorse for his own shortcomings. Yet Alcibiades's desperate need to become a great leader and win glory for Athens exceeded any shame he felt over admitting his ignorance. And he grieved that he was not the man he ought to be.

Socrates waited in silence for a few moments, then used his staff to draw an outline in the sand. It was a rough map of the known world, based on those created by the Ionian philosophers. He asked Alcibiades to point out Athens, which he easily did. "Now show me where your houses are," added Socrates. Alcibiades owned a lavish townhouse in Athens and two rural estates nearby in the Attic countryside. He struggled, though, to pinpoint their exact locations. "You see," said Socrates, "they don't add up to even a tiny fraction of the world, and yet you hold them in such high regard!"

"Do you really believe that you can put your trust in your good looks, noble birth, and property," asked Socrates, "so long as you lack wisdom and virtue? If you were to follow the advice inscribed at Delphi to *Know thyself*, you would care for your soul more than your property, and outdo, in that regard, even the kings of Sparta and Persia." Socrates explained that as our true nature lies in the mind and not the body, to know oneself surely means to know the mind. Alcibiades looked intently at him. "We need to be clear about what we are, and how best to care for ourselves, if we're to follow that famous maxim," said Socrates, "but I think we've failed to understand its true significance." "What can you possibly mean?" asked Alcibiades.

Socrates furrowed his brow and peered out from under his bushy eyebrows. "The inscription, it seems to me, advises us to know ourselves in no ordinary way," he said, "and I can only compare it to an unusual feature of the human eye." He leaned in a little, raised his head, and looked directly at Alcibiades. "Suppose," he continued, "that instead of instructing you to *know* yourself, Apollo instructed your eye to *see* itself." "I would imagine he meant," said Alcibiades, "that the eye must look at something in which it could perceive its own image, such as the reflection in a mirror." "Indeed," replied Socrates, "but an image of our face may also appear when we look at the face of another person." Alcibiades thought for a moment before exclaiming, "Yes, that's right, if we look closely enough, we can sometimes glimpse our own reflection in the pupil of their eye!" Socrates was impressed. "So an eye looking at an eye, indeed at its very center," asked Socrates, "would see its own image?" Alcibiades nodded in agreement. Amused by this idea, he began shifting a little as they spoke, trying to glimpse his own reflection in Socrates's eyes.

"Indeed, the eye sees itself only when it looks directly into the other's pupil, the very part capable of vision," said Socrates. "Likewise, the soul knows itself only when it looks directly into the soul of another, at the part capable of knowledge. When we examine another's capacity for wisdom, we provide ourselves with the purest mirror available among mortals," said Socrates. Alcibiades was fascinated. "By this means," concluded Socrates, "we may best do as the Delphic maxim advises and come to know ourselves."

"Where one lacks knowledge, however," said Socrates, "it is better to be led by experts." Alcibiades, somewhat reluctantly, nodded in agreement. Socrates argued that ignorance of ourselves therefore condemns us to a slavish existence, inappropriate for anyone who wishes to be free, let alone anyone who would lead others. "Do you recognize this as your condition?" he asked gravely. Alcibiades, still with tears in his eyes, replied that he was becoming painfully aware that this was his problem. "How then can you escape from the slavery of ignorance?" asked Socrates. "God willing," said Alcibiades, "I will be saved, for I will be following you, and from this day forward you can be sure that I will begin to study the nature of justice, and I will not let up until I learn how to be a great statesman." "I hope you do," said Socrates ominously, "but I am afraid for you. Not because I do not trust in the goodness of your nature but because this city may be powerful enough, in the end, to destroy us both."

THE PRACTICE OF ILLEISM

AESOP SAID THAT WE'RE BORN with two sacks hanging around our necks: one large sack, right under our noses, containing everyone else's flaws; and a small one, hidden behind our back, which contains our own flaws.[4] Self-knowledge, in other words, is difficult. Our worst character defects, or biases, are visible to others, but we have a blind spot for them ourselves. As the New Testament put it: you can see the tiny fleck of wood in someone else's eye but not the great beam of wood in your own.[5] Without a mirror for our soul, we're often simply oblivious to ourselves. Blindness to our own errors presents a serious challenge, of course, for anyone concerned with self-improvement.

Modern psychology may help shed some light on Socrates's proposed solution to this problem. Igor Grossmann, the head of a research center at the University of Waterloo in Canada, specializing in the psychological study of wisdom, has found evidence that we exhibit better judgment when considering other people's problems rather than our own.

> We chose the term Solomon's Paradox to identify the contradiction between thinking about other people's problems wisely, but failing to do so for ourselves. The Biblical King Solomon, known for his keen intellect and unmatched wisdom in guiding others, failed to apply wisdom in his own life, which ultimately led to the demise of his kingdom.[6]

In one study, Grossmann and his colleagues described a hypothetical relationship problem to participants in two groups. One group was asked to imagine it was a friend's problem, the other group's participants, to view it as if it were their own.[7] The group examining the problem as if it happened to a friend scored 22 percent higher on ratings of intellectual humility, 31 percent on open-mindedness, and 15 percent on compromise.

What if we could help ourselves to overcome the psychological limitations associated with Solomon's paradox by studying our own reflection? Socrates reputedly advised some of his followers to contemplate themselves in mirrors, as a way of examining their own moral character.[8] However, he also believed that we can see our reflection in the character of others. Socrates appears to have imagined being in his interlocutor's shoes, sharing their assumptions and making similar errors to theirs. The Socratic method uses the person answering as a mirror, reflecting the image of the questioner. Philosophical dialogue with others helped Socrates to examine his own beliefs with greater detachment and objectivity. When we read philosophical dialogues, or, better still, engage in a *real-life* dialogue, we gain a broader perspective from which to consider our own way of thinking. By observing someone else's reasoning, we can more easily imagine the consequences of holding a particular belief, such as how it might affect one's character and actions, whether it conflicts with other beliefs, and how it might relate to a variety of different situations.

Moreover, it looks like Socrates himself adapted the philosophical method employed in the dialogues for *solitary* use. When someone asked one of his followers what benefit he had obtained from studying philosophy, he replied, "the ability to hold conversations with myself."[9] Indeed, we find several references to Socrates having philosophical conversations with himself, which may help to explain this intriguing remark. In Plato's *Hippias Major*, for example, Socrates keeps referring to a strange man who relentlessly pesters him with questions—a close relative, who even shares his home. He waits there to challenge Socrates when he returns from his conversations. This man reminds Socrates that he should be ashamed to use words such as *wisdom*, *justice*, and *beauty*, if he can't even define their meaning.

"And yet how are you to know," he will say, "either who produced a discourse, or anything else whatsoever, beautifully, or not, when you are ignorant of the beautiful?"

He tells us that the questioner who waits for him is "Socrates, the son of Sophroniscus, who would no more permit me to say these things carelessly without investigation than to say I know what I do not know." In other words, the strange man is Socrates himself, viewed as if he were *another person*. It seems that even after Socrates had finished having a dialogue with a Sophist, or one of his own friends, he would continue the discussion with himself in private, in his imagination.[10]

A closely related method involves referring to our own thoughts and actions as if we were talking about those of someone else. Third-person self-talk is known as "illeism" (pronounced ILL-ee-ism), from *ille*, the Latin pronoun for "he." We don't even need to use our imagination for this, just our *words*. For example, rather than thinking "*I'm* really upset and I don't know what to do!" (in the first person), I might say to myself "*Donald* is really upset and he doesn't know what to do!" (in the third person).

A recent pair of studies on illeism asked a total of 555 participants to record their thoughts in a journal for four weeks.[11] To test whether wise reasoning could be cultivated in daily life, participants were to write about various social experiences that happened each day, one group using first-person and the other third-person language (illeism). Those employing illeism were found to have improved on ratings of "wisdom," measured in the same way as above. The study also found that in some cases illeism reduced negative emotions, such as anger or frustration, in participants' relationships.

Similar verbal techniques have long been used in cognitive

psychotherapy. Aaron T. Beck and his colleagues advised clients suffering from anxiety disorders to practice detached self-awareness: "Look at your thoughts, feelings, and actions as if you're a friendly, but not overly concerned, bystander."[12] They describe this as learning to "watch myself watch myself," in language highly reminiscent of Socrates's analogy of the eye that looks at itself. Moreover, using third-person language can, they claim, help a client to "increase self-awareness by voluntarily choosing to distance himself from his anxiety."[13]

Beck and his colleagues also recommended an exercise in which someone observes his thoughts and feelings throughout the day in order "to gain a more objective picture of himself." He is instructed to replace first-person pronouns with third-person pronouns and his own name ("Bill," for example). He therefore gives himself a running commentary, as if observing the thoughts of another person, such as, "Bill seems to be scared. His heart is beating. He seems to be concerned that others are thinking poorly of him. Bill is focusing on the impression he is making." Similar techniques have become increasingly common in more recent "mindfulness and acceptance" approaches to CBT, such as Acceptance and Commitment Therapy (ACT).[14]

Socrates certainly employed illeism, referring to himself in the third person, but he *began* by searching for his reflection in *other people*. He found an *unlikely* mirror for his soul in the form of Alcibiades. For when Socrates asked him about justice, the son of Cleinias gave honest answers and made honest mistakes: the kind Socrates could imagine making himself. Neither did Alcibiades run away from Socrates's questions. He almost became hooked on this process, later saying that Socrates's questions, having troubled him at first, finally possessed him—making his heart beat faster than a Corybantes in a trance. "His words make my tears flow," the young noble said, "and I have seen a great many others affected by him in the same way."[15] He claimed it was impossible for him to go on as he once had, thinking only of himself, once Socrates had forced him to dedicate himself to justice in the affairs of Athens.

Socrates saw in Alcibiades the potential to become a philosopher and also, because of his ability to influence his fellow citizens and the need he felt to achieve excellence, a great statesman. Whatever others may have thought of Alcibiades, Socrates clearly saw him as a young man who, at some level, wanted not only to *appear* wise and just but to actually *be* so. Together they would embark on a philosophical journey that neither man could have accomplished alone.

THE BATTLE OF POTIDAEA

SOCRATES'S HEART FELT AS IF it had stopped beating. Time froze. He watched helplessly as Alcibiades was struck in the thigh by a javelin. His shield dropped from his grasp, and he fell roughly to the ground.[16] The young noble, glimpsing an opportunity for glory, had charged among the enemy.[17] He fought like a lion and succeeded in taking down several Corinthians. Enemy skirmishers quickly surrounded him, though, pelting him with their weapons from a distance, while he struggled to defend himself. The opening words of the ephebic oath taken by all of Athens's citizen-soldiers could not have been far from Socrates's mind as he looked on: "I will never bring reproach upon my hallowed arms, nor will I desert the comrade at whose side I stand."

Somehow, Socrates managed to reach Alcibiades's side. There he stood with his sword drawn, staring down the enemy, poised to single-handedly protect his young friend. As more Athenian hoplites ran to their aid, Socrates got the wounded Alcibiades back on his feet and retrieved his sword and shield. Together they were able to join the Athenians making a tactical retreat, back to the safety of their fortified camp on the beachhead.

They had been sent to besiege the city of Potidaea in the Chalcidice peninsula, where northern Greece bordered the "barbarian" realm of Thrace.[18] Originally a colony of Corinth, Potidaea had become one of Athens's tribute-paying allies. In 432, Athens, fearing that the city was on the verge of rebellion, sent a military expedition to reestablish control. This backfired by triggering an open revolt. The Corinthians sent a large force of hoplites to the region. The situation quickly escalated, with the Athenians bringing in several waves of their own reinforcements. They proceeded to besiege the heavily fortified city of Potidaea but found themselves under attack by the Corinthians and cavalry from nearby Macedonia. After some initial skirmishes, a stalemate ensued. Athens sent another contingent of reinforcements. This happened to include both Socrates, by this time a veteran hoplite, aged thirty-eight, and Alcibiades, who, aged twenty, was seeing active military service for the first time. In the summer, they fought the pitched battle in which Alcibiades was wounded. Although the Athenians won, they now found themselves engaged in the longest and most expensive siege of the war.

Socrates should have been awarded the military prize for bravery, having risked his own life to save a fellow hoplite. Alcibiades had also exhibited conspicuous courage, however, and the generals wanted the prize to go to a noble. Socrates enthusiastically agreed with their decision, knowing that, in any case, it was better to deserve an award than to receive one. Alcibiades therefore accepted the customary crown of golden laurel and suit of armor. He would forever remain indebted to Socrates for having saved his life during his first military expedition. The philosopher's selflessness in allowing his young friend to take the decoration also set Alcibiades on the path to an illustrious military and political career.

From that day on, whenever they served together, although the philosopher should have messed with his demesmen, Alcibiades insisted that he and Socrates share the same tent, eating, sleeping, and taking their exercise together. As a result of this proximity, Alcibiades, for the first time, observed his friend entering a trance. One summer morning, while the Athenians were still preparing to return from the siege, Socrates became lost in thought and remained standing in the same spot on the beach without moving a muscle. After taking their evening meal, some Ionian soldiers became so captivated by his odd behavior that they laid out their camp beds beside him and kept watch over him throughout the night. Behavior of this sort contributed to Socrates's reputation for being an *atopos* individual, someone highly eccentric and out of the ordinary.

Socrates stood there, cataleptic, for no less than twenty-four hours. He only emerged from his meditation at daybreak the next morning, when he abruptly turned toward the rising sun and said a short prayer before returning to his tent. Unlike Anaxagoras, who merely thought of it as a fiery mass, Socrates appeared to regard the sun with a kind of reverence. When Alcibiades asked him what he had been doing, Socrates replied that after having spent some time questioning the Sophists and other men who were reputedly wise, he had come to feel that Apollo, speaking through the Pythia, had meant to pose him a question. "What question?" asked Alcibiades. The philosopher lowered his voice slightly: "Would you prefer, Socrates, to remain as you are, having neither the knowledge nor the ignorance of these men, or would you rather become like them, knowing nothing but *believing* that

you are wise?" Socrates had answered immediately that it was better to remain as he was. No sane man, he said, would choose to be
ignorant of his own ignorance.[19]

This question, however, continued to trouble him. How could
he hope to avoid falling into the same trap as the Sophists by
falsely believing that he was wise when he was not? Having con-
templated this at great length, he now arrived at the conclusion
that he should continue to examine others. Witnessing Alcibiades's brush with death on the battlefield also seemed to have affected Socrates. He increasingly saw it as his divine mission to
practice his philosophy in public, on the streets, in collaboration
with his friends and, indeed, anyone else who would join their
conversations. On his return home, he would increasingly turn
his attention from the Sophists, or teachers, toward their students, the young men of Athens, such as Alcibiades.

Knowing oneself is extremely difficult, perhaps impossible,
without the use of something analogous to a "mirror for the mind."
We often lack self-awareness because we make assumptions, and
we exhibit the sort of biases that are easier to spot in other people
than to notice in ourselves. First and foremost, though, looking
in this mirror requires a type of *courage*. When Alcibiades had a
mirror held up to him by Socrates, what he saw reflected was not
a dashing and eloquent noble but a confused and foolish young
man, misled by his own conceit. By contrast, Socrates, because
of his virtue, seemed beautiful and divine to Alcibiades—like an
image of a god hidden inside the statuette of a grotesque satyr.

Just before the Battle of Potidaea, one of Alcibiades's tutors had
become jealous of the young noble's admiration for Socrates. He
denounced the philosopher's character on the streets of Athens
by claiming that his outward features revealed that he was a dim-
witted and vicious man, adding that Socrates had the look of

someone obsessed with women. Socrates's young friends found this ludicrous, and Alcibiades laughed out loud. To their surprise, though, Socrates replied that the man had a point. In fact, he turned the criticism into a compliment by saying that he was, indeed, by nature a very flawed and wretched individual, but that through philosophy he had improved his own character beyond recognition. It was one of many occasions when his friends got the uncanny impression that Socrates was joking and being ironic while nevertheless also making a serious point.[20]

With this incident in mind, it's easy to imagine how Socrates might have stared deep into the eyes of Alcibiades and concluded, paradoxically, that he was looking at his own mirror image. Yet what he glimpsed in the eyes of his beloved was not the image of the Socrates that we know. He saw his own potential vices and errors in Alcibiades, but also a capacity for virtue. At least, he hoped that was what he saw. Speaking of the young noble, Aristophanes quipped:

> *It is best not to rear a lion in the city,*
> *But if one is reared, minister to its ways.*[21]

After introducing him to philosophy and saving his life in battle, Socrates now became responsible for rearing a lion in Athens.

7

THE PELOPONNESIAN WAR

IT WAS EARLY EVENING WHEN the transport ships carrying troops returning from Potidaea sailed into Piraeus, the port city neighboring Athens. The campaign had kept them away from home for nearly three years. Alcibiades and Socrates, who had become almost inseparable, disembarked together. As the ships had rounded Cape Sounion, sailing along the coast toward the harbor, they saw nothing ahead except scrubland where once had been olive groves, vineyards, and barley fields. Farmhouses lay abandoned and derelict. Athens's victory in the north should have been a cause for celebration. Upon disembarking the ship, however, they found Piraeus crammed with refugees from the surrounding countryside, and the streets lined with beggars, often showing the scars of disease.

Each summer since the siege of Athens began, the Spartans had invaded Attica, the region containing Athens and Piraeus, razing the crops. Each summer, Pericles ordered the countryside evacuated. At its peak, the population of Attica was roughly a quarter of a million; about fifty thousand lived in the city of Athens and almost as many in Piraeus. A fortified corridor known as the

Long Walls connected Athens with its port so that even when besieged, supplies could reach the city by sea. During the annual invasion, the rural population withdrew behind the city walls, which Sparta lacked the siegecraft to penetrate. The city's inhabitants would therefore almost triple in number.

In the second year of the war, with food already in short supply, a terrible illness swept through the city.[1] It began with a high fever, inflammation of the eyes, and swelling in the throat and tongue, after which symptoms spread throughout the body: sneezing and coughing, vomiting and diarrhea, rashes and pustules on the skin. Groups of sufferers, reeling and confused, crowded around fountains, desperate to quench the raging thirst brought on by the disease—they probably contaminated the water in doing so. Within eight days, about a quarter of the infected lay dead. Physicians were powerless to help. Over three years, the plague would claim many tens of thousands of Athenian lives, perhaps even exceeding the number of casualties from fighting in the war.

The plague had also changed society. Since Athens's enemies were largely unaffected, the gods, it seemed, had singled out their city for punishment. As desperation took hold in Athens, so did political cynicism and corruption; at the same time, religious disillusionment and superstition were on the rise. The Spartans who roamed the Attic countryside watched the funeral pyres burning from a safe distance. Between warfare and disease, the Athenian military was significantly weakened, and the soldiers' troubles were only just beginning.

Socrates and Alcibiades had received word that Pericles had succumbed to the plague not long before their ship docked at Piraeus. They marched, eyes downcast, into Athens, via the Long Walls, along with the rest of the returning hoplites. During their lengthy absence, the glorious city of Pericles had been reduced to a pitiable condition. Alcibiades entered the city wearing the hero's crown, awarded to him for valor at Potidaea. When they reached the city gate, he was met by his kinsmen, and together they walked to the Kerameikos and the tomb of his famous guardian. First his father and now Pericles had been taken in their prime. Alcibiades only made it home from Potidaea thanks to Socrates. He must have felt the gods spared him for some great purpose. The legacy of his clan, the Alcmaeonids, and the future of the Athenian democracy founded by them, now rested on his shoulders.

Socrates also came home a hero but found himself walking a very different path from the young man whose life he had saved. The philosopher trod through the city alone. He stopped at a small wrestling school near the Acropolis, to see if anyone he recognized was there. Sure enough, familiar faces immediately surrounded him: surprised, they called out and welcomed the philosopher home. Suddenly, Chaerephon appeared. Lunging forward like a madman, he grabbed his friend's hand and shrieked "Socrates, by the gods, are you all right? How did you fare?" "I arrived home in one piece," said Socrates, smiling, "as you can see." "We have heard the fighting was much worse than expected," frowned Chaerephon, "and many Athenians were lost." "That I can confirm," replied Socrates. "Sit down, then, and give us news, my friend," urged Chaerephon, "for we have yet to hear the whole story."

Chaerephon led Socrates to a group of young men, which included Critias, the noble who had accompanied Alcibiades when they watched Socrates question Protagoras. Like several of his aristocratic friends, he now grew his hair long, in the Spartan style, and wore it in braids. The young men gathering around Socrates desperately wanted to know how the war in the north was going. He explained that the initial fighting had been intense.

Nevertheless, the Athenians had managed to blockade Potidaea. However, when additional reinforcements arrived from Athens the previous summer, they brought the plague, which killed over a thousand of his fellow soldiers. Socrates was one of the few unaffected. During the second winter of the siege, Potidaea's starving inhabitants turned to cannibalism, but eventually they were forced to surrender. The Athenian generals sent by Pericles showed mercy, however, and permitted the rebels to evacuate, carrying a few possessions.

Socrates asked how things had been at home. Chaerephon explained that no sooner had the siege of Potidaea begun than Sparta summoned her allies to hear their latest complaints against Athens. The Corinthians, Sparta's most powerful ally, were furious, as Potidaea, like Corcyra, was a former colony of theirs, but this time one with whom they retained friendly ties. The two Spartan kings were reluctant to escalate the conflict, but their allies insisted that Athens had repeatedly broken the peace treaty. A vote was held in Sparta, and war was declared.

When the Spartans sent their hoplites to invade Attica, Pericles argued before the Assembly that Athens had no hope of winning a pitched battle against such elite infantry. He urged the population to retreat behind the city walls, even though it meant sacrificing their farmland. Pericles assured the people that their navy, which was vastly superior to any Spartan fleet, could make up for the damage by raiding enemy cities along the Peloponnesian coast. Following the first summer of the Spartan invasion, Pericles was required to deliver a funeral oration in honor of those who had fallen in battle. The speech he gave, which it was rumored Aspasia helped him write, became famous for extolling the virtues of the democracy that men had given their lives to protect. "Our government does not copy that of our neighbors," he said solemnly, "but it is an example to them. We are called a democracy, for the administration is in the hands of the many and not of the few."

He told them that "Athens is the school of Hellas," and that its citizens were more adaptable than their enemies. His words also hinted at a weakness, though. "Our enemies have not yet felt our united strength," he said, "as manning such a great navy divides our attention, and on land we are forced to send our own citizens into battle." His powerful voice sent shivers down their spines. "Such is the city for whose sake these men nobly fought and died," he continued. "They could not bear the thought that she might be taken from them, and every one of us who survive should gladly take up the fight on her behalf." Most of all, though, he used the occasion to call upon their sense of patriotism: "I would have you fix your eyes upon the greatness of Athens day by day, until you become filled with love for her, and when you are impressed by the spectacle of her glory, reflect that this empire has been acquired by men who knew their duty and had the courage to do it."

Pericles's military strategy was indeed wise, but he could not have foreseen that a plague would strike the overcrowded city and claim so many lives, including his own. Chaerephon explained that after Pericles's death, the Assembly had split into two rival factions led by Nicias and Cleon. Nicias, a moderate of noble birth, had inherited a share in the hugely profitable silver mines at nearby Laurium. He lacked the eloquence of Pericles but remained popular with the people because of his reputation for moral integrity and religious piety, and for his generous financial contributions to the city. He would prove to be a talented general but, unlike Pericles, was notoriously superstitious and at times hesitated to take decisive action. He favored negotiating peace with Sparta, which appealed to the oligarchic faction in Athens, though the terms he was willing to accept struck many of the poorer citizens as too favorable to their enemies.

Cleon, a businessman whose wealth came from his family's tannery, emerged as a political outsider, a demagogue who quickly gained popularity by attacking the ruling elite. He evolved into a radical populist, appealing to the lower classes with a distinctive approach in the Assembly, characterized by his cynicism, aggression, and forthrightness. He often whipped up public hostility toward Sparta but lacked the military experience to lead an army himself. Despite his popularity, he was dogged by allegations of corruption. Both men came from the same generation as Socrates. Alcibiades felt certain that they lacked the strategy and ambition to win the "Peloponnesian" war, and perhaps he had a point. Neither Cleon nor Nicias could ever unite Athens in the way that Pericles had.

Socrates soon wearied of discussions about the war and shifted the conversation toward his preferred topic: philosophy. Did any of Athens's youths, he wanted to know, show any aptitude in this regard? Critias was among those most eager to discover what they could learn from the eccentric philosopher, whose reputation had grown since the pronouncement of Apollo, especially with the news that he had saved the life of Alcibiades.

At first, Critias seemed as promising as Alcibiades, although he was more committed to writing than to politics. He was particularly interested in comparing the virtues of the Athenian and Spartan constitutions and had been studying the concept of virtue, which he felt could be reduced to "doing your own work." Although Socrates thought this sounded rather like looking out for one's own interests, he was impressed that Critias seemed to care enough to attempt a definition. After Alcibiades and Critias, Socrates attracted more young followers, whether he bumped into them at the gymnasia, in the shops of Agora, or in the homes of his more affluent friends. He hoped that training in philosophy might improve their characters and protect them against being corrupted by rhetoric and conceit, maybe even preparing them to become the next generation of leaders their city needed.

The war that followed the Battle of Potidaea exceeded any previously recorded in Western history. Whereas the Trojan War, if we are to believe Homer, had lasted ten years, this war between Athens and Sparta would last twenty-seven. The two main combatants were at the peak of their martial powers. Sparta had become the great beast of the land, with an infantry feared by every other nation. Athens had become the great beast of the sea, ruling the waves with a fleet of around three hundred ships. Most of the other Greek cities were forced to ally themselves with one side or the other, joining the Delian League of Athens or the Peloponnesian League of Sparta. The war would engulf the whole Mediterranean world and even drew in the neighboring "barbarian" races of Thrace and Persia.

The Athenians called it the Peloponnesian War after the region in which Sparta and most of her allies were located. The Spartans must have thought of it as the *Athenian* War and, although its first phase is named after the Spartan king *Archidamus*, we might also think of it as the War of Pericles, the Athenian statesman under whom it began. The Periclean war strategy was clearly stated and well known to every citizen: Athens must refrain from further expansion, hold her existing empire together, avoid fighting the Spartans on the land, trust in her navy, retain total control of the waves, and endure patiently until her enemies grew exhausted and sued for peace. Though distasteful at first to many Athenians, who would rather have gone out to fight and defend their farmlands, this strategy was based on sound knowledge of Athens's strengths and weaknesses as well as those of her adversaries.

Pericles was now dead, however, and the course of the war would soon be shaped by the influence of political orators pushing for a change of strategy.

Although Pericles was a Democrat, and something of a populist, he tried to reconcile the interests of common people and aristocrats for the greater good of Athens, and he would challenge the will of the people where necessary. Cleon was also a Democrat, but more radically populist, and in some ways the opposite of Pericles. If Pericles was a moderate, Cleon was an outright firebrand. To garner support, he denounced the prudent but unpopular strategy of withdrawing the population within the city. Although he inherited a lucrative business, critics claimed that he entered politics heavily in debt. He used the war, they said, as a cover for enriching himself by extorting money from Athenian aristocrats and foreign allies, accepting bribes, and embezzling public funds.

Pericles had appealed to what was best in the people; Cleon to what was worst. He would yell insults at his opponents in the Assembly, running to and fro, hitching up his robe and slapping his thigh, for dramatic effect. It worked. The people found his unusually brash style more entertaining than the polished rhetoric of established statesmen such as Nicias. In the aftermath of the plague, as Athens tried to reassert herself, Cleon's rhetoric became more violent, crude, and aggressive, as he attacked his critics rather than refuting them, but most often he carried the Assembly with him. Soon, this kind of outlandish behavior became normalized, and the political climate at Athens degenerated into partisan bickering. Genuine statesmen gave way to demagogues, who stoked the fear and anger of the citizens and pandered to their greed and other vices.

The change became evident the year after Pericles's death, when

Mytilene, the major city of the island of Lesbos, was discovered to have plotted a revolt against Athens, with aid from Sparta. Mytilene was one of the few members of the Delian League who avoided paying tribute to Athens by providing the coalition with crewed ships. In response to the revolt, the Athenians sent a fleet to blockade the city, while troops laid siege by land. When Spartan ships finally reached the northern Aegean, nine months into the campaign, Mytilene had already fallen. The Athenian Assembly was divided about what to do with the captives, presumably numbering tens of thousands. Cleon fumed that a show of strength was required: these foreigners are a threat to our state, he said, and they must be crushed. He moved that the entire male population of Mytilene should be put to death, and the women and children enslaved. The demagogue whipped up such outrage and lust for revenge among his fellow Athenians that they voted to send a trireme with orders for the troops surrounding Mytilene to carry out a massacre.

After reflecting on the decree overnight, however, many Athenians regretted the cruelty of the decision that Cleon had convinced them to make. They insisted on reconvening the Assembly. Cleon mounted the rostrum again and gave a speech that became infamous. The days of Pericles, in which sober debates about justice were the norm, were gone. Cleon launched into a shameless diatribe against the moderates who opposed him and, despite his own reputation for corruption, accused them of taking bribes. Yelling loudly above the opposing voices, he raged against the Mytileans, invoking every prejudice to blacken their name. An example must be made of their city, he boomed, warning other cities against contemplating revolt. The Athenians, he cried, were fooling themselves if they believed the Periclean myth that their empire was a civilized alliance of friends, held together by justice and diplomacy. They should realize it was pure despotism and their subjects were slaves, who must be forced into submission by punishing them until they learn to *fear* their masters. He induced terror in the assemblymen, stoking their fear of losing control and then working that fear up into anger and a lust for revenge. If Athens didn't have the strength to punish her enemies, he said, they would punish her. Teach them, he roared, *that the penalty for rebellion is death!*

After Cleon finally stepped down from the rostrum, the son of one of Pericles's former advisers, a moderate, stepped forward and called for reason. The two things most opposed to good counsel, he said, were haste and anger. The Assembly should give themselves time for sober debate. Cleon, he said, was fearmongering and manipulating the vote by attacking the character of anyone who disagreed with him rather than answering their objections. There was no logic to his strategy. The punishment he had demanded was so extreme that it would blacken the reputation of Athens for many years to come. Support for democracy among the lower classes in other cities, he said, was their greatest political asset. By punishing not only the powerful but the entire population, Athens risked losing its moral authority, which was the glue that held its fragile empire together.

The Assembly voted, by a hair's breadth, to change its decree. A second trireme raced through the night to catch the first ship, which had left a day earlier. Miraculously, it arrived just in time to avert a genocide. Cleon's opponents would later accuse him of using the threat of a massacre to extort money, for his own pockets, from the residents of Mytilene.

Cleon had stood before the Athenian Assembly and castigated the democracy itself for being incapable of governing an empire. He complained that the debates permitted by the Assembly led to delay and indecision. The Assembly was too easily swayed by rhetoric and changed its mind too easily, he said. Weak laws, he argued, which are subject to change, were worse than bad ones applied consistently. During a war, he claimed, the Athenians needed a strong leader like him, to save them from the chaos caused by indecision. Of course, by accusing his political opponents of corruption and escalating conflicts with other states, he could make this need appear more urgent.

It should have been obvious that Cleon was doing the very thing he accused his enemies of doing: manipulating the debate, through appeals to emotion rather than reason. Like many authoritarians, he managed to combine demagoguery *and* antidemocratic rhetoric. Socrates watched from a distance, observing how easily Cleon was able to conceal his own corruption by accusing his critics of corruption, undermining the democratic process, while posing as a champion of the people and promising to be their savior. Democracy worked if the people behaved rationally, but once they fell completely under the spell of a demagogue, rule by the people became a form of tyranny in disguise.

THE DIALOGUE WITH GORGIAS

THE MOST CELEBRATED ORATOR IN all of Greece arrived in Athens shortly after the Mytilenean debate, and caused quite a stir. Gorgias had been dispatched as an envoy from the Greek colony of Leontini, in Sicily, a large island located far to the west, off the tip of the Italian peninsula. Thanks to his rhetorical skills, Gorgias won Cleon's support in persuading the Assembly to send twenty warships to Sicily, commanded by a general named Laches. These Athenian warships were to help friendly cities who were fighting against Syracuse, an ally of Sparta, and the most powerful city on the island. Cleon was desperate to take credit for a military victory, but in the end the expedition achieved little. Laches and the other generals were later accused of being traitors and taking bribes, by Cleon and his faction, who sought to punish them for their perceived failure.

Socrates had heard that Gorgias resembled Protagoras and others Sophists, except that he focused not on the attainment of wisdom or virtue but on the art of oratory and the closely associated discipline of rhetoric. These skills were becoming important in Athens, not only because the power of persuasion could save one's life in the law courts but because it could sway the Assembly, causing them to vote for or against military campaigns. The fate of Athens itself and the lives of millions of people living in other Greek cities might hang on an orator's choice of words.

Rhetoric, Gorgias therefore believed, had an almost divine power, which could exceed that even of military might, because it can persuade men to agree to peace or declare war. Language is an all-powerful drug, he claimed, as words can cause us pain or pleasure, evoke fear or anger, fill us with courage, or bewitch our minds and lead us astray. It is more important than any other art because it allows a person to persuade anyone of anything, something a skilled orator may accomplish with surprisingly little effort.

"They say it's better to arrive late for a battle," said Critias wryly, "but early for a feast."[2] Since Socrates and Critias had first become acquainted, the haughty young aristocrat had shown some enthusiasm for philosophy, though his natural talent was poetry. Recently, both he and Alcibiades had begun taking lessons from Gorgias in order to advance their political aspirations, and both young men had shown a talent for oratory. Socrates and Chaerephon had arrived late at the Lyceum where an audience, including

Alcibiades and Critias, was listening to the Sophist finish a long and elegant speech. "That's Chaerephon's fault," said Socrates. "He wouldn't stop talking to our friends and kept us lingering in the Agora."

Socrates usually looked quite disheveled: he went barefoot and his favorite cloak was threadbare. However, today his clothing was torn, and his body was cut and bruised. As he had become bolder about questioning strangers, following his return from Potidaea, he not infrequently found himself being accosted in the street. Only this morning a wealthy Athenian businessman, indignant at the philosopher's questions, had kicked and beaten him. Socrates, as always, was unshaken. When witnesses urged him to sue the man for assault, he chortled, "If a donkey had kicked me, should I have dragged him into court?"[3] To many, his indifference to these attacks seemed like weakness, though, and it gave them the impression that he was afraid of speaking up in court, because despite his obvious cleverness, he lacked the eloquence to win a case.

Chaerephon offered to make up for their lateness by asking Gorgias the question that had been troubling his friend Socrates: "The art practiced by a physician is called medicine," he said, "but what is the proper term for the art in which Gorgias is an expert?" Critias interjected, defensively, that the great orator was exhausted from delivering a long speech. Hearing this, Alcibiades tried to answer on Gorgias's behalf with a half-serious digression about how oratory was the finest of all arts. This satisfied nobody. After some hesitation, Gorgias finally agreed to answer himself. Socrates, preemptively, insisted that the orator should refrain from making speeches and try instead to give an answer that was unambiguous and concise.

Gorgias smiled warmly. "My art is oratory, or public speaking," he said, "and I am one of the finest practitioners alive." "And you teach others to be orators like yourself?" added Socrates casually, as he reached down to rub his bruised leg. "Yes," replied Gorgias, "in Athens, and other cities."

Socrates paused for a moment, narrowed his eyes, and looked Gorgias up and down, from under his thick eyebrows, as though inspecting a horse. "Now, physicians aim to produce bodily health by the art of medicine," he said, "but what does the art of oratory or rhetoric produce?" "Speech," replied Gorgias pointedly. Critias and his friends sniggered. "That's wonderfully concise," smiled Socrates, "but perhaps you could elaborate." Gorgias replied that rhetoric was concerned with knowing how to speak well on any subject. Socrates objected that experts in other fields, such as medicine, must learn how to speak well by putting their knowledge of whatever subject they have studied into words. So what made rhetoric different—what did it study? "It has to do with the very greatest of human concerns," replied Gorgias, as he looked toward his students and smiled.

Socrates shrugged and remarked that if a physician were present, he would surely also claim his art dealt with the greatest of human concerns, and likewise a gymnasium instructor or a businessman. Gorgias, however, was not referring to health, beauty, or wealth, so what made him believe that his art was concerned with a greater human good than theirs? "Because rhetoric," said Gorgias, "not only confers *freedom* to those who possess it but also gives them the power *to rule over* others." Socrates asked him to elaborate, and Gorgias finally explained that, in his eyes, the art of rhetoric was of supreme importance because it allowed one to influence one's fellow citizens, by means of persuasion. "If you have enough expertise in oratory and the art of rhetoric," said

Gorgias, smiling, "that physician will end up as your slave, as will the gymnasium instructor, and the businessmen you mentioned will not be making money for himself but for you!" This elicited a few cheers from the young men listening.

Socrates asked Gorgias if he could be more precise. Teachers in every subject, after all, persuade their students to believe certain things. Gorgias answered that oratory was mainly concerned with persuading a group of citizens, such as a jury or political assembly, that one course of action is just whereas another is unjust. "So through the art of rhetoric an orator influences the beliefs of others concerning what is *right* and *wrong*?" said Socrates, summing up. "Precisely," said Gorgias.

Socrates asked Gorgias whether learning and persuasion were both capable of producing belief in listeners. He agreed that they were, although he was forced to concede that rhetoric differed from learning in that it produces belief in the absence of knowledge. "Then the orator persuades men on juries and the Assembly to *believe* that certain things are just or unjust, as opposed to teaching them to *know* what is just," concluded Socrates, adding, "he could hardly teach so many people something as important as the nature of justice in such a short space of time." "Of course not," said Gorgias.

"A group has gathered here to listen to you," said Socrates, indicating Critias, Alcibiades, and the other young men who stood around them, "and I think some must be considering whether they should become your students. So please tell us how orators gain so much influence over the Assembly with regard to matters such as shipbuilding, construction, or medicine, given that they are not qualified in them." Gorgias, laughing, said that if a rhetorician and a medical expert should compete against one another to influence citizens voting on some public health measure, the rhetorician would win every time. The same would be true for any expert when pitched against the power of rhetoric.

The art of rhetoric is so remarkably effective, said Gorgias, that a skilled orator may easily discredit an expert on medicine or ship-building. If he chose to do so, he could even cause great mischief in the city. Gorgias noticed some of his listeners frowning at this. So he added, somewhat hurriedly, that just because a man has been well trained in combat does not mean he should go around killing people indiscriminately. By analogy, he explained, if a man who has been trained in oratory should bring about harm, that is his own doing, and there is no reason to blame his teacher.

While Gorgias praised the art that he taught, Socrates listened carefully. He paused to think for a moment, then, appearing to change the subject, noted that Gorgias must have witnessed many debates that ended up in pointless wrangling because competing parties took for granted different definitions of the subject. "Bystanders often leave feeling that they have wasted their time listening to such exchanges," said Socrates. It was therefore essential, he added, to arrive at a common definition of important terms, such as *rhetoric* or *justice*. Gorgias nodded slowly, raising an eyebrow.

"Why do I say this?" asked Socrates. "Because something you just mentioned appears to be at odds with something you said earlier. I do not wish to question you further in case you believe that I am merely trying to pick holes in your argument for entertainment. If you are the same sort of man that I am, though, I will go on." Gorgias already regretted being drawn into a conversation with this scruffy-looking eccentric. "What sort of man do you mean?" he asked, sounding puzzled. "One of those who is glad to point out the mistakes of others," replied Socrates, "but also glad to have his own mistakes pointed out. Indeed, I consider being refuted the greater good." "Why?" asked Gorgias. "Because it is better to be cured of an evil oneself than to cure another," replied Socrates, "and as far as I am concerned, no greater evil can befall a man than to be mistaken about matters as important as the ones we are now discussing. So if you are anything like me, in that regard, I would like to continue questioning you, but otherwise, let us leave it there."

Most of Gorgias's young students assumed that it was best to be on the winning side of a debate, and they wondered if Socrates was joking. The goal of philosophical debate, or *dialectic*, which is about truth and knowledge, is typically at odds with that of *rhetorical* debate, which is more about "winning" approval from an audience. Socrates believed that, when it comes to philosophical debate, it was better to *lose* an argument, for the simple reason that the loser is the one who is most likely to benefit by having their errors corrected, and thereby gaining in knowledge.

Gorgias looked baffled and became a little defensive. This way of thinking went against everything he taught. He answered that he would like to believe that he was the sort of person Socrates described. Yet, he said, he was concerned the audience might be growing weary of their discussion. "I would like to hope that I would never abandon a conversation as important as this," cried Chaerephon. Alcibiades, Critias, and the others likewise begged them to continue. Gorgias, to please the crowd, agreed to hear Socrates out.

"In that case," continued Socrates, "what surprised me was that you said that you can teach someone to be an orator, and that he will become so persuasive, through the art of rhetoric, that he will be more convincing even than a physician, say, with regard to matters of health." "Yes, at least in front of a large audience," replied Gorgias. "Not when speaking to another physician then?" asked Socrates with an air of curiosity. "Of course not," said Gorgias, "and the same is true regarding other areas of expertise." Alcibiades, and one or two others looked uncomfortable with this answer, but Critias and the rest merely nodded in agreement.

"In other words," said Socrates, "you teach the ignorant how to appear more convincing than experts but only when they are speaking to audiences who are equally ignorant of the subject." "That can no doubt happen," Gorgias admitted hesitantly. He then turned to the audience, smiled, and quipped, "Yet is it not pleasing to know that by studying rhetoric *alone* you can win a debate against an expert in any other art without even having to study it?" At this, a few of the youths watching began talking excitedly among themselves.

"So does a rhetorician learn to fake having knowledge with regard to justice as you said he does with regard to health and other subjects?" asked Socrates. "That is, must a young man have prior knowledge of justice before he becomes your student? Otherwise, are you saying that you will teach someone who possesses neither wisdom nor justice how to acquire a popular reputation for them?" This question made Gorgias shift uneasily. "I suppose he will learn about justice from me, if he happens not to know anything already," replied Gorgias. In truth, he did not profess to teach justice and had even questioned whether it was possible to do so.

Socrates knitted his brow. "Do you remember a short while ago," he said, "when you told us that if a man trained in combat were to kill people, there would be no reason to blame his teachers?" Gorgias nodded slowly. "And you said that the same holds true of oratory, so that if one of your own students were to employ rhetoric in a way that caused harm, we should not blame you, his teacher," added Socrates. "I did," said Gorgias. "But now you make it sound," said Socrates, "as if no orator would ever do any harm because you claim he would either know what is just already or learn it from you." Gorgias was silent.

"Do you recall," said Socrates, "how we agreed earlier that oratory was concerned with delivering speeches about what is right and wrong?" "I do," said Gorgias. "When I heard that, I assumed oratory could never cause any harm because it was about persuading others to do what is right," said Socrates. "Shortly after that, however, you stated that an orator might use rhetoric to do great harm. That was why I asked if you, like me, were a man who took pleasure in having his own mistakes pointed out to him; otherwise, I would not have pointed out the inconsistency. Because as our conversation continued, we were both led to agree that it is impossible for an orator to use his art in order to inflict wrongdoing and injustice on others." Gorgias fidgeted uneasily. "So, by the dog, Gorgias," said Socrates, "it may take a much longer discussion to get to the bottom of these contradictions!"

Gorgias posed as someone teaching his students how to become great statesmen and orators, who could easily persuade the citizens which course of action was right and which was wrong. Unlike Pericles, and his advisor Protagoras, though, neither Gorgias nor his students cared very much about discovering the most wise or just course of action. They only wanted to influence people, to advance whatever their own interests happened to be. It was no coincidence that as Gorgias and other Sophists like him were growing in popularity, Athenian politics, following the example of Cleon, was becoming more cynical and manipulative.

THE WAR UNDER CLEON

THE PELOPONNESIAN WAR HAD BEEN a stalemate for about six years. Nicias advocated Pericles's strategy of retreating within the city walls when threatened by the Spartan invaders, to focus instead on maintaining control at sea. It was taking longer than expected, however, to wear down the enemy, and the plague had inflicted a heavy toll on the citizens of Athens. Socrates had not fought in a major battle since Potidaea, as Athenian policy was to keep most of their hoplites in reserve and rely instead on the navy. That was about to change as soon as the war hawks, led by the demagogue Cleon, got the upper hand in the Assembly.

In the summer of 425, the Athenians successfully executed a daring plan to establish an outpost at Pylos, on the west coast of the Peloponnese. This would change the course of the war. Pylos provided an excellent natural harbor for Athenian ships and was strategically located about two days' march west of Sparta. A small force landed during a storm and quickly fortified the promontory. The Spartans responded by attacking from both land and sea. The Athenians had thrown up a temporary palisade, though, which kept back the enemy infantry, and Sparta's ships were driven from the harbor when the Athenian navy arrived. To make matters worse for the Spartans, a company of their soldiers, including 120 elite infantry, were left stranded on a small adjacent island, called Sphacteria, surrounded by Athenian ships.

The Spartans were desperate to secure the freedom of these men trapped on the island, as many members of their ruling class were among them. After initial negotiations collapsed, Cleon ridiculed Nicias before the Assembly, for lacking the nerve to take the island. Nicias tried to persuade the citizens that an assault on the Spartan position would be extremely dangerous. Cleon accused him of cowardice and brashly asserted that Sphacteria could be captured within a mere twenty days. This seemed preposterous, as Spartan nobles would never surrender, and the dense foliage on the island made it easily defensible.

To everyone's surprise, Nicias called Cleon's bluff by stepping aside and offering the demagogue, who lacked military experience, command of the mission. Cleon had no choice but to accept and, by a remarkable stroke of luck, he succeeded. One of the Spartans accidentally started a wildfire, while trying to cook a meal. The fire burned down most of the bushes on the island, leaving Spartan positions exposed. The Athenians launched an attack and, to their immense surprise, the Spartans, after being surrounded, eventually threw down their weapons and surrendered. Cleon took the credit, which probably belonged more to Demosthenes, the general who had secured the harbor in the first place. With so many captured nobles held hostage, Athens now forced Sparta to cease its annual invasion of Attica. Sparta's humiliation signaled a new phase in the war. The demagogue, Cleon, at the height of his popularity, could take an increasingly active hand in future military campaigns.

The Athenians' greatest setback, up to this point, had occurred when the Spartans besieged Amphipolis, their colony on the border of western Thrace. The arrival of Spartan troops in this region threatened crucial imports of timber and grain to Athens, as well as revenue from tributary cities. To reach Amphipolis, the Spartans had marched through Boeotia, a region north of Attica dominated by the city of Thebes, another member of the Peloponnesian League. Buoyed by his apparent success in Pylos, Cleon therefore persuaded the Assembly to mobilize every able-bodied man, whether foreigner or citizen, for a land invasion of Boeotia. A high-risk strategy, it signaled a radical departure from the military policy of Pericles, who had advised the Athenians to avoid endangering the lives of their precious hoplites by facing the enemy on land. It would be the first major battle the Athenians had fought against the Boeotians since Coronea, over two decades earlier, where Alcibiades's father had been slain.

The Athenians hoped that, by seizing control over parts of Boeotia, they might cut off the Spartan army to the north. They seized the temple of Apollo at Delium, overlooking the Gulf of Euboea, and converted it into a temporary fortress. This gave them another coastal stronghold within enemy territory, which could potentially serve as a base for a full-scale invasion. They stationed a small garrison at the fort and sent most of their poorly equipped light troops back home to Athens. As the rest of their main army was preparing to leave, however, a huge Boeotian army arrived. Each side had seven thousand hoplites. The Athenians, however, had far fewer horsemen. The Boeotians also had over ten thousand well-equipped light troops, whereas the Athenians had none remaining of which to speak. Socrates had been deployed among the ranks of the Athenian hoplites; Alcibiades served in the cavalry. They would both witness firsthand the consequences of Cleon's rashness, which had thrown huge numbers of inexperienced soldiers into battle, on enemy territory, without an adequate defense.

While the Athenian general, Hippocrates, was still delivering his speech to the troops, the Boeotians launched a surprise charge from the top of a nearby hill. Caught off guard, the Athenian hoplites were suddenly ordered to charge uphill toward the enemy. This was an extremely dangerous tactic. An uphill charge would potentially be exhausting for hoplites wearing heavy armor, and it would also become difficult for the light troops to throw their javelins accurately. Socrates must have felt in that moment that he, his phalanx, and the thousands of fellow hoplites around him, could well be charging toward their deaths.

The Theban right wing, which was a staggering twenty-five men deep, three times greater than the norm, must have hit them like a hammerblow when it came racing downhill. Somehow the Athenian hoplites held their ground. For a moment, therefore, it seemed Athens might be winning but after encircling the enemy's crumbling left wing, some of their men became confused, victims of the fog of war. Athenians began attacking Athenians by mistake. Once they fell into disarray, a surprise attack from the Boeotian cavalry easily routed them. The whole Athenian army broke ranks and fled in different directions, pursued mercilessly by enemy horsemen.

Socrates was part of a small company who joined the former Athenian general Laches during this bloody retreat. Laches later said that if only the other men had fought like Socrates, to whom he probably owed his life, Athens would have avoided defeat at Delium. As dusk fell, though, they were still being harassed by the Boeotian cavalry, and many Athenians had already fallen around them. Most of their companions would have felt their morale dwindling as they realized the dire nature of their situation. Suddenly, they heard a horse galloping toward them through the surrounding chaos. From the darkness, a familiar voice called out: *Take heart!*

As if by some miracle, Alcibiades had found them. He swore to remain with them, watching their backs until they reached safety. While Laches had been starting to panic, Socrates kept guard fearlessly and scanned the environment for friends and enemies. "He made it plain," said Alcibiades, "that if anyone came near him, he would defend himself vigorously. When you behave in war as he did, the enemy fears to approach you, for they pursue those who turn and flee instead."[4] Though hundreds of their comrades were slain at Delium, Laches and Socrates made it home alive. Alcibiades now having saved the life of the man who rescued him at Potidaea, was no longer in his debt, although the bond between them can only have deepened as a result.

Delium would be the largest land battle of the war. Athens had gained nothing, and lost well over a thousand men, including the general in command. Most of the Athenians fled back home, but some retreated to the fortified temple at Delium. Shortly after, the Boeotians attacked it with a flame-throwing siege engine, which used giant bellows to blast fiery pitch and sulfur down a tube, burning the wooden palisades to the ground. Some of the garrison were killed or captured, but most fled back to Athens.

Socrates and Alcibiades had experienced the disaster in person. Cleon and his war hawks had persuaded the Assembly to plunge the whole of Athens into exactly the sort of risky infantry campaign that Pericles had warned them to avoid. Athens was incapable of matching, for any length of time, the number of light-armed troops available to its most powerful enemies, such as Boeotia. This problem was due to the simple fact that most of these men were already needed to serve as oarsmen in Athens's vast navy, and even when called upon to fight they often lacked adequate weapons and armor to be of much value in a land battle. The defeat at Delium came about because experienced men, with sound knowledge of Athens's military strengths and weaknesses, had been drowned out by the persuasive voice of a firebrand demagogue.

THE PRACTICE OF
COGNITIVE DISTANCING

ONE OF THE MOST INNOVATIVE concepts in the field of psychotherapy was introduced by Aaron T. Beck in the 1970s.[5] Known as "cognitive distancing," it refers to our ability to view our own thoughts with greater detachment and objectivity, as if observing the thoughts of another person. For instance, under normal circumstances, if I have a thought such as "This man is my enemy," I may simply *perceive* the man as if he is my enemy. This is especially true if the thought is accompanied by strong feelings of fear or anger. Alternatively, I might pause, step back, and *observe* myself having the thought "This man is my enemy"—I may even notice myself saying those words in my mind. In this perspective, the thought becomes separate and distinct from the object or person to which it refers.

Most of the time, we do not look *at* and examine our own thoughts; rather, we take them for granted and look at events *through* them. Beck compared this to wearing colored glasses—let's say with blue lenses for sadness. Gaining cognitive distance would be like taking off the glasses and looking at them, or just realizing that the blueness (sadness) resides in the lenses. If I were clinically depressed, however, I might forget that I'm wearing lenses, and assume that the world itself is sad and blue. In this way, our thoughts, especially our value judgments, easily become *fused* with the events to which they refer.

Beck noted the overlap with philosophy when he said that this concept is related to *epistemology*, or theory of knowledge.

Distancing involves being able to make the distinction between "I believe" (an opinion that is subject to validation) and "I know" (an "irrefutable" fact).[6]

The client's ability to make this distinction, he says, is of "critical importance" in cognitive psychotherapy. Socrates, of course, was one of the pioneers of epistemology, and a similar distinction between opinion and knowledge is central to his philosophy.

Beck believed that it was important to teach clients cognitive distancing *before* proceeding to ask them what cognitive therapists call Socratic questions. To begin questioning our own beliefs, we must first be able to view them as hypotheses rather than facts. Beck said that a person has gained cognitive distance if he can examine his beliefs "as a psychological phenomenon rather than as identical with reality," which means seeing them as capable of being refuted.

If he automatically equates the thought with reality, his distancing is poor. If he can regard the idea as a hypothesis or inference, rather than accept it as fact, he is distancing well.[7]

Rhetoric, as Gorgias implies, is basically the art of persuading one's audience to accept certain ideas uncritically. If cognitive therapists teach other people to notice the colored lenses through which they're looking at life, rhetoric does the opposite.

When politicians use verbal manipulation to make you frightened or angry about something, they don't want you to *notice* that's what they're doing. In the art of persuasion, the goal is for one's audience to fuse opinion with reality. The aim of an orator, such as Gorgias, is to "win" the debate, by persuading the audience that he is right. Socrates, though, in typically paradoxical fashion, claims that he would rather be proven wrong, especially regarding the most important matters in life. Those are two fundamentally different attitudes, and perhaps even opposing ways of life. The orators wanted to sound as confident as possible that they knew what was right, and seldom stopped to question their own assumptions. Socrates continuously examined his own beliefs, which required being able to imagine they could possibly be *false*. Often when people behave as though their own beliefs are self-evidently true and beyond question, that can be taken as a warning sign that they lack cognitive distance and have fused their opinions with reality.

In the dialogues, Socrates generally places philosophy in opposition to rhetoric. At times he did acknowledge that rhetoric and philosophy could work together, for our good, by persuading us of the truth.[8] However, in most cases, rhetoric, like storytelling, is designed to create an emotional effect by *decreasing* cognitive distance. When we are completely engrossed in a novel or movie, we suspend critical thinking and allow ourselves to become lost in the story for a while, as if it were real. Political oratory sweeps us along and carries us away, in a similar fashion, without any pause for analysis, so that opinions are experienced as though they are facts. Powerful rhetoric can resemble, if you like, a form of *hypnosis*. Socrates, therefore, won't allow the Sophists to cast their spell over our imagination but keeps interrupting them with questions. The Socratic method could be called a form of *dehypnosis*. It is designed to awaken us from the trance of rhetoric.

THE PEACE OF NICIAS

TWO YEARS AFTER ATHENS'S HUMILIATING defeat at Delium, Cleon placed himself in direct command of a major military expedition. He set sail with thirty ships, hoping to take back Amphipolis and salvage his reputation. Socrates, who served on this campaign, aged forty-eight, was by now a veteran of several battles. He had acquired a reputation for exceptional courage and endurance, and he exhibited enough knowledge of training, strategy, and tactics for generals to seek out his advice.[9] Amphipolis would be his third, and perhaps his last, major battle. Most of the men fighting alongside him would have been younger. Although citizens could see active service until they reached sixty, so many Athenians had been killed or incapacitated by warfare and disease by this time that there must have been relatively few men of Socrates's generation left on the battlefield. Alcibiades, who appeared set to become Cleon's rival for the affections of the people, was, perhaps for that reason, not called on to fight in this campaign.

After some initial victories, the Athenian force under Cleon, which consisted of twelve hundred hoplites, plus several thousand lightly armed foreign troops, marched on Amphipolis. The city was defended by the slightly larger but less experienced Spartan army led by Brasidas, who commanded two thousand Spartan hoplites, plus around four thousand light-armed foreign troops. The Athenians noticed that Brasidas, the most daring and talented Spartan general, and fifteen hundred of his troops had taken up position on a hilltop beside Amphipolis, from which he could better observe Cleon's movements. This presented a good opportunity to attack the city, while some of its defenders were outside the walls, but instead, Cleon insisted on waiting for the arrival of mercenaries whom he had sent for from nearby Thrace and Macedonia. His troops grew frustrated at the delay and accused him of weakness and incompetence. Cleon responded by marching them up to the city walls, to inspect its defenses. While he stalled, waiting for the reinforcements, he insisted that there was no danger of the enemy emerging to attack them. This gave Brasidas enough time to return to the city.

Cleon's scouts noticed that the Spartan troops were gathering inside. He became afraid that they were about to charge out and attack, so he ordered a tactical retreat. As he tried to get his men to change formation, however, they became disorganized. Seizing this opportunity, Brasidas led 150 of his most experienced hoplites out of the south gate, in a surprise attack against the Athenian center. This caused Cleon's men to panic, which was the cue for the remaining enemy troops to charge from the north gate and attack the Athenian rear. They were completely routed and lost around six hundred men, whereas the Spartans lost merely seven. During the intense fighting, Cleon was killed and Brasidas mortally wounded. The Athenian survivors, including Socrates, were forced to abandon the expedition, board their ships, and sail home with news of another costly defeat, due to the arrogance of a leader who lacked any military competence, but could be very persuasive.

The deaths of Cleon and Brasidas, the two leading war hawks on either side, brought the first phase of the Peloponnesian War to a close and opened the way for peace negotiations between more moderate factions. The Peace of Nicias, as it came to be known because Nicias had led the Athenian side of the negotiations, was signed in 421 and was meant to last for fifty years. It stipulated that everything should be returned to the prewar status quo, including Pylos being handed over to the Spartans and Amphipolis to the Athenians. However, most of Sparta's allies refused to sign, and a loophole was exploited to retain control of Amphipolis, so the treaty began crumbling from the outset.

With Cleon dead, the path was clear for a new champion of

the Democrat faction, who could appeal to the masses. Alcibiades, by tricking some Spartan envoys, was able to thwart Nicias's attempts to settle further terms with them. He was now actively working against Nicias and the treaty, which many common Athenians considered to be too much in the interests of wealthy aristocrats and against their own.

Around this time, perhaps shortly after returning from Amphipolis, Socrates married a young woman called Xanthippe, about thirty years his junior.[10] By all accounts, she had a quick temper, and Socrates's friends liked to joke about her being a shrew. When Alcibiades complained that her scoldings were intolerable, Socrates merely laughed and said that he had become used to the sound just as, years earlier, he had become used to the clattering of ropes and pulleys, lifting heavy blocks, in the stonemason's workshop. He asked Alcibiades, who kept geese on his estate, whether the noise they made upset him. Alcibiades replied that he had accepted it and gotten used to it, because they provided him with eggs and goslings. Socrates, smiling, replied, "And Xanthippe is the mother of my children." Despite her fierce temper, he seems to have thought of her as a good wife, and she would give him three sons.

Alcibiades also took a wife, called Hipparete, the sister of Callias, the wealthiest man in Athens.[11] He could now begin his political career in earnest. As soon as he reached the minimum age of thirty, Alcibiades stood for election and was appointed general for the first time, which effectively made him a statesman in the Athenian Assembly. Although a bond remained between the young noble and the philosopher who saved his life, Alcibiades spent less time in Socrates's company as he pursued his political ambitions. He became more interested in how he could use his military cunning and undeniable talent as an orator to achieve glory for himself and Athens.

Despite the supposed peace treaty, the war between Athens and Sparta continued, albeit initially through indirect means such as political maneuvering and proxy conflicts. These culminated in the Battle of Mantinea, which took place in 418, thirteen years into the war. Argos, the most powerful neutral state in the Peloponnese, leaned toward democratic rule and away from the oligarchic regimes favored by Sparta. With encouragement from Alcibiades, the Argives (as the people of Argos were known) formed a coalition with the nearby cities of Elis and Mantinea, members of the Peloponnesian League who were persuaded to revolt against Sparta and change sides. Argos and her allies were joined by a small Athenian force led by Alcibiades. They attempted to take control of the town of Tegea, which would have allowed the allies to blockade Sparta by land. Sparta managed to win the battle and break up the coalition. Nevertheless, Alcibiades had shown that, through cunning and diplomacy, he could place Sparta in real danger, with little direct risk to Athens.

In the summer of 416, following a failed attempt by Nicias ten years earlier, the Athenians sent a fleet of thirty-eight ships, carrying over three thousand hoplites, to besiege the wealthy island-state of Melos.[12] Although Alcibiades's star was rising, he does not seem to have been involved in the decision to undertake this campaign.[13] In fact, he was busy preparing his charioteers to compete in the famous race at Olympia that year. Alcibiades entered an unheard of *seven* teams, probably with four horses per chariot, a display of extraordinary wealth and ambition, which would put most kings in the shade. He won first, second, *and* fourth place. Alcibiades hoped that gaining such celebrity would help advance his political career, although it played into the hands of his enemies by fueling envy of his success and accusations that he wanted to set himself up in Athens as a king. Meanwhile, his political rivals had convinced the Assembly to vote in favor of a notoriously brutal attack on a neutral state.

Though originally colonized by the Spartans, Melos had chosen not to take sides in the recent conflict. The Athenians, in defiance of the Melians' neutrality, blockaded the main city and laid waste to the surrounding countryside. They wanted to make an example of the Melians that would deter their subject states from rebelling, by showing them how severely they were willing to treat non-members of the alliance. Conquering the only major island in the Aegean that was still holding out against them would also secure Athenian naval dominance in the region.

What followed was one of the darkest incidents in the history of Athens's foreign relations. When the Athenian envoys met with their Melian counterparts, they exhibited a degree of political cynicism and self-interest exceeding even that for which Cleon had been known. The poet Hesiod had written of a hawk who seized a nightingale in his claws. As she wept pitifully, he spoke to his prey, "Foolish bird, why are you crying out?" One far stronger has captured you, he said, and however you struggle, it is up to him whether he lets you go or carries you away for his dinner.

> Stupid he who would wish to contend against those stronger than he is:
> for he is deprived of the victory, and suffers pains in addition to his humiliations.[14]

The Athenians likewise argued that it is futile for the weak to try to negotiate with the stronger—because *might is right*.

They dropped any pretense that they had been injured and were seeking justice, or had any moral justification whatsoever for the invasion.

The Athenians warned the Melians not to waste their breath saying "we have done you no wrong" and to instead concentrate on negotiating the best terms they could realistically expect in defeat. If they surrendered and paid tribute to Athens, they might live; otherwise, they would face annihilation. You know as well as we do, the Athenians said, that justice, in the real world, is only a matter for discussion between those equal in power. "The strong do what they can," they added, "and the weak suffer what they must." Like Cleon, the unnamed Athenian politicians leading this campaign, whoever they were, clearly viewed themselves as despots, and foreign subjects as slaves to be cowed by fear.

Having failed to appeal to justice, the Melians sought to persuade the Athenians that aggression was inconsistent with their own nation's interests. "How can you avoid making enemies," they said, "of all the other neutral cities, who will conclude that one day you will attack them too?" The Athenians brushed this aside, shortsightedly, saying that they were concerned solely about islands who could give them trouble, among whom Melos was the only remaining neutral state of note.

The Melian envoys said they considered it cowardice for a free state to voluntarily submit its people to a yoke that others had risked so much trying to escape. The Athenians replied that it was no shame to surrender to a superior force but rather dishonorable to attempt a futile battle and lose. The Melians hoped, however, that their cousins, the Spartans, would send aid. Despite facing overwhelming odds, moreover, they told the Athenians they saw themselves as just men fighting against the unjust and that they were willing to put their trust in the gods.

The Athenians replied once more that it was a law of nature and the will of the gods that the strong should rule the weak. On that basis, they did not fear that any god would grant good fortune to their enemies. Nor did they believe that the Spartans would risk helping the Melians. After going away to consider the terms, the islanders sent their response: "Our resolution, Athenians, is the same as it was at first." They were unwilling to surrender the freedom of a city that had been inhabited for seven centuries. They would put their trust in fortune, the gods, and the hope that Sparta would come to their rescue. They chose to stand their ground and fight.

The Athenian generals began laying siege, blockading the island so that nothing could get in or out. At first the Melians fought back, making daring nighttime raids. However, Spartan assistance never materialized, whereas reinforcements from Athens soon joined the siege. In the winter of 417, after months of famine, the Melians finally surrendered. At the beginning of the war, Athens had shown mercy toward conquered cities such as Potidaea. More than a decade had passed since the demise of Pericles, and the policies of the Assembly had by now grown desperate and the actions of its generals cruel. At Melos, they did what Cleon had been prevented from doing at Mytilene: they enslaved all the women and children and slaughtered every adult male they could find. It would be one of the most notorious genocides in history. The city was handed over to Athenian colonists. The rhetoric of democracy and justice had been replaced with the rhetoric of tyranny and violence. For now, Athens was victorious, though the arguments her envoys had used to threaten the Melians would soon come back to haunt her.

8

THE SICILIAN EXPEDITION

IN EARLY 415, DIPLOMATS FROM the Sicilian city of Segesta arrived in Athens to plead for military aid. They were accompanied by exiles from the neighboring Greek colony of Leontini, which had previously sent Gorgias. Leontini had been seized by Syracuse and its democracy replaced with an oligarchic regime. Athens was sworn to defend its allies, including these far-flung cities to the west. Thousands of Athenians gathered on the hillside of the Pnyx to hear the Segestan envoys present their case. They warned the Assembly that the whole of Sicily might end up under the control of Syracuse, its most powerful city, which was an ally of Sparta.

The envoys had the support of Alcibiades, who was eager to be placed in command of a new military expedition. The Segestans claimed they could pay the Athenians a fortune for military aid, sixty talents of silver with the promise of more to come.[1] The Assembly members were so easily persuaded that they immediately voted to send a fleet of sixty triremes. However, they decreed that Alcibiades must share command with the more cautious Nicias and another general called Lamachus. The Assembly granted their generals authority to "conduct themselves in Sicily in whatever way seemed most in Athens's interests."

Nicias was appalled by this decision. He disapproved of the campaign and did not wish to be dragged into serving alongside Alcibiades, his main political rival. Five days later, an even larger crowd of citizens convened to finalize the preparations required for the expedition. Nicias used the opportunity to complain that they had not adequately debated whether the fleet should be sent at all. Despite having been appointed one of the generals in command, he pleaded with the citizens to reconsider the whole plan.

Nicias said he was alarmed by the military risk and implored his fellow Athenians to rescind the decree. The fragile peace that he had negotiated with Sparta was, he claimed, being jeopardized by Alcibiades, who was simply hungry for glory. In addition, Athens was still recovering from the plague. The Athenians were not safe enough at home to risk sending so many troops overseas. It was foolhardy, Nicias said, not only to leave Athens short of men for its defense but to risk their lives far from home in a campaign doomed to failure. He dismissed as groundless the claim that unchecked, Syracuse would grow stronger and join forces with the Peloponnesians against Athens. He pointed out that, as Pericles would have said, they should not grasp at another empire before securing the one they already have.

Finally, Nicias launched into a scathing attack on his young rival's character and that of the faction who supported him. Alcibiades, he sneered, was full of youthful arrogance, having been appointed general, and plotted this campaign for his own selfish ends. He had, notoriously, squandered his family fortune on expensive racehorses and was now looking for a way to pay off his debts. He lacked experience and was behaving impulsively, in a way that placed all of Athens at risk.

Nicias was appalled at Alcibiades, still only in his midthirties, being granted a share in the command of such a major expedition. He also feared that the campaign to aid Segesta would become a pretext for conquering the whole of Sicily. Although the decision had already been made, he tried to persuade the assemblymen that the campaign was too dangerous. They had, he said, been misled by Alcibiades. He begged them to put it to the vote a second time. The duty of men holding public office, Nicias asserted, was not only to do their country as much good as they can but also to avoid doing it any harm. Privately, he feared that sending a fleet to Sicily would compel the Spartans to revoke the treaty he had painstakingly negotiated. The collapse of the peace agreement would not only tarnish his reputation as a politician but also jeopardize his business interests, including his lucrative silver mines in Attica.

As the officials struggled to maintain order, Alcibiades took to the rostrum, with the Segestans and Leontinians at his side. By now an accomplished orator, he first defended his own reputation, in his typical fashion, by turning the weaknesses used against him into strengths. It was true, he lisped, that the money he lavished on racehorses brought him fame, but all of Athens shared the glory of these victories. His private life was not, he said, the concern of the Assembly, whereas in public life he had exhibited largess at home and diplomatic success abroad. His youth and energy were virtues that perfectly complemented the experience of older statesmen. "Having united the most powerful cities of the Peloponnese," he said, "without any real danger or expense to you, I forced the Spartans to risk their all in the Battle of Mantinea. And though they prevailed, they have not yet recovered their confidence after coming within a hair's breadth of defeat."

Regarding the substance of the motion, Alcibiades had come prepared. He demonstrated a clear grasp of Syracuse's military strengths and weaknesses, derived from lengthy conversations with the Sicilian envoys. He made his case for deterrence: "It is not enough for us to parry the attacks of such a powerful enemy," he said, "but we must strike the first blow and prevent their attacks from ever being made. We cannot settle for what we have but must expand our domain," he continued, "for if we cease to rule others, we shall be in danger of being ruled ourselves. In short," he concluded, "my conviction is that a city that is active by nature could not choose a quicker path to ruin than adopting a policy of inaction, and that the safest rule of life is to take the character and institutions of one's city, for better or worse, and to live up to them as best one can." Sicily was also rich in cornfields, control of which could free Athens from its dependence on grain supplies shipped from the Black Sea via the Hellespont—arguably the city's greatest vulnerability.

Pericles had built Athens into a power rivaling Sparta, through alliances with many smaller Greek cities in the Aegean and other nearby regions. Their navy must actively protect these friendly cities at all costs if they wish to maintain the security of their empire. The envoys from their allies in Sicily came forward to remind the Athenians of their oaths. Alcibiades assured the Assembly that, as he was confident of making allies and obtaining reinforcements in Sicily, twenty ships would suffice instead of sixty. Athens would not need to risk much. He wished to be given sole command over a smaller force, without having to worry about interference from Nicias. Alcibiades then made way for his rival to speak.

Nicias mounted the rostrum a second time, in a desperate bid to damp down the enthusiasm for war. Alcibiades, he argued, had greatly *underestimated* the number of men required. There were, he said, seven fortified enemy cities on the island. If Syracuse managed to unite with its neighbors, their collective wealth would be immense and their military power unstoppable. His argument backfired, though, when one of the assemblymen asked him to be more specific about the numbers. Without thinking, the reluctant general blurted out that at least a hundred ships and five thousand hoplites would be required.

Nicias watched in horror as, instead of abandoning the motion, the Assembly voted to commit *even more* resources to the campaign. What had started as a modest expeditionary force had expanded into a full-blown armada, comprising almost half the ships available to Athens. Such a large fleet could not be entrusted to one man alone. So the Assembly insisted, once again, that command must be shared between Alcibiades, Nicias, and Lamachus—even though Nicias had tried his utmost to have the whole plan scrapped.

This was the pinnacle of Alcibiades's power. Although forced to share command, it was clear to everyone that he was the architect of the expedition. His dream was, after the imagined fall of Sicily, to take the cities along the Italian coastline and to subjugate Carthage and the north of Africa. With the resources acquired, including additional troops, money, and timber to build more ships, he could mobilize an army powerful enough to invade the Peloponnese and finally defeat the Spartans. Athens would rule over an empire that encompassed the entire Hellenic world and most of the Mediterranean. With Greece united, they could even plan an invasion of Persia, their most powerful "barbarian" enemy.

Athens was immediately gripped with war fever. Everywhere, there was talk of the great adventure ahead: glory to be won and vast wealth to be pried from enemy hands. Alcibiades's ambitions frightened the older, more conservative, aristocrats, who would bear most of the cost. The young and the poor, however, who had most to gain from conquest, felt inspired by his vision. They had all heard that Sicily was wealthy and filled with valuable resources.

Most of them probably found it difficult to comprehend the scale of their expedition, though. The island on which they were about to wage war was larger than all of the Aegean islands combined.

Socrates had, at first, encouraged Alcibiades in his ambition. He believed that his natural courage and love of glory could be channeled, through philosophy, into the study of wisdom and justice. Perhaps he could become a great statesman. As Alcibiades became more engaged with politics, though, which meant trying to win support in the Assembly, he was increasingly drawn to the Sophists who taught rhetoric, the art of persuasion. He seemed torn between wanting to *become* a great leader and wanting to *appear* like one.[2]

THE SCANDAL OF THE HERMS

ONE MORNING, WHILE THE SHIPS were being readied, the Athenians awoke to find that every herm in the city, except one, had been defaced. These statues, which stood in the doorways of many homes and temples, consisted of a rectangular pillar topped with the head and shoulders of the god Hermes. The pillar below was featureless except for a set of male genitals. Dozens of herms had been mutilated during the night. It was an act of sacrilege against Hermes, the patron god of voyagers, and a terrible omen for the fleet preparing to depart.

The crime was widespread enough that it had to be the premeditated work of a group working together in secret. Suspicion was directed toward the *hetaireiai*, secret societies of powerful individuals who banded together to advance their own political interests. The most obvious motive was to frighten the ships' crews from setting sail for Alcibiades's campaign. Panic spread throughout Athens, as sabotaging the expedition, upon which many believed victory in the war depended, was seen as a plot against the state itself. Perhaps it was the prelude to an oligarchy, or tyrant, staging a coup. Cleon's accusations against the aristocrats fuelled an atmosphere of heightened suspicion and recrimination at Athens, and its legacy was increased fear of the secretive political clubs.

An investigation was launched, led by a young aristocrat named Charicles. It inevitably became an opportunity for bitter political enemies to seek revenge against one another. At one point, two of Nicias's brothers were accused. It is surprising then that the finger of blame ended up being pointed at Alcibiades, his greatest rival, who seems to have had the least to gain and most to lose from this crime. Nevertheless, accusers started to come forward willing to testify that they knew of his involvement, once immunity from punishment, and rewards, were offered.

Days before the fleet was due to leave, a young man appeared before the Assembly with accusations of another religious crime. He alleged that Alcibiades and his friends had defiled the Eleusinian Mysteries, the secret initiation rites of the goddess Demeter, by performing a reenactment of them in the presence of an uninitiated slave. This was a grave profanity, as the sanctity of these rites was jealously guarded. The annual festival held at Eleusis, which neighbored Athens, was also a major source of foreign revenue. The slave was called to testify and was able to describe secret rituals, of which he should have had no knowledge. Presumably, the political clubs were believed to engage in acts of sacrilege because they carried such a severe penalty—to betray the club's pledge of secrecy would potentially mean incriminating oneself in a serious religious crime.

The case was taken up by Alcibiades's enemies, who claimed that his extravagant private life showed that he aspired to overthrow Athens's democracy and install himself as tyrant. Cleon had left Athenian politics in a degenerate state, where sensational accusations and extreme knee-jerk responses were indulged and could lead the powerful to be condemned for treason on the basis of quite negligible evidence. Alcibiades repudiated the allegations against him and demanded a trial to clear his name, though being found guilty might mean a death sentence. His enemies responded with a masterstroke. They argued that his trial should be postponed to avoid delaying such a huge military expedition. The young men were so keen to set sail that the vote was easily carried. The timing of the trial had been engineered, as Alcibiades realized, so that it might take place while most of his supporters were on campaign and unavailable for jury service. Under circumstances so contrived, and so unfavorable to Alcibiades, it seems obvious his political rivals were planning to use the Athenian system of justice to destroy him.

THE SECOND DIALOGUE
WITH ALCIBIADES

AT DAYBREAK ON THE DAY of the fleet's departure, thousands of parents accompanied their sons to the docks. The whole city came down to Piraeus, including Socrates. Although the philosopher was now in his midfifties, he was still eligible for military service. He recalled the disasters he had witnessed at Delium and Amphipolis as well as the long and brutal siege of Potidaea. He also recalled the Battle of Coronea, where Alcibiades's father had been slain. Cleinias was no older then than his son was now. This time, the philosopher's inner voice warned him against joining the expedition. He sought out Alcibiades, on the docks, by his flagship, and advised him not to go, but it was clear nothing would change his mind. Alcibiades knew something was amiss.

He could have refused to set sail because of the trial hanging over him. He saw victory in Sicily as his opportunity, however, to go down in history as one of Athens's greatest leaders.

"The Athenians voted for such a large and well-equipped armada because they felt it guaranteed their safety," said Alcibiades. "Of course," said Socrates, "a smaller force, like the one you initially requested, would have arrived sooner and given the enemy less time to prepare." Alcibiades nodded. Their fleet was too large. Extensive preparations and frequent stops for supplies would slow their progress considerably, robbing them of the crucial advantage of surprise. "My main concern," Alcibiades added, "is that with three generals instead of one, every decision will be a debate, leading to delays when action is necessary." "Those debates are not the ones you should fear most," said Socrates. "You easily persuaded the Assembly to give you the fleet you requested, and answered the allegations against you so convincingly that the citizens decreed you should retain your command." His voice became graver: "Once you set sail, they will no longer feel your influence. Other speakers who wish you harm, and use the courts as their weapons, will have the people by their ears."

"I am reminded of your conversation with the Sicilian orator, Gorgias," said Alcibiades.[3] "Yes," said Socrates, "it was many years ago, but I remember he claimed that rhetoric gave his students great influence over their fellow citizens—though he was unsure whether what they had learned was just, or good for the city." "At the time, I was eager to leap to Gorgias's defense," said Alcibiades with a laugh, "as was my friend, Critias." "Yes," said Socrates, "by admitting, rather boldly, that he and his fellow orators had no interest in justice—I suppose you were trying to help him."

Alcibiades recalled his frustration at listening to Gorgias being tied in knots by Socrates's questions. The great orator had contradicted himself repeatedly. Gorgias was merely afraid of losing face, Alcibiades had claimed. He should have had the courage to admit that he wasn't an expert on justice and didn't attempt to teach it to others. Nobody wants to admit that he is ignorant of justice, and Socrates, Alcibiades had complained, exploited this to make Gorgias appear foolish.

"Alcibiades, my dear friend," Socrates said, "perhaps you can help Gorgias and me back to our feet, if we have tripped up in our thinking." Socrates insisted that his friend should also refrain from launching into long-winded speeches. So Alcibiades turned the tables on the philosopher, and invited Socrates to answer some questions, beginning with what sort of art he took rhetoric to be.

"I don't think of it as an *art* at all," replied Socrates, "but as something more like a *knack* acquired through trial and error." "What sort of knack?" snorted Alcibiades. "One that seeks to produce feelings of pleasure or gratification in others," replied Socrates. Alcibiades retorted that surely it was a *good* thing for an orator to gratify his audience. Socrates, however, said that this meant orators resembled *confectioners*. At first this perplexed everyone, but Socrates explained what he meant. "Confectioners," he said, "come up with recipes for sweets, which appeal to the tastes of their customers. They learn, through trial and error, how to give people what they want regardless of whether it's good for them or not." Socrates said that he therefore considered both rhetoric and confectionery to be forms of *pandering* to others, by attempting to gratify them: one with sweets, the other with fine words.

"Physicians study the science of nutrition," said Socrates. "They prescribe diets intended to be good for our health, based on an understanding of the human body. The treats supplied by a master confectioner, in contrast, are based merely upon whatever people tell him tastes most pleasant. If an audience of children, lacking any knowledge of nutrition, were asked to choose between eating the treats of a confectioner or the healthy food prescribed by a physician, the confectioner would win their vote every time."

"Pandering," said Socrates, "pays no attention to the best interests of its subjects and instead catches the foolish with the bait of pleasure, tricking them into esteeming it more highly than their own good." On this definition, of course, the vast majority of "politicians" would be *panderers*, or demagogues, rather than genuine statesmen. These men employ rhetoric in order to gain power, instead of studying justice and learning how to benefit society.

Sophists and orators, according to Socrates, were lumped together in the minds of the public. These men teach their students how to influence the votes of assemblymen and jurors by persuading them that some course of action is right or wrong. They are far more concerned with appearance than truth, and they create the impression of possessing wisdom and virtue despite being ignorant of their nature. "Rhetoric is to the mind," said Socrates, "as confectionery is to the body—both are knacks that their practitioners have developed for pandering to the desires of the ignorant, and neither pays any attention to what is in *anyone's* best interests."

"Do you seriously believe that highly regarded orators, such as Gorgias, are mere panderers?" cried Alcibiades. "I don't think they should be held in any regard at all," shrugged Socrates. "What are you talking about?" Alcibiades exclaimed. "Aren't they the most powerful men in the city?" "Not if by power you mean the ability to achieve what is good for them," replied Socrates. "Because if that is the case, orators are among the *least* powerful men in the city." Alcibiades laughed. "Hang on, can't skilled orators kill whoever they like, confiscate other men's property, and banish anyone they please—like tyrants?" It was true. By exerting their influence over the Assembly and courts, demagogues could indeed do all these things.

"Yes," replied Socrates, "and yet, just like tyrants, orators are the *least* powerful men in the city." Alcibiades was perplexed. "Did you not just say that great power gets whatever is good for its possessor?" asked Socrates. Alcibiades nodded. "Do you believe it is good for a man who is foolish to do what appears best to him?" Socrates added. Alcibiades said no. "Then unless you can prove that orators and tyrants are wise," said Socrates, "how does it follow from the fact that they can have men killed that they possess great power?" "This fellow—," Alcibiades blurted out. "Says that such men are powerless to achieve what is good for them, or what they really want," said Socrates, smiling.

"No, no, you said that they can do whatever appears best to them!" huffed Alcibiades. "But they are ignorant of what is *actually* best for them," said Socrates, "which means that they may *appear* powerful to themselves, and perhaps others, but are in reality completely powerless." "That's outrageous, Socrates," lisped Alcibiades, "you're talking the most monstrous rubbish!" "Rather than using such bitter words," said Socrates, "prove to me where I am mistaken." Alcibiades appeared lost.

Socrates explained that when we undertake most actions we do so for some other end. For instance, when someone drinks medicine, they don't want the bitter taste, but they endure it for the sake of their health. "Tyrants and demagogues do whatever they do believing that it will somehow help them, not harm them," added Socrates. "So can they be said to do what they want, and to have great power, if their actions turn out to be bad for them?" he asked. Alcibiades, reluctantly, agreed that they could not. We might say that someone armed with a sword appears more powerful than an unarmed man, but if we add that the swordsman is blindfolded and cannot see whom he is attacking, he is *less* powerful. By analogy, a tyrant who is blind to what is in his own interest is utterly powerless no matter how many armed men are under his command or how much harm he believes he can do to others, because he does not understand what he is doing.

"You make it sound, Socrates, as if you do not envy the man who can kill, rob, or imprison anyone he likes," said Alcibiades, frowning. "Do they do so justly or unjustly?" asked Socrates. "It makes no difference!" exclaimed Alcibiades. "Consider what you are saying, my good man," said Socrates, "because those who do such things unjustly are not to be envied, surely, but pitied." "You honestly believe that a tyrant who holds your life in his hands," scoffed Alcibiades, "can be called miserable and pitiable?" Socrates nodded. "It is obviously the man who is put to death unjustly that you should pity," exclaimed Alcibiades. "I pity him less than the tyrant who kills him," said Socrates, "because to do wrong is a greater misfortune than to suffer wrong."

"You wouldn't rather have the power of a tyrant to kill and banish and have everything his own way?" interjected Critias, who was equally incredulous. Socrates asked him to imagine that they'd met in a crowded marketplace and he'd said, "My young friends, I have in my possession a wonderful means of tyranny, a concealed dagger, with which I may potentially kill whomever I choose from the people around me!" Indeed, with merely a dagger, anyone could murder someone in the street, if he set his mind to it. He could, moreover, light a torch and with that alone burn down the whole Athenian fleet while it sits in the harbor. "Why do you not call that great power?" asked Socrates. "Because," replied Alcibiades impatiently, "if anyone except a great tyrant committed such crimes he would most likely be arrested and severely punished."

"And you think that being punished is bad?" asked Socrates. "Of course!" replied Alcibaides. "In that case," said Socrates, "once again, you appear to be saying that having power means being able to do what is in your best interests, as opposed to doing what harms you." Alcibiades hesitantly agreed. "And you assume that killing other men, and so on, is not always in the tyrant's interests, but sometimes good and sometimes bad for him," said Socrates, "so where do you draw the line?" "Why don't you answer your own question," said Alcibiades, who was growing quite frustrated. "Well, if it's more pleasing to hear it from me," replied Socrates, "then I would say that killing, banishment, and so on, are good when they're done justly and bad when done unjustly." "Even a child could refute you," said Alcibiades. "Then I would be most grateful to that child," said Socrates, smiling, "for curing me of my error."

"Really, Socrates," exclaimed Critias in frustration, "only recently a tyrant seized power in Macedonia—do you call him fortunate or unfortunate?" "I don't know," replied Socrates, "having never met him." "Are you serious?" spluttered Critias. "Next I suppose," he added, with a sneer, "that you're going to tell us you have no idea if the great king of Persia is fortunate, despite his vast wealth and influence!" "Not without knowing more about his education and the nature of his character," replied Socrates, shrugging. "Having a good life depends *solely* on that?" asked Alcibiades. "Yes," said Socrates, "because a person is fortunate if wise and virtuous but miserable if foolish and vicious." Alcibiades cocked his head to one side in disbelief: "So according to you, Socrates, this tyrant, being a criminal, is unfortunate, his victims are somehow the fortunate ones, and you would rather be in their shoes and dead than his and alive—come now, no man of reason would agree with such utter nonsense!"

"My dear friend," sighed Socrates, "this really does seem like a childish objection on your part. You are not trying to refute me with reason but with rhetoric. You feel that most of Athens would agree with you," he added, "and you are probably right— even many influential men would take your side. Yet though I am but one individual, I do not agree with you, because you have produced no reason why I should. Our disagreement," he added, "rests on the fact that you believe it is possible for a man who is wicked to be called fortunate, whereas I do not." Alcibiades nodded, although he looked a little confused. "Let me ask you this," said Socrates, "do you believe that a man who does wrong will be fortunate if he is brought to justice and punished?" "Of course not," replied Alcibiades. "He will be most unfortunate." "So you maintain that a wrongdoer who avoids being brought to justice is more fortunate than one who is punished?" asked Socrates. Alcibiades agreed. "My view," said Socrates, "is that a wrongdoer is unfortunate in either case but especially so if he evades justice."

"What are you talking about, Socrates?" snorted Alcibiades. He took a deep breath and then tried to express his concerns: "Let us suppose that a would-be tyrant is arrested for plotting to seize power. His body is broken on the rack, he is castrated with hot irons, and he will be forced to watch his wife and children suffer the most horrific forms of torture before having his eyes plucked out for good measure. He is then crucified until near death, at which point his body is finally burned at the stake, and his remains disposed of with no funeral rites. Would this man, according to you, be more fortunate than one who evades justice and manages to set himself up as a tyrant in a city where he does whatever he likes until he dies peacefully in old age?"

"My dear Alcibiades, you'll fare no better trying to prove me wrong by frightening me with bogeymen," Socrates replied, smiling, "than you did a moment ago when appealing to the mob. Neither the man who establishes an unjust tyranny nor the man who is caught and punished for trying to do so can be called fortunate, although of the two the one who gets away with it is worse off." At this, Alcibiades turned away from Socrates toward Critias and the others, and he burst out laughing. "Is laughing at someone instead of giving reasons a new form of refutation, Alcibiades?" said Socrates. "What reasons are needed," replied Alcibiades, "when you say things that nobody else believes? Ask anyone present."

"Which is more shameful, doing wrong or suffering wrong?" asked Socrates. Alcibiades, without hesitation, said *doing* wrong, although Critias and the others seemed unsure if they would agree. "If it is more shameful does that not mean it is worse?" asked Socrates. At first, Alcibiades wanted to say he didn't consider good to be identical with what is honorable, or bad with what is shameful and dishonorable. However, the more Socrates pressed this point, the more he wavered. Having appealed so often to the court of public opinion, he felt uneasy making the assertion that what is shameful and dishonorable can be good—most audiences would, of course, disapprove of things they consider *shameful*.

Socrates summed up his paradoxical claims as follows. First, wickedness and wrongdoing are the greatest evils. Second, punishment is just whenever it cures this evil in us, whereas avoiding such punishment makes the evil permanent. Third, the greatest evil of all must therefore be to commit wrongdoing and yet evade punishment altogether, such that we are never cured of our wrongs. Of course, the mildest and best punishment that can improve our characters would be to have our errors exposed by philosophy, which is what Socrates dedicated his life to doing.

While Alcibiades had been arguing lightheartedly, for the most part, Critias was scowling and seemed quite exasperated.

"By the gods," he suddenly exclaimed, "tell me, Chaerephon, is your friend Socrates playing the fool?" "He seems earnest to me," replied Chaerephon. "Socrates, do your words not turn life upside down and leave us doing the opposite of what we should?" spluttered Critias.

Both Alcibiades and Critias had been attracted to the study of rhetoric, by its promise of political power. Nevertheless, Alcibiades differed from Critias and most of his other peers, in that he at least felt genuine shame when Socrates questioned him about justice and forced him to admit his ignorance. Nevertheless, he was notoriously lacking in moderation and often found himself overplaying his hand. Socrates liked to remind his friends of another famous inscription at the temple of Apollo, which counseled "Nothing in excess." He, like many older Athenians, feared that the hubris and vast excess of the Sicilian Expedition was tempting fate and would perhaps end in tragedy.

THE EXPEDITION SETS SAIL

THE CROWDS WHO LINED THE road from Athens to Piraeus were flushed with confidence. Even more of the city's inhabitants had crammed themselves along the quayside, or spilled onto the shore, to celebrate the departure of their fleet. Alcibiades stood proudly on the deck of his flagship, the trireme *Eleutheria*, or *Freedom*.[4] Although Athens had deployed large fleets before, this expedition was like no other. The ships departing from Piraeus that day looked beautiful and invincible to the families who waved their sons goodbye.

It was the most expensive and well-equipped force ever mobilized by a Greek city, and the most distant theater in which Athens had ever gone to war. As the generals stopped at friendly ports along the way, more triremes joined them. By the time the fleet approached the region known as Magna Graecia, in the south of Italy, it had swollen to 134 warships, accompanied by roughly as many supply ships and smaller boats. There must have been at least twenty-six thousand fighting men onboard, mainly oarsmen, some of whom could double as light-armed troops, but also archers, slingers, and thousands of heavily armed hoplites. They included allies, loyal to Alcibiades, mostly from Argos and Mantinea. Thousands of noncombatants accompanied them, such as bakers, carpenters, and stonemasons, who earned a living helping to maintain the huge armada.

However, when they stopped at the ports of Greek cities they assumed would be friendly, they found none willing to offer them much aid. The citizens were fearful of being looted, or even enslaved, by such an imposing army. Worse still, the Athenians had been duped regarding the financial resources of their Segestan allies. Now, Alcibiades was left in joint command of a huge armament, bigger and more unwieldy than he had requested, without sufficient funds to pay his men.

The three generals, inevitably, disagreed about strategy. Lamachus favored a lightning attack on Syracuse. Nicias wanted merely to complete their mission by attacking Selinus, fulfilling their obligation to the Segestans, to make a show of strength, and then sail home at the first opportunity. Alcibiades's plan was more ambitious. Now that the element of surprise had been lost, he proposed that they build alliances with as many cities in the region as possible. He hoped to secure grain, horses, and additional troops in Sicily. They would proceed to establish a base at Messana, on the northeastern tip of Sicily, besiege Selinus, and then take the city of Syracuse. Nicias and Lamachus reluctantly agreed. Messana, however, and other nearby cities, gave them a cold reception and little or no support, being frightened by the imposing size of the Athenian fleet.

Alcibiades's men managed, with the aid of local partisans, to set up a base in the town of Catana, about halfway between Messana and Syracuse, on the eastern coast of the island. Like the Leontinians and Segestans, the citizens of Catana had embraced elements of democratic rule, making them natural allies of Athens. Unfortunately, Catana was too small for the Athenians' needs, and they had to camp outside in a temporary stockade, which left them somewhat vulnerable to attack. Meanwhile, Alcibiades's enemies back in Athens had been fomenting outrage. To clear the way for their own attempt to seize power, they had persuaded the citizens that the religious scandals were evidence of a coup that had intended to install Alcibiades as tyrant of Athens. The campaign in Sicily was barely underway when the *Salaminia*, one of Athens's two state ships, arrived unexpectedly at Catana. With more informers suddenly coming forward to testify against him, Alcibiades had been recalled to stand trial in Athens and face a potential death sentence.

The Athenian authorities could not arrest a general of Alcibiades's stature without risking a mutiny of the many soldiers devoted to him. He agreed to return voluntarily to Athens and stand trial, his flagship escorted by the *Salaminia*. Along the way, they put ashore overnight at a Greek colony on the Italian coast. Alcibiades, having weighed his options carefully, decided to slip away from his guards. He was smuggled onto a ship and disappeared under cover of darkness. Before embarking for Sicily, he had volunteered to defend himself in court but was denied the opportunity to do so. His enemies clearly meant to ensure that he would not face a fair trial.

As soon as the news of his escape reached Athens, Alcibiades was condemned to death *in absentia*. He was now an outlaw and a hunted man. He eventually turned up in Sparta, by invitation of King Agis II, one of the few places where he could seek refuge. Back home, in Athens, the son of Cleinias was ritually cursed and his property seized and publicly auctioned, which raised a fortune of one hundred talents of silver for the state. A bounty was put on his head and that of his confederates. Decades earlier, when Alcibiades was little more than a baby, and Anaxagoras received word of his death sentence, the philosopher calmly replied that both he and his accusers had been condemned to die long ago by nature. When the news reached Alcibiades that his rivals in Athens wanted him dead, he whispered darkly: *I will show them that I am alive!*

THE WAR UNDER NICIAS

THE ATHENIANS, NOW UNDER THE command of Nicias, with Lamachus as deputy, sailed around the coast and marched through the interior of Sicily to make a show of strength. The enemy waited, refusing to engage them for now. Alcibiades had enjoyed a special relationship with the Segestans and Leontinians. With him gone, they must have doubted Nicias's commitment to their goals and their defense, leaving them less inclined to risk supporting his campaign. Nicias, in any case, achieved little else in the first year, before his troops settled down to winter in Catana. The Athenians, reluctant to ship their own horses such a long distance, had assumed they could obtain horses from cities on the island. However, lacking Alcibiades's skill as a negotiator, Nicias was unable to persuade the local rulers that such a vast armament meant them no harm. Without cavalry, in this terrain, his troops were left severely hampered in their ability to engage in land battles. The enemy had many horsemen who could outflank infantry, pursue and pick them off when retreating, or defend their own troops in retreat. Over time, they began riding up to the Athenian camp and taunting them: "Have you come not to fight, men of Athens, but merely to settle down in our country?"

The Syracusans eventually marched to Catana, believing an opportunity had arisen to surround the Athenians and catch them off guard, only to discover they had been tricked. The Athenians had sailed along the coast during the night and were fortifying a position adjacent to Syracuse, beside some hills and marshland, which gave them protection against enemy cavalry. After burning the deserted camp at Catana, the Syracusans began the day-long march home. The two armies lined up for battle the next morning, formed into opposing phalanxes: handpicked veteran troops on the Athenian side against novices levied by the Syracusans to defend their homeland.

The battle was in stalemate until a storm broke overhead, which so badly disconcerted the inexperienced Syracusans that the Athenians were able to rout them. The enemy cavalry, over a thousand strong, prevented any pursuit, however, limiting their losses to only a few hundred men. After that hollow victory, Nicias withdrew to Catana, to have his troops rebuild their encampment and resupply for the spring campaign. The Syracusans used the winter months to build fortifications and provide their soldiers with better arms and training. They also sent for military aid from Sparta.

In the spring, the Athenians managed to capture some high ground overlooking the city of Syracuse, which they fortified, in order to begin a siege. Next, they started to erect a wall of circumvallation around the city, to prevent anyone from getting in or out and to protect their own troops. Their efforts were hampered by the Syracusans building counterwalls, between their city and nearby forts. After some intense fighting, however, the Athenians were able to blockade the city of Syracuse by both land and sea, sending their fleet into the harbor, though one of their generals, Lamachus, was slain in battle. The Syracusans, demoralized, began to discuss terms of surrender. It appeared the expedition was finally about to succeed.

Sparta, in response to Syracuse's pleas, had made the surprising decision to send a small fleet commanded by an undistinguished general named Gylippus, whose mother was a slave. Nicias, viewing this as a mere token gesture, took no precautions. The Spartans, however, by sending a general with a small force were mirroring the prudent strategy initially proposed by Alcibiades. They would unite their allies, train and organize them, without making the mistake of intimidating them by sending in too many troops. Nicias was about to discover that despite Gylippus's humble birth, he would prove himself to be one of the most formidable generals of the war.

Gylippus landed with a modest force of one thousand hoplites and around two thousand auxiliary troops. He announced that if the Athenians agreed to depart Sicily in five days, they would escape harm. Nicias treated his offer with contempt, so Gylippus began to engage the Athenians in battle. After some initial setbacks, by bringing Spartan military expertise to the aid of the beleaguered Syracusans, he soon turned the war around. The Syracusans were able to complete a counterwall, which rendered the Athenian circumvallations useless. With Nicias's hopes of blockading the city completely dashed, enemy reinforcements arriving by sea, and horsemen patrolling the surrounding countryside, the Athenians were forced into a defensive posture. Suddenly, they had become the ones besieged.

To make matters even worse, Nicias's health began to fail, apparently due to kidney disease. His troops were weary and the hulls of his ships, after more than a year at sea without suitable harbors for repairs, were in dire condition. Over the winter, he wrote to Athens, asking the Assembly to consider recalling the expedition and allowing him to step down from his post. They refused to accept his resignation and chose instead to send a large contingent of reinforcements. The Athenians and their allies had now committed over two hundred warships in total, carrying more than forty thousand troops. All of Athens's previous campaigns now seemed to pale in significance beside the scale and complexity of the Sicilian Expedition.

When the reinforcements arrived, their general, Demosthenes, immediately attacked, hoping to frighten the enemy with a show of force. After failing to take the counterwall using siege engines, he concentrated all his forces in an audacious nighttime offensive. The Athenian side became disorganized in the darkness, however, leading to the loss of a great many lives. After this setback, he reluctantly advised Nicias to call off the expedition and return home. The Athenians were in a poor condition, battle weary and infected by disease, having been forced to camp at length beside marshland. They were caught in a stalemate and running out of resources. Worse, while they were absent, the Spartans had seized the opportunity to invade Attica and occupy a fort at Decelea, about midway between Athens and Boeotia. This allowed them to control the region surrounding Athens year-round instead of just in the summer. Besieged now both by the Spartans at home and by the Syracusans in Sicily, Athens found itself fighting, and losing, a war on two fronts. It was time for the Athenians to cut their losses and run.

Although Nicias had opposed beginning the expedition, he

stubbornly refused to leave. He was afraid the Assembly would punish such a colossal failure by accusing him of cowardice and taking bribes, and execute him for treason. He therefore insisted, against all counsel, that the Athenians should remain in Sicily, nurturing the vain hope that a faction within the walls of Syracuse might somehow aid them. For Alcibiades, defeat in Sicily would, at worst, have meant some losses and a humiliating retreat. He never expected that Nicias would risk the lives of so many men by keeping them there to die.

When, instead of partisans throwing open the gates, more reinforcements arrived from the Peloponnese, the other generals finally persuaded the ailing Nicias that they had to leave. As the Athenian army was packing its bags, however, an unexpected sight filled them with awe. The night sky began to darken, as the full moon appeared to slowly fade, before turning blood red. Pericles would have faced his cowering troops and explained with authority that it was merely a natural phenomenon; the earth's shadow had eclipsed the moon. Indeed, the dimmed moonlight was a blessing, as it might help conceal their flight from the enemy. The notoriously superstitious Nicias insisted it was an omen that warned them to stay for another month, until the moon had completed its cycle. Meanwhile, Gylippus helped the Syracusans to train their fleet.

While they were waiting for Nicias to order the retreat, the Athenians suffered a surprise naval defeat at the hands of the Syracusans inside the harbor. The men were sick with malaria, and their ships were badly in need of repairs. Once masters of the waves, they were now being bested by novices. The Syracusans strung a barrier, a mile wide, across the harbor mouth, by fastening boats together with chains. Nicias, realizing that their food supply had been cut off, ordered every able-bodied man aboard their ships to attempt a desperate breakout. Their lives, he said, and the safety of Athens would turn on the outcome of this one battle. About a hundred ships on each side clashed in the cramped harbor, preventing the Athenians from being able to maneuver and ram their opponents. Instead, they were forced to fight from the decks by throwing javelins, as if engaged in a land battle on the water. Nicias had hoped to capture enemy ships with grappling hooks, but the Syracusans cleverly thwarted this strategy by modifying their decks to prevent anything from gaining purchase.

The battle was gruesome and long. Everywhere rowers entangled their oars, as chaos ensued among the largest number of ships ever to fight in such a confined space. The Athenians became confused, being unused to such chaotic naval fighting. Eventually they were driven ashore, and the crews abandoned their ships, fleeing back behind the fortifications of their camp. They panicked and decided to retreat without recovering their dead, an act considered so disgraceful it could have led to them being severely punished on their return to Athens. As both sides had lost half their ships, however, the other generals advised Nicias to launch a second attack. He told his men that if they ever wanted to see Athens again, they *must* break their ships out of the harbor. The crews, completely demoralized and fearing a massacre, refused. Nicias's only option was to abandon his entire fleet, leaving it in the hands of the enemy, and retreat by land to the nearest friendly city that might offer him refuge. There were around forty thousand Athenians left alive, including a great many noncombatants. They became, effectively, a city on the march, fleeing from their pursuers.

The Syracusans, to make things worse, tricked Nicias into delaying his march long enough for them to send out scouts and build roadblocks further inland. When the Athenians finally broke camp, they were forced to leave many wounded behind and their dead unburied. This was such an offense to their honor that they wept and beat their heads in grief while they walked away, turning their backs on their dead and dying comrades. Once again, they discovered the danger of an infantry march through terrain filled with enemy cavalry. They were weak, frightened, confused, and constantly harried by hit-and-run attacks. On the march, they lamented how their high hopes at the splendor of their armament setting out had plummeted into such despair after their humiliating defeat. It was undoubtedly the greatest reversal of fortune ever suffered by a Greek army. Nicias tried to improve morale by giving a speech in which he claimed their collective misfortune meant the gods were bound to take pity on them, given his many years of devotion to the state religion. That must have seemed like weak medicine in their plight.

Eventually, during a nighttime march, the Athenians became divided into two groups. The first surrendered, after being encircled by the enemy and pelted with missiles. The second fell into total disarray, in the rush to obtain drinking water, when it came upon a river under the blazing sun. The Syracusan army, which was waiting in ambush nearby, surrounded and slaughtered most of the Athenians by the riverbanks. A few managed to flee this chaos to reach the safety of Catana, but by now more had died during this march than in any single battle of the expedition.

The remaining seven thousand were taken captive by the Syracusans, who imprisoned them in quarries near their city, packed together without shelter from the sun, and surrounded by armed guards. Nicias surrendered and begged the Spartan general for mercy, something many Athenians considered a disgrace. His pleas fell on deaf ears, and the Syracusans had him executed. His troops were left to rot in the quarries, among piles of corpses, where they died slowly of disease and starvation. After eight long months, the few who survived were auctioned as slaves, apart from the remaining Athenians, who were simply butchered like animals.

One day, back home, a stranger arrived at Piraeus. While sitting in a barber's chair, he began to gossip about the disaster in Sicily, assuming the news had already reached Athens. Nobody could believe what he was saying. It caused such uproar that he was accused of spreading enemy propaganda. They tortured him on the wheel, trying to make him say it wasn't true. Over the following days, though, other travelers arrived who confirmed his story and the shameful downfall of Nicias.

The Sicilian disaster and the Spartan occupation of Decelea, near Athens, marked the beginning of the Peloponnesian War's third and final phase. The Athenian armada had suffered an unimaginable defeat. At least ten thousand hoplites and thirty thousand sailors had been slain, plus noncombatants. Almost half the Athenian Empire's entire fleet had been captured or destroyed. These losses included their most experienced troops. The crippling financial cost of the expedition had all but ruined the city. Perhaps worse, Syracuse had now been brought into the war, allied with Sparta, and its emerging naval power would continue to threaten Athens.

Rhetoric was a double-edged sword that could be used to transform strengths into weaknesses and vice versa. Socrates had repeatedly warned Alcibiades that the Assembly of Athens could be turned against him by skilled orators, appealing to the fears and prejudices of the masses. In his absence, the son of Cleinias had been powerless to defend himself before the courts. Alcibiades's apparent strengths—his great wealth, popularity, and military prowess—became *weaknesses* because they were used by his enemies to instill fear that he planned to overthrow the democracy and impose himself as a tyrant. Ironically, though, having been stripped of his command and forced into exile by his enemies, to avoid being put to death, Alcibiades was the only general to survive the Sicilian Expedition.

THE PRACTICE OF SPOTTING THINKING ERRORS

SOCRATES BELIEVED THAT RHETORICIANS AND dema-gogues used several ingenious contrivances to win an argument by persuading people of things that weren't necessarily true. In our dialogue above, Alcibiades resorts to several of these tactics while trying to persuade Socrates that rhetoricians and tyrants are the most powerful men in politics. First, he attacks Socrates's character in order to discredit him, next he appeals to popular opinion, then he tries to scare him by describing graphic scenes of violence, and finally he mocks him in an attempt to portray what he's saying as ridiculous. Not one of these tactics would be capable of proving Socrates *wrong*. They are, if you like, ways of winning an argument by *manipulating* the audience or, put bluntly, *cheating*.

The consequences of such cheating could be devastating. No sooner had Alcibiades and most of his supporters reached Sicily than his political enemies persuaded the Athenian citizens to reverse their earlier decision and recall him for trial. This was, for Athens, perhaps the single most catastrophic setback of the war. Yet it wasn't due to the action of hoplites wielding spears on the battlefield but rather orators wielding rhetoric in the Assembly.

One of the greatest challenges we face today is how to defend ourselves against rhetoric. Today's Sophists are called "influencers," and arguably most of our politicians behave more like demagogues than true statesmen. We're easily manipulated into believing things that we don't know to be true. We are the victims, not only of other peoples' rhetoric but also of *our own*. We frequently exaggerate, trivialize, and generalize, and are selective with the facts, thereby persuading *ourselves* to believe things that may be false. For instance, research shows that people who are anxious tend to overestimate risk, whereas those who are angry do the opposite, like the Athenians who called for this expedition, underestimating the dangers they would face.

Socrates protected himself against rhetoric by questioning the Sophists and exposing the contradictions in their thinking. He also questioned himself, as we've seen. Cognitive therapy has developed a wide variety of techniques, which can help us to examine our thinking for what researchers call "cognitive distortions," informally referred to as "thinking errors." These resemble some of the most common logical fallacies employed by rhetoricians.

When Aaron T. Beck first introduced cognitive therapy, he presented its basic strategy as follows: "The therapist helps a patient to unravel his *distortions in thinking* and to learn alternative, more realistic ways to formulate his experiences."[5] The most common technique of early cognitive therapy was simply to ask, regarding our own distressing beliefs, "Where's the evidence for that?" Most people find this easier to learn with the help of a therapist. An even simpler technique consists in the habit of spotting our own cognitive distortions—you can learn to do this quite easily *without* the help of a therapist. Just by noticing our thinking errors and realizing that they *are* errors, we can gain a more detached perspective, the "cognitive distancing" mentioned in an earlier chapter. Training ourselves to become mindful of cognitive distortions can also make it harder for *others* to deceive us by leading us into such errors in our thinking.

Books on CBT contain various lists of common thinking errors. Each one may overlap with the others. However, Beck originally described *four* common types:

- **Exaggerating or trivializing.** Beck called this "extreme thinking," which, for example, includes what many therapists call "catastrophizing," or overestimating the severity of a threat and blowing it out of proportion. We also tend to speak of people minimizing or trivializing certain things. Beck likewise referred to thinking in *polarized* extremes, such as believing that someone is either a friend or an enemy, and nobody falls in between, a tendency that is sometimes called "black and white" or "all or nothing" thinking.
- **Selective thinking.** We've all encountered people who exhibit "selective memory," "selective hearing," and the like. These are examples of a more general problem, which Beck called "selective abstraction," because it involves taking information out of context by ignoring, or possibly dismissing, relevant facts—you might also call it *cherry-picking* information or failing to look at the whole picture. For instance, a depressed person may only remember the criticisms made in an appraisal of their work, while forgetting any compliments.
- **Jumping to conclusions.** Beck refers to this as "arbitrary inference," which means making *unfounded assumptions*. For instance, cognitive therapists label it "fortune telling"

when someone presumes to know things in advance without sufficient evidence, such as overestimating the probability of a threat. Another common example would be "mind reading," in which we jump to conclusions about what other people are thinking.

- **Overgeneralization.** This is the term Beck used for another common error, in which we assume that something true in one situation is true in general. For instance, clients in therapy often talk in *sweeping terms* about certain things "always" or "never" happening. Overgeneralizations are the basis of many stereotypes and prejudices against other groups, such as "All philosophers corrupt the youth!"

As you can see, there are several variations of these errors and many others we could add to the list. Most people don't experience all of them at once, of course. There's nothing to stop you from identifying other types of cognitive distortion and choosing to work on those. It's often helpful, though, to analyze your emotions carefully in order to spot what your most significant thinking errors might be. You may want to begin by thinking of several recent examples of situations where you have exhibited one of the errors above. Imagine how fateful decisions could have been made differently in the Athenian Assembly if the citizens were trained to notice when these sorts of distortions were being exploited by demagogues. Would they have voted to recall Alcibiades for trial, or even to invade Sicily in the first place, if they had been more on the lookout for political rhetoric encouraging them to make errors of reasoning?

You'll obtain the most benefit from learning about thinking errors if you can get into the habit of spotting them wherever they occur, or at least whenever they appear to be associated with anxiety or some other problem. The easiest way to do this is to keep a count or tally of thoughts that exhibit a specific type of thinking error. That alone may suffice to help you achieve cognitive distance, which can often reduce the frequency, intensity, and duration of upsetting thoughts. Beck, for instance, wrote,

Counting [one's own irrational thoughts] allows the patient to distance himself from his thoughts, gives him a sense of mastery over them, and helps him to recognize their automatic quality, rather than accepting them as an accurate reflection of external reality.[6]

There are several variations of this technique. You could keep a written tally or use a counter, of the sort used by golfers or doormen. Keep track, for instance, of how many times a day you catch yourself engaged in catastrophic or *exaggerated* thinking. Beck advised accepting the thought rather than fighting it, and merely saying to yourself: "There's another fearful thought. I'll just count it and let it go." Likewise, you could keep track of how many times each day you catch yourself making *overgeneralizations*, whether in thoughts or speech, or how often, each day, you make *unfounded assumptions*, or exhibit a negative bias and engage in *selective thinking*.

You'll probably find it's easier to focus on one type of thinking error at a time rather than tracking all of them. Often when people start doing an exercise like this, they notice an initial increase in the frequency of troubling thoughts. That's normal. Over the following days, if you're consistent, you'll probably find the negative thoughts occurring less often. You'll also start to experience them as more boring, as if viewing them from a more detached perspective. If you can spot your own biased thinking, in this way, and distance yourself from distorted thinking, you'll stand a much better chance of protecting yourself against the rhetoric of others, including influencers and politicians.

THE WAR UNDER ALCIBIADES

IN SPARTA, ALCIBIADES HAD BOLDLY claimed that rather than having any animosity toward his new hosts, he saw himself merely as a patriot defending Athens. He proposed allying himself with Spartan political moderates, represented by King Agis II, and helping them to defeat Nicias and the faction who now controlled Athens. When the king's wife became pregnant the following year, however, it was rumored to be Alcibiades's doing. He was forced to seek refuge a *second* time, fleeing from Sparta to the Persian Empire, under the protection of Tissaphernes, the satrap, or governor, of Ionia and Lydia, in Asia Minor. It was here that the news reached him of Nicias's death and the destruction of the Athenian fleet in Sicily.

With Alcibiades gone, and Athens in turmoil following the Sicilian disaster, a handful of wealthy aristocrats finally seized their chance to take control. Athens had been a democratic state for almost a century. The nobles, however, blamed the Democrats for perpetuating a war that had crippled them financially. In the summer of 411, the navy was told that there were no more funds coming from Athens and their generals would have to go and raise money from allied cities to pay them.[7] By this time, most of the ships were stationed in the port of Samos, a large island near Miletus on the coast of Asia Minor, governed by a democracy that was closely allied with Athens.

A plot was hatched by certain nobles to overthrow the democracies simultaneously in Athens and Samos, and replace them with oligarchic regimes, wresting power from the common people and placing it instead in the hands of a select group of wealthy aristocrats. Prominent among these Oligarchs were Charicles, the young radical who had investigated the scandal of the herms, and a moderate named Theramenes, who happened to be a former student of Socrates. In Athens, they staged an armed coup and rewrote the constitution, establishing a council of four hundred nobles, who would in turn choose five thousand citizens, from the hoplite class, to whom the vote would be restricted. This transformed the Assembly from a democracy into an oligarchy, where the lower classes, who provided most of the oarsmen for the navy, lost their political voice.

The plot in Samos, however, was uncovered, which led to a rebellion, championed by the Athenian general, Thrasybulus. The generals involved in the oligarchic conspiracy at Samos were deposed and the rebel sailors swore allegiance to Thrasybulus and the democracy. The city of Athens may have been in the hands of an oligarchy, but Samos, where the Athenian fleet was stationed, remained a democracy.

The first act of Thrasybulus as the leader of the Democrat army in exile was to move that they grant Alcibiades immunity from prosecution, recall him from exile in Persia, and elect him general, with immediate effect. The vote was easily carried. Alcibiades had heard Socrates say many times that a wise man is never distressed by apparent setbacks because he realizes that there are countless reversals of fortune in life, especially during war. What we call misfortune may turn out to be good fortune, and vice versa. It was only by losing control of their city to the Oligarchs that the Athenian navy were free to elect the generals they loved the most. They clearly believed Alcibiades might turn the tide of war.

Meanwhile, internal fighting broke out in Athens, between the moderates, led by Theramenes, who wanted most of the hoplite class to be enfranchised, and the extreme Oligarchs who wanted to restrict the vote to the original four hundred. The situation worsened when the radical Oligarchs were found to be constructing a fortress in Piraeus, into which they moved the grain supply. The moderates alleged these men were preparing to hand the city over to Sparta. This led to a minor conflict, in which the leaders of the extreme faction were overthrown, and the moderate oligarchy of the five thousand was finally instated. Theramenes, one of the leaders of the moderate Oligarchs, began to call for the return of Alcibiades from exile. However, Athens was effectively left in a state of civil war between the Oligarchs who controlled the city and the Democrat generals who commanded their fleet.

When Alcibiades arrived in Samos, he was greeted as a hero. The sailors crowded around him, begging him to lead them back to Athens. The rebels were furious and wanted nothing more than to liberate their city and their loved ones, and take revenge by slaughtering the remaining Oligarchs. Envoys from the moderate regime now controlling Athens appeared at Samos, promising that the families of the sailors were unharmed. The men remained so enraged, however, that they wanted to launch an immediate strike on Athens, in order to topple the oligarchy.

Alcibiades was perhaps the only man alive who could stand before the Athenian navy in their moment of blind fury and dissuade them, without facing a mutiny. They would be making a fatal mistake, he said, to sail for Athens now. The Spartans would be free to take over not only Ionia but also the Hellespont. About half of Athens's grain supply was shipped down the strait from the

Black Sea coast. If the Spartans controlled the region, the city's throat would be cut, and its people would starve. Athens would be wrested from the Oligarchs, only to fall to Sparta within the year. No, if they wanted to restore the democracy at home, they would have to do the opposite of what the Spartans expected, and sail north to attack them.

Alcibiades went from man to man, through the streets of Samos, gathering support for his daring plan. At times, the cries of opposition grew so deafening that he needed to enlist the famously powerful voice of his friend Thrasybulus. Alcibiades sent word back to Athens that he wanted to make peace with the moderate oligarchy led by Theramenes and avert the looming civil war. Rather than Athenians fighting Athenians, the Democrat and Oligarch factions must unite against the Spartans, or Athens would face certain destruction.

The historian of the war, Thucydides, would look back on this as Alcibiades's finest hour, and the first truly great service he did Athens—a feat of leadership "of the most outstanding kind."[8] Plutarch, reflecting centuries later on the life of Alcibiades, wrote that a lesser man who had been raised suddenly to power by the multitude, especially after returning from exile, would have been tempted to become a demagogue pandering to public opinion. Alcibiades, however, "chose to act in a manner befitting a great ruler who opposes those who are swept along by anger, and prevents them from committing a grave error," and, on that day, he distinguished himself as the savior of their city.[9] He was still an outlaw, though, a rogue general who had been taken in by the Spartans and Persians. Even many of the rebel Athenians were unsure how far they could trust him.

In 411, the Spartan general Mindarus tried to instigate a decisive sea battle, by bringing up reinforcements to his base at

Abydos on the Hellespont. These ships, however, were ambushed en route by the Athenians, a move that forced the main Spartan fleet to sail to their rescue. Mindarus now fielded ninety-seven triremes against the main Athenian fleet under Thrasybulus, which had only seventy-four ships. The battle wore on until late afternoon, when a stalemate set in. Suddenly, a fresh squadron of eighteen triremes from Samos appeared in the distance, under the command of Alcibiades. The Spartans stopped in confusion, uncertain to whose aid he had come.

As Alcibiades's ships drew nearer, the crews raised bright purple flags, signalling that they were there to fight for Athens. The Spartan fleet panicked and turned to flee toward the safety of their base. The Athenians pursued them and managed to seize thirty enemy ships and recover fifteen of their own, which had been captured during a previous battle. Alcibiades was back in the fight and, with characteristic flourish, had immediately restored the hopes of the whole Athenian navy.

The Athenians, however, were so financially crippled that they were unable to press their victory. So when, shortly after this, the Persian satrap Tissaphernes arrived at the Hellespont, Alcibiades gladly sailed out to meet him, eager for his friend's support in financing the war effort. Instead, to his surprise, he found himself under arrest, as the king of Persia had ordered Tissaphernes to aid the Spartans. Alcibiades was transported to a prison deep in Persian territory. The Spartans took this opportunity to recapture the city of Cyzicus with the help of another Persian satrap, Pharnabazus, and reinforcements from the Syracusan fleet.

A month later, however, Alcibiades reappeared on horseback at Clazomenae, on the Ionian coast. He was with a fellow prisoner, both having managed to break out one night under cover of darkness. Word had reached him that the Athenians suspected

Mindarus was about to launch another major attack against their naval base on the Hellespont. Alcibiades rushed to their aid, once again, with a small squadron of triremes. When reinforcements under Thrasybulus (the leader of the Democrats at Samos) and Theramenes (the leader of the moderate Oligarchs at Athens) arrived to join them, Alcibiades suddenly found himself in command of an imposing fleet, numbering eighty-six sails. It was an extraordinary moment: Athens had been on the verge of civil war, but Alcibiades had managed to persuade the Oligarchs and Democrats to set aside their differences and fight side by side in a combined force capable, once again, of defeating the Spartans.

Alcibiades saw his chance and took it. First, he impounded every vessel, large or small, that could cross the Hellespont. The Spartans would not learn about the size of the fleet that was about to launch against them until it was too late. The next morning, he gave a rousing speech to the men under his command, explaining their plight but filling them with hope. Following the catastrophic defeat of Nicias in Sicily, Athens was now destitute. The enemy was rich, its coffers filled with Persian gold. All the better, for Athenians would "fight at sea, fight on land, and fight against fortresses" in order to take back whatever they needed from the enemy. That day the sky was dark with clouds and heavy rain fell, weather that triremes would not normally choose to set sail in. Instead of delaying, Alcibiades used it as the opportunity for a surprise attack. Sure enough, as his ships emerged from the storm they caught the Spartan fleet off guard, on maneuvers by the shoreline. Alcibiades led a decoy squadron, which drew the Spartans out to sea, while Thrasybulus and Theramenes cut them off from the safety of their harbor.

The Spartans panicked and fled to the nearest shore, where they moored all sixty of their triremes, side by side, to prevent them being rammed by the Athenians. Alcibiades landed on the shore with a contingent of hoplite marines, who fought their way along the beach to outflank the enemy. Mindarus led a desperate counterattack on the shore but was slain in the fighting. The entire Spartan fleet was captured, except for the Syracusan ships, which were burned by their own crews. The Spartan officer left in command sent home a notoriously laconic message: "The ships are gone. Mindarus is dead. The men are starving. We know not what to do." They were down but not out. Although the Spartans had lost their main fleet, they still had the vast resources of the Persian Empire behind them.

The next day, Alcibiades sailed into Cyzicus unopposed, as the Peloponnesians and their new Persian allies had evacuated. He secured a massive bounty from the city. Next, the Athenian fleet recaptured Byzantium, which controlled the Bosporus and access to the Black Sea. Alcibiades sailed from one city to another, exacting tribute, collecting taxes, building fortifications, and gradually restoring Athenian domination of the Hellespont. After witnessing him achieve a string of stunning victories, the short-lived oligarchy at Athens collapsed, and democracy was reinstated. Eight years had passed since the son of Cleinias had bid farewell to his friend Socrates and set sail from Athens. It was time, at last, for Alcibiades to go home.

9

THE FALL OF ATHENS

ALCIBIADES'S SMALL FLEET OF TRIREMES rowed trium-
phantly into Piraeus, the port of Athens, in the summer of 407
BCE. The twenty ships were decked with battle trophies: captured swords and spears, helmets, and shields bearing the Spartan
lambda. The figureheads ripped from over two hundred defeated
enemy vessels were towed along in their wake.

Alcibiades stood at the prow of his flagship, whose bright purple sails were rivaled in beauty only by the flowing robes in which
he was dressed. Now in his forties, although he retained his famously youthful looks, a few strands of gray hair were starting to
appear. On his arm, he bore a golden shield, which depicted Eros
armed with the thunderbolt of Zeus. A celebrated actor led the
chant, keeping the oarsmen in time, accompanied by a famous
flutist. The crowds, intoxicated like revelers at a party, cheered
the man they hoped would be their savior. Fathers pointed out
the returning hero to their youngest sons, who had never before
glimpsed his face.

As Alcibiades disembarked, the mob pushed aside even his
fellow generals, Theramenes and Thrasybulus, rushing to sur-

round the tall nobleman. Those who got closest grabbed at his clothes and adorned him with ribbons and golden wreaths. It was obvious the moment he set foot on Attic soil that many Athenians, especially the men of military age, welcomed him as their leader. Some even wanted him to be named king over what remained of their empire. Tears stained his cheeks as the praise with which his fellow Athenians now showered him stood in such marked contrast to the condemnation they had once heaped upon him. Homesick, after so many years in exile, he could not resist the temptation to return to Athens in glory.

"Remember, my friend, that it was *my* motion in the Assembly that brought you back," a grinning Critias whispered in his ear. Critias had grown into an accomplished orator and was becoming one of the most influential speakers in the Assembly. He and the other young nobles hoped that Alcibiades's presence would help consolidate their influence over Athenian politics. Alcibiades's reputation among much of the ruling class had been restored by his stunning victories in Abydos, Cyzicus, and Byzantium, which seemed to be turning the tide. More importantly, by reconciling the moderate Democrats and Oligarchs, and persuading them to fight as one against Sparta, he had averted a civil war, which threatened to tear Athens apart. His popularity among the common people had barely waned, despite his troubles, and was now higher than ever. The sailors adored him as one of their own, and would follow him anywhere, boasting that their general had never yet been defeated in battle.

After the Athenians had celebrated his recent victories, they began recounting to one another, with tear-filled eyes, the catastrophic misfortunes they had suffered during his exile. Many lamented that they would never have lost the war in Sicily and suffered such dire catastrophe if only the Assembly had granted

Alcibiades supreme command and trusted him as they had trusted Pericles. With her navy almost vanquished from the sea, enemy soldiers marching through her farmlands, and political rivals at each other's throats within her walls, Athens had seemed on the verge of collapse. Yet Alcibiades had seized victory by convincing the opposing factions to set aside their differences for the common good. The main Spartan fleet had been destroyed at Cyzicus, its general killed, and Athens had regained control of the Hellespont. Democracy had been restored in Athens, and now the Spartans were forced to sue for peace.

Nevertheless, Alcibiades was a former exile, and a divisive figure, with powerful enemies among the Athenian aristocracy. He only agreed to leave his ship and come ashore when he witnessed his kinsmen and friends approaching the harbor to greet him. They offered him safe escort into Athens, where he hastened to the Pnyx, in order to address the Assembly. Standing on the rostrum he spoke to a huge crowd, perhaps numbering tens of thousands. They lamented the miscarriage of justice that had forced him into exile, placing him at odds with his homeland. Alcibiades spoke with great temperance and diplomacy, quite the opposite of Cleon's fiery rhetoric. Instead of complaining bitterly about his fate and blaming his fellow citizens, he calmly described his previous downfall as a matter of personal misfortune. Rising above partisan squabbles, he led by example, showing his fellow Athenians the magnanimity he also needed them to find within themselves. His message was that they should set aside thoughts of revenge and work together to rebuild their empire. Nobody, that day, saw fit to speak against him.

Alcibiades had long been prepared to answer the charge of impiety, not through words alone but also through his actions. For the past eight years, the Spartans had occupied the fort of Decelea, giving them control of northern Attica all year round. This stopped processions taking place from Athens to Eleusis, forcing celebrants to sail along the coast instead. Alcibiades's first act was to pledge before the Assembly that in early autumn, he would ride to Eleusis, leading an armed escort, and provide security for those attending the Greater Mysteries of Demeter. In the eyes of the people, this made the former accusations against him for defiling the mysteries seem ridiculous—either he was innocent or the goddess had forgiven him. The Assembly therefore ordered the priests to revoke the curses they had laid upon him, which named him as a traitor, and to throw the pillars on which they had been inscribed into the sea. His fellow citizens then voted to return to him all his former property in the region, which the state had seized when he was exiled.

Having addressed the past, Alcibiades turned his attention to the future. He began to detail military weaknesses among the Spartans and their allies, which he believed would provide Athens with further opportunities for victory. His speech was designed to give the people courage, as he, once again, asked them to follow him into war—and it worked. The Athenians were so enthusiastic that they put a golden crown on his head, a glamorous but not unusual award for military achievements. More importantly, they elected him *strategos autokrator*, or supreme commander of all their forces on both land and sea. The Assembly ordered a fleet of one hundred triremes to be prepared for him, crewed by twenty thousand men, including fifteen hundred hoplite marines.

Even as the victor's crown was placed on his head, however, Alcibiades knew gossips would be whispering that he had put into harbor on an ill-omened day. The multitude may have greeted him and led him into the city with fanfare, but the goddess veiled herself from him and refused him welcome. Images of Athena had been covered up throughout Athens, while they were being cleaned, as part of the annual summer festival of Plynteria. The temples were therefore closed. As the city was temporarily without its patron deity, no business was supposed to be conducted. Over two centuries earlier, Alcibiades's ancestors had defiled the Acropolis by killing rebels there who were involved in an attempted coup meant to install a tyrant over the city. The notorious curse laid upon the heads of the Alcmaeonid clan, for shedding blood before Athena's sacred altar, was still brought up against them. It appeared strange, therefore, that his old friend Critias had proposed a motion for Alcibiades to be recalled from exile during this solemn religious holiday. The timing would cast a shadow over his arrival and leave any authority he was granted by the Assembly's vote in question.

It was at the Pnyx, on the day of his return, that the son of Cleinias sighted an old friend whose memory had haunted him ever since he left Athens.[1] Despite everything, Alcibiades felt that his homecoming would be incomplete, perhaps even worthless, unless he could set eyes once more on Socrates. Indeed, if Socrates had not, a quarter of a century earlier, saved his life on the battlefield of Potidaea, Alcibiades would never have witnessed the start of the war, let alone become Athens's supreme commander in its final phase. It must have seemed like a lifetime since they last spoke, eight years earlier, when Socrates warned his beloved friend not to take command of a fleet crossing the Ionian Sea, for the doomed expedition to Sicily. The crews of over two hundred triremes had been lost on that campaign, and it was perhaps only by a quirk of fate that Alcibiades was not among the dead. Socrates and Alcibiades looked at each other for a moment, through the crowd, but no words were exchanged. Alcibiades felt too ashamed. Instead, he turned away, embraced his kinsmen and companions, and joined their celebrations.

THE THIRD DIALOGUE WITH ALCIBIADES

SEVERAL WEEKS PASSED BEFORE ALCIBIADES found the courage to approach Socrates. He came across him in one of his favorite haunts in the Agora. Although Socrates was notorious for going around barefoot, he liked to pass time in the workshop of his friend Simon, the shoemaker. Alcibiades, by contrast, was very fond of a good shoe, and had made an unusual new design fashionable, which bore his name. Over the sound of nails being hammered into leather soles, the conversation of this odd couple soon returned, as always, to the nature of justice. Although he held the Assembly in the palm of his hand, as long as he remained in Athens, Alcibiades knew that he fell short of the wisdom required to be a truly great statesman. Nevertheless, he exceeded the fame of any living military or political leader in Greece. What he craved most was to outshine even Pericles, and he seemed on the verge of achieving that.

Pericles, though, had accomplished a delicate balancing act. Despite being the ruler, in effect, of a large and powerful Athenian Empire, he maintained the appearance that he was a man of the people, upholding democracy. How could Alcibiades exceed Pericles's power and status except by crossing the line that separated an elected general from a lawless tyrant? Yet, although there were rumors of him conspiring with the oligarchic faction, Alcibiades always professed his allegiance to the Democrats, never participated in an oligarchic regime, and never became a tyrant. Indeed, he helped restore the democracy after the civil war. The citizens of Athens elected him *strategos*, and he stepped onto the rostrum, offering his services as their commander, during their hour of greatest need.

"The very first time we spoke," lisped Alcibiades, "two decades ago, you told me to set my sights upon rivaling the greatest
Spartan and Persian kings for wisdom. I had barely been outside
of Attica, but I've since traveled widely and come to know all
of Greece, including Sparta, and even the barbarians of Thrace
and Persia—more intimately, I dare say, than almost any man
alive."[2] "Are you suggesting," said Socrates, raising an eyebrow,
"that exile, deemed among the greatest of evils and meted out by
the Athenians as punishment, may actually have benefited you?"
"War and exile, indeed, have been my teachers since we parted
ways," said Alcibiades, smiling. "It is a remarkable thing," said
Socrates, "if circumstances considered by many to be the greatest
of evils can be turned to some good." Indeed, he liked to compare
his beloved Alcibiades to the followers of Dionysus, known as
Bachants, whom legends said were able to draw milk and honey,
miraculously, from wells that had run dry.

"Are you not also known for your eloquence?" asked Socrates.
"It is true," answered Alcibiades, "that I have made a study of
oratory, in order to cultivate what natural ability I may have had,
attending closely to the lectures of Gorgias and other fine rhetoricians, but I would be ashamed to step upon the rostrum if I did
not also believe that I had acquired knowledge that may be of
some benefit to my fellow citizens."

"You have certainly proven yourself capable in the arts of war,"
nodded Socrates. "That may be true," said Alcibiades, frowning,
"but, as you often say, it requires more to be a leader, for to know
when to go to war and when to negotiate peace, one must understand many things, not least what it means to govern with justice."
"Do you believe, best of men, that you have that knowledge?"
asked Socrates. "I know only that I do not yet know what justice
is," sighed Alcibiades, "although I have assuredly learned some-

thing by keeping the company, in my former years, of wise men such as yourself." "Then come with me," said Socrates, "and we shall continue to explore these questions together."

Alcibiades, pained by the knowledge that he lacked wisdom, would continue to seek out Socrates whenever he was able. For this reason, and because his magnanimous return from exile had saved Athens from civil war, Socrates favored Alcibiades over the other great statesmen of his era. Alcibiades realized that Athens's survival depended on its opposing factions setting aside their desire for revenge against one another and working together. Despite his many flaws and the controversy and misfortune in which he became embroiled, he had *wept* when he realized that he lacked wisdom. Others avoided Socrates or turned against him in anger, but Alcibiades was among the few devoted students who had kept returning to him, although they were separated for many years due to Alcibiades's exile. Whereas other statesmen believed that they knew what justice was, Alcibiades knew that he did not, and he yearned to better himself. He wanted, unlike his rivals, not only to lead Athens but to *deserve* to do so.

Several months had passed since Alcibiades's return, and the fleet was on the verge of setting sail to engage that of the new Spartan general, Lysander. Socrates, walking by the River Ilissos, heard a voice calling his name. He turned to see Axiochus, Alcibiades's uncle and best friend, hurrying toward him.[3] Axiochus, with tears in his eyes, began pleading with Socrates to come to his house, where he said Alcibiades was waiting. "He won't eat or sleep, he beats his hands noisily against his breast, and there is only one name on his lips, but I fear he is too proud to approach you himself. Now is the time," urged Axiochus, "for you to show the wisdom of which you are always talking. Come with me, Socrates, and console your beloved friend." Socrates seldom accepted invitations to the homes of powerful men. This time he smiled, nodded politely, and followed Axiochus along the road by the city wall toward an elegant townhouse by the Itonian gate.

When they arrived, Axiochus was pleased to find his friend was on his feet. Although Alcibiades still seemed disturbed, and from his frail appearance it was clear he had been unwell, he smiled and greeted Socrates. When Alcibiades was a child, his father had been slain, in his prime, at the Battle of Coronea. Since that day, the son of Cleinias had been consumed by the need to cover himself in glory before meeting a similar end. As a young man, he grew up in the shadow of Pericles, constantly competing for attention with his famous guardian's sons and desperate to be remembered as an even greater leader than the foremost man in Athens.

His love of fame and glory had defined him, making him into a larger-than-life character—both he and Socrates, though different in so many ways, would be remembered as *great souls* by their contemporaries. The *philotomia* that had consumed Alcibiades made the many dangers he faced throughout his life seem trivial to him. Since returning from exile, though, the fickle nature of public acclaim had become more apparent to him and shaken his belief that it could ever make his life, and death, worthwhile. "Once I laughed at death," he murmured, shaking his head. "Remembering your words, Socrates, I thought of it as a child wearing a bogeyman mask, which frightened fools, to be sure, but seemed ridiculous to the wise."

"What is this, my friend," said Socrates, "and whatever has become of your boastful nature, your talk of virtue and your famous courage? Are we to assume that you have become one of those worthless men," he added, smiling gently, "who exhibit their strength in the training grounds only to lose their nerve and run away in the field of battle? Remember that you are an Athenian and have rubbed shoulders with men of wisdom since you were a beardless boy. After having cast your eye over nature for forty years, will you not now agree with the old saying that life is merely a sojourn on earth? You should pass your time here as a rational man, ready to depart in good spirits at any moment. Otherwise, you condemn yourself to the life of a coward, who ends his days being torn away roughly from existence, weeping like a child." Alcibiades seemed momentarily taken aback, but then the remark seemed to strengthen his desire to recover his former courage and vigor. He laughed, albeit softly.

"Well spoken, my friend," said Alcibiades, "and you're right, as usual. Yet it seems every wise saying slips from my grasp now that I am face-to-face with what I dread most: to die no longer trusting that I will be remembered for my achievements." Although he believed that Athens could be saved, Alcibiades knew that the glory she experienced under Pericles could never be recovered, let alone exceeded, since the disaster at Sicily. Despite the power handed to him, and the adulation poured upon him, he began to fear for his legacy. He saw how easily reputations could change when political regimes were overthrown and knew that he might be remembered by future generations of Athenians as a villain and a traitor. "Fear grips my mind," he said, "and tears me into pieces, when I imagine being removed from the light, and everything good, and left rotting, wherever that may be, unseen and forgotten, being eaten by worms and other foul creatures."

"You are speaking at odds with yourself," remarked Socrates. Alcibiades looked slightly puzzled. "Are you not making the error," explained Socrates, "of confusing consciousness with unconsciousness?" "How so?" asked Alcibiades. "You are grieving over the loss of consciousness that comes at death," said Socrates, "while at the same time you lament the idea of your body rotting, and being deprived of what is pleasant. How can anyone be pained by these experiences, though, if after you die your fate is to be in a state of complete insensibility no different from the one you were in before you were born?" "We cannot, I suppose, experience what our bodies suffer after death," said Alcibiades hesitantly. "You are right, my friend."

Socrates smiled. "As for your reputation after death, consider, noble man, the many difficulties faced over a hundred years ago by your great ancestor. Cleisthenes was vilified and exiled *several* times before he succeeded in founding the institutions of our democracy." Alcibiades's expression was growing somber once again. Fear of the legendary curse upon the heads of the Alcmaeonid clan had been used by Cleisthenes's enemies to turn public opinion against him a century earlier. The same superstition had been used to undermine and attack Alcibiades, throughout his whole career. "Although it may trouble you now to think of the injustice that befell your ancestor," said Socrates, "it certainly did not trouble you when it happened, because at that time you did not exist. So your own present troubles will not affect you in the slightest after your death," he added, "as there will no longer be any Alcibiades in existence to recall them."

"Then again," said Socrates, "according to some the soul continues to live after the body dies, and they become separated from one another. As the body is afflicted throughout by pains, diseases, and other ills, which tarnish what little pleasure we experience in life, the soul grows homesick for heaven and the blissful existence free from sorrow that awaits it there. If such stories are true, then to depart from this life would be to exchange evil for good," he concluded, "something worth desiring rather than fearing."

Alcibiades looked unconvinced. Scowling, he replied, "Really,

Socrates, if you truly considered life on earth to be such a bad thing, then why would you, who exceed us all in wisdom, ever choose to remain here?" "You are not testifying truthfully in the case against me," said Socrates with a laugh, "because like most Athenians, you still confuse a philosopher, who *loves* wisdom, with one who claims to *possess* wisdom!" Socrates explained that it was the Sophist Prodicus, a student of Protagoras, who was the source of these teachings. Socrates did not presume, himself, to know what awaits us in the afterlife. "Nevertheless," he said, "when I heard Prodicus give a speech at the house of Callias, he spoke so eloquently and convincingly against living that I drew a line through the very word, in my mind, marking it as a thing of such little value that I began to yearn instead for death." "Whatever did he say?" asked Alcibiades.

"Let me tell you what I can recall," said Socrates, as he began to gesture and declaim like an orator. "What part of life is free from pain? The infant cries as soon as it is born. Its life thus begins with suffering. And it continues to cry. It cries because it is deprived of food, because it is too hot or too cold, or because it is afflicted by some other cause of discomfort. Being unable to speak, it cries aloud almost constantly. After enduring all this, upon reaching its seventh year, it finds itself under the tyranny of various instructors. Before long, it is being taught grammar, music, geometry, military tactics, and countless other subjects. Things become worse for him as a youth, when the physical trainers in the Lyceum and the Academy begin to discipline him with a stick. Miserable as these experiences are, they are viewed as childish trifles compared with what follows, when he embarks upon adulthood and faces military service, health problems, financial worries, and his life bcomes one constant struggle.

"Before long, old age will have sneaked up on him, and ailments,

which prove increasingly hard to remedy, join forces in the prelude to death. Some pay back quickly the life that is on loan to
them. Others give it back one piece at a time, as though Nature
stood over them like a moneylender demanding the payment due,
as they approach old age. Bit by bit, eyesight, hearing, and the
strength of limbs are taken from them. Even if their bodies remain vigorous, their minds weaken and they become children for
the second time, in their senility.

"What of those, like yourself, who set out across the ocean, and
spend all their days aboard ships? Such men exist neither among
the living nor the dead. Having abandoned their native land, and
cast themselves upon the water, as though transformed into am-
phibious creatures, they commit themselves wholly to the whims
of fortune, and staggering danger. Something you are now on
the verge of facing, yet again. Political power, likewise, is held
in high regard and certainly also brings many pleasures, but in a
fevered state, accompanied by anxiety. That, as you know, is because the fall of an ambitious statesman is full of suffering, worse
than a thousand deaths. Who then can be happy who lives for the
approval of the mob? Even if they receive him with loud cheers
as the plaything of the people, afterward they will reject him,
hissing disapproval, fining him, casting him into exile or putting
him to death," said Socrates in conclusion, "and he is remembered
either with pity or as a villain."

"That is precisely my fear," replied Alcibiades. "Nothing seems
more disagreeable to me now than to stand on the rostrum and
speak to the Assembly and yet it is also my desire to win glory for
myself and my country. You judge the whole business accurately
by looking at it from a distance, Socrates, but we who have tried
our hand at politics know from our own bitter experience how un-
grateful, cruel, envious, and ignorant the people can be. By its very

nature, the Assembly itself is composed of the most worthless med-
dlers, who are only brought together into such a formidable body by
the strength of their collective fear and anger. Those who must pander to it are the most miserable creatures of all." "You make the case
well," said Socrates, "that the most powerful position in Athenian society is the one for which a man should pray the least." "It
does not surprise me," said Alcibiades, frowning, "to discover once
again that we have arrived at such an odd conclusion. Tell me, what
other paradoxes do you and Prodicus have about life and death?"

"That death exists neither for the living nor for the dead," replied Socrates. "How can that be?" asked Alcibiades, looking
more puzzled by the minute. "As regards the living," answered
Socrates, "they are not yet dead, and so the experience of death
does not exist for them. Regarding those who are dead," he added,
"they do not exist themselves, and so cannot experience anything.
You cannot suffer because of death while alive, because it does not
exist for you, nor can you suffer after death, because you will be no
more." The troubled nobleman solemnly agreed. Socrates went on
to explain that when we fear our own death, as if being dead was
somehow an event in our life, we behave as if we knew the value
of something that neither is nor will ever be. Fearing death is like
worrying about dragons, centaurs, or other mythological creatures. Although we can talk about these and other such fantastic
creatures, we never actually encounter them during our lives. The
experience of own death is no less elusive. "Vain is the sorrow," he
said, "in Alcibiades grieving for Alcibiades. For what is fearful is
so to those who exist but to those who do not exist, how can it be
fearful?"

Alcibiades was growing skeptical. "This is fine talk," he said, "of
the kind that wins acclaim from the young boys in the gymnasia,
who like to gather around the Sophists. What grieves me, though,

is not the thought of experiencing suffering after I am dead, something I admit to be impossible, but rather of losing the good things of life and never again knowing any pleasures." What troubled him most, in fact, was the thought of dying a failure in the eyes of his countrymen, which he still considered dishonorable. "The distinction you are trying to make between the experience of pain and deprivation of pleasures is mere wordplay, though," said Socrates. "You are forgetting that you will be dead, and so you will not be able to experience the suffering of deprivation. Are you not therefore contradicting yourself," asked Socrates, "by fearing both that you will be deprived of consciousness and that you will be conscious of being deprived of pleasure?" Alcibiades agreed. He seemed more taken with the argument now and somewhat less preoccupied with the dangers he faced.

"Then again," said Socrates, "there are those who believe that at the end of life, rather than oblivion, we may look forward to immortality. They say the body is like a tomb or prison, from which the soul is released at death, in order to enjoy a pure and blissful existence in heaven." "If the soul does endure," asked Alcibiades, "how can we be sure it is bliss rather than sorrow that awaits us after our death?" "That will depend on your character and where you take your pleasure in life," answered Socrates. "How so?" said Alcibiades. "For a true philosopher, who loves wisdom more than anything, requires nothing besides the ability to reason in order to be happy," said Socrates. "As long as he is asking someone questions, perhaps even himself, and examining their character and values, he is engaged in the highest activity that life has to offer. Whatever happens to him after death, if he is conscious at all, and able to think about his situation, he will be able to reason and continue to do philosophy, in death just as in life." In other words, for a person who is self-sufficient and gains satisfaction entirely from his own conduct, regardless of his environment or other people, any form of afterlife would be a blessing, just as he would be able to prosper in any foreign country. He does not need to know in advance what the place in which he will find himself is like because he already knows that every good he requires comes from within himself.

"You see," said Socrates, "either death is nothing, an endless sleep, in which case it is not evil but indifferent, or our soul continues to exist, and we have the opportunity to do philosophy, in which case death is something good, or at least no worse than living. Indeed," he added, "we have reason enough to hope that it may be better than our life on earth, as we will have the opportunity to experience a realm purified of earthly pains and pleasures, in which I like to think we may have the opportunity to converse with the great men of the past, including your famous ancestors, and perhaps even with the gods themselves. Death is therefore either something indifferent or something good," he said, "and in either case it is something the wise man fears least of all."

Alcibiades, as always, seemed humbled after speaking with Socrates. "You must let me know now if there is anything I can do for you before I leave," he said, smiling, "as we are not certain to meet again." "There is a favor I would ask you," said Socrates. Alcibiades suddenly became as attentive as a soldier awaiting orders; he knew Socrates rarely accepted let alone asked for favors. "Recently," said Socrates, "I was approached by a youth, who begged me most pitiably for assistance. His noble birth and beauty have become his misfortune because he was taken captive and sold to a brothel in Athens—his life there is wretched, as you can imagine." "War leaves many young men in the hands of those who would abuse them," said Alcibiades, with a frown, as he lowered his voice. "Like you," said Socrates, "he came to me in great earnest, seeking nothing more than to improve himself." Alcibiades smiled as he reminisced about his first encounters with Socrates. Then quite abruptly he replied, "His owner will receive payment; he will be free by tomorrow." "Crito has agreed to provide him with a home," said Socrates. "What is his name?" asked Alcibiades. "They call him Phaedo," replied Socrates, "from the city of Elis."[4]

THE BATTLE OF EPHESUS

IN THE SPRING, ALCIBIADES SET sail from Piraeus, with a fleet of one hundred triremes, crewed by around twenty thousand men. His goal was to draw out the main Spartan fleet, of ninety triremes, which Lysander had stationed at Ephesus on the coast of Asia Minor. Alcibiades immediately blockaded the enemy, trapping them in the harbor. The Athenian fleet made its base at the nearby city of Notium. However, a stalemate ensued, with neither side willing to initiate a battle.

Knowing that it would be best to wait for the right opportunity to attack, Alcibiades sailed north with twenty ships, to lend support to his friend and ally, the Athenian general Thrasybulus, who was engaged in a nearby siege. He made the fateful mistake of leaving the remainder of his fleet under the command of not a general but Antiochus, his personal helmsman. Alcibiades gave him strict orders not to engage the enemy. Unfortunately, Antiochus appears to have been tempted by the lure of glory, perhaps seeking to emulate the daring of his captain. In defiance of his orders, Antiochus sailed out to draw the enemy onto the open main, where they could be ambushed by the rest of the Athenian fleet. The plan backfired. The Spartans were ready and managed to sink Antiochus's ship, killing him. They raced to Notium, where the rest of the Athenian fleet was caught by surprise. Seven more Athenian triremes were sunk and fifteen captured by Lysander, although most of their crews escaped.

On receiving the news, Alcibiades promptly returned with enough ships to restore the stalemate. The losses suffered by Athens were a modest setback in military terms. The battle had catastrophic *political* consequences, however, for Alcibiades. His enemies at Athens leaped at the opportunity to blame him. In person, he held the Assembly in the palm of his hand, but once again, orators had taken advantage of his absence. The simplest and perhaps oldest trick of rhetoricians is to present information selectively. They dwelled at length on his notoriety and failings, and said nothing of his talent for leadership and brilliance as a strategist, his rich experience, and his many victories. They brought up the Alcmaeonid curse and the old charges of impiety made against him. In order to sow fear, they claimed it was a mistake to hand Alcibiades so much power, as he intended to overthrow the democracy and impose himself upon them as a tyrant.

What happened was, in some ways, a repeat of his previous ousting during the Sicilian Expedition. Most of the common people who supported Alcibiades were unable to vote because they were in Notium serving as rowers in the fleet, along with many of his personal friends and allies who served under him as officers. The Assembly had been left in the hands of his enemies, particularly older men from wealthy and aristocratic families, with more oligarchic sympathies. They whipped up anger, fear, and resentment toward Alcibiades, who stood in the way of agreeing terms with Sparta. He had already escaped punishment for one disaster, they claimed, but Athens could not survive a second dose of Alcibiades. They voted to strip him immediately of his command and remove him from the office of *strategos*. Around this time, his friend Critias, whose Spartan sympathies were becoming more apparent, was exiled to Thessaly. Alcibiades, in total dismay, withdrew voluntarily from public life. He had fathered a child during his return from exile, but his wife died shortly after giving birth, and his baby son, Alcibaides the Younger, was left in Athens to live as though an orphan.[5] Alcibiades, effectively once more in exile, sailed to his stronghold in the Thracian Chersonese, the peninsula on the western side of the Hellespont. The very democracy that he had just helped to restore had, ironically, brought about his downfall once again.

THE PRACTICE OF OVERCOMING DEATH ANXIETY

WE LEARNED IN AN EARLIER chapter how Socratic philosophy can be utilized as a cognitive therapy for fear. In this chapter, we saw how Socrates used his philosophy to conquer perhaps the greatest fear of all, for many people, the fear of death. The essence of a Socratic therapy for the fear of death appears in Plato's *Apology*, quite prominently, but the mention is tantalizingly brief. A later pseudo-Platonic dialogue called *Axiochus* elaborates on the argument, key parts of which it portrays Socrates attributing to the Sophist Prodicus.[6]

For many people, overcoming the fear of death can change everything. The Stoic philosopher Seneca went so far as to say that as long as we are afraid of death, we shall never do anything worthy of life.[7] At least, reducing this one fear may diminish countless others. Socrates realized that, as with all fears, the first step in mastering our dread of death is to understand that it is largely *cognitive*. We fear death because, despite our uncertainty about its nature, we *believe* that it may be something catastrophic. Animals withdraw from pain, and they have evolved many instincts that protect them from danger. They do not, however, *fear* death, at least not in the sense that humans do. How could they? They have no concept of death. We barely have a concept of death ourselves, and yet we assume that it is something to be feared.

One of the most famous passages in all of classical philosophy comes from the Stoic *Handbook* of Epictetus: "Men are not disturbed by events but by their opinions about them." It was quoted by Albert Ellis and Aaron T. Beck, the pioneers of cognitive-behavioral therapy, in order to explain the cognitive model of emotion. This became a slogan, of sorts, taught to many thousands of CBT clients and repeated in countless books on the subject. However, they did not go on to quote the next part of the passage. The complete saying should read as follows:

> Men are not disturbed by events but by their opinions about them: for example, death is nothing terrible, because if it were, it would have seemed so to Socrates; for the opinion about death, that it is terrible, is the terrible thing.[8]

As you can see, Epictetus immediately applied this concept to what he considered the most pressing psychological issue we face. He refers to Socrates's attitude toward death because, I presume, he is aware that this insight into the psychology of emotions did not originate with Stoicism but goes all the way back to Socrates himself. If generations of psychotherapists had not gotten into the habit of quoting this passage out of context, they would have been forced to reply to the question that it implicitly raises: *How much benefit is there in overcoming our other fears if we continue to be afraid of death?*

For Socrates, the fear of death is a dangerous *conceit*. We believe that we know something that we do not, in fact, know—that death is awful. We base our fear not on knowledge, however, but opinion. This realization is a form of cognitive distancing. We can learn to "distance" or separate our judgment that death is awful from death itself, the event to which it refers, by noticing that it is just an opinion and not a fact. Learning to tolerate uncertainty about the nature of death permits us to suspend our judgment, which will normally reduce the intensity of our distress, especially if this way of thinking becomes habitual or second nature to us.

Today, we know that several different techniques can be used to help psychotherapy clients achieve cognitive distance. We have mentioned some in preceding chapters. For instance, you might begin by observing your feelings about death carefully, noticing how your thoughts shape your emotions, from a detached perspective. Socrates was doing this, in a sense, when he conversed with *other people*, and studied how their beliefs about death and other such important things influenced their emotions and behavior. By observing these processes at work in others, we can sometimes learn to view our own thoughts and feelings with greater objectivity.

In cognitive therapy, we often teach clients to place their thoughts in quotation marks, as it were, by articulating them in a particular way. This combines well with illeism, the technique of referring to ourselves in the third person. Therapists don't often apply these techniques to the fear of death, but if we did we might say: "I notice right now that Donald is thinking 'death is awful!'" or words to that effect. By tactics such as these, we can learn to separate our thoughts about death from the event of death itself, in a way that dilutes our emotional response, while still permitting us to contemplate the idea that death could, potentially, be awful—or perhaps not. The main thing is that we gain cognitive flexibility and the ability to think about death in new ways.

As Socrates said during his trial, we can't know for sure if death is bad, but we can know that acting with injustice is bad, and so are other vices. So perhaps *how* we live our lives, whether badly or well, is more important than the fact that we must die, sooner or later. If we are true lovers of wisdom, who value our own enlightenment above wealth, reputation, physical pleasure, or anything else, our chief good is within rather than outside us. This transforms our relationship with death. We can no longer be deprived of our highest good, except by being deprived of reason altogether, in which case we'd be oblivious rather than suffering. As Socrates realized, therefore, philosophers *cannot* fear death, as long as they genuinely love wisdom.

THE DEATH OF ALCIBIADES

WITH ALCIBIADES GONE, HIS ALLIES were also removed from office, and ten new generals were elected who shared command of the Athenian fleet. At the Battle of Arginusae, they destroyed seventy Spartan ships. This victory more than made up for Athens's defeat at Ephesus, and hopes increased that the war was going in their favor once more. By the following year, however, the Spartan fleet under Lysander had taken Lampsacus, on the Hellespont, threatening to cut off grain supplies to Athens.

A huge Athenian armada, under the new generals, managed to blockade Lysander's ships. Although the Athenians had managed to rebuild their fleet, and reputedly mustered 180 ships for this battle, they could not so easily replace men. Their triremes were now crewed mainly by relatively inexperienced sailors.

Rather than stationing themselves in the harbor of a nearby city, they set up camp on a beach in order to remain close to the enemy. In years to come, sailors would tell how Alcibiades rode into the Athenian camp, dressed in furs, like a "barbarian," with his hair unbound. Although the generals in command were hostile toward him, he offered them his services, advising them to move to a safer location as their camp was a deathtrap. He could raise a force of Thracian horsemen and javelineers, attack the Spartans by land, and force their ships into open waters, where the Athenians would have the advantage.

The new generals, who had been appointed by his enemies, laughed at him and insulted him. They told him to remember that they were in charge and that he had been stripped of his rank. They refused his help, not wanting him to have any share in the credit for the victory they anticipated. Rather than greet him as a fellow Athenian statesman, they banished him from their presence as an outcast. His words of warning must, however, have spread like wildfire among the Athenian camp.

A few days later, in what became known as the Battle of Aegospotami, Lysander launched a surprise attack, catching the Athenian vessels unguarded, without their crews onboard. Save for a handful of ships that had fled, the Spartans captured the entire fleet. Lysanders had the corpses shipped back home so that the Athenians could count their dead. Athens had finally lost the Peloponnesian War. At the outbreak of the conflict, under the rule of Pericles, Athens was at the height of its power. During the course of the war, as a result of battle, famine, and plague, Attica's population had shrunk by one third. Now, at the end, in 404 BCE, having lost both its empire and its navy, Athens was left a shadow of its former glory. Once a symbol of the city's intellectual enlightenment, and its Golden Age under Pericles, the spot where Anaxagoras's celebrated meteorite had fallen from the heavens now became associated with the calamitous fall of the Athenian Empire.

With no navy to defend it, Athens fell into the hands of the Spartans. Lysander placed a military junta, known as the Thirty Tyrants, in charge. One of their first acts was to send Alcibiades's three-year-old son, Alcibiades the Younger, to a city where he could be kept hostage, in peril of his life.[9] The Thirty saw Alcibiades as the biggest threat to their rule, and exiled him from all of Greece, most of which was now under Spartan control. He fled from his Thracian stronghold, across the Hellespont, into Persian territory, and ended up seeking refuge in an obscure Phrygian town. An outlaw, hunted throughout Greece by his own people, he was now forced to beg for protection from foreigners the Athenians viewed as barbarians. Alcibiades is said to have been consumed with the desire to free his country and restore democracy once again. He reputedly hoped that the Persian king Artaxerxes might support him in another war against the Spartans. He never got a chance to try his luck; his name was already on a kill list.

Alcibiades was the last great member of the noble house, who founded the Athenian democracy, led Athens at the height of its empire, and was now blamed for its fall. For the Spartans to be confident of replacing Athenian democracy with a government controlled by their Oligarch allies, the Alcmaeonid line would have to be extinguished.[10] Pindar, in praising the ancestors of Alcibiades, had ominously proclaimed:

> Great exploits spark great envy, and the saying is true:
> good fortune, flowering for all time, brings with it
> not just happiness but tragedy.

They came for him long after darkness had fallen. Having finally hunted him down in rural Phrygia, they cloaked their lamps. A dozen assassins fanned out to encircle the house, silently piling brushwood against the walls. At the signal, they sparked the fire that set it all ablaze. They waited, eyes glinting in the darkness, by the light of the growing flames, as the fire began to roar loudly. At first, it seemed like nothing more would happen. Then the door flew open and out rushed Alcibiades into the night, armed with a dagger, naked except for a cloak thrown over his arm to shield him from the flames. For the briefest of moments he stopped, looking here and there, calculating his chances. Suddenly, he bellowed a war cry and dashed straight toward the closest of his assassins. Before he'd taken two strides, the first javelin slammed into his chest, then another, and another.[11] He collapsed at their feet, in a dark pool of blood. They cut his throat and took his head as a trophy.[12]

At least that was how the sailors told the story. They heard it from some foreign mercenaries who said they had heard it from one of the two prostitutes who had shared Alcibiades's bed on the night he died. The older men said the Persian satrap Pharnabazus had ordered his execution at the behest of Lysander, the Spartan general. Alcibiades had many enemies who envied his great family and would have relished seeing his life end in tragedy. The rumor that most outraged the young sailors, however, was that their exiled commander's death had been insisted upon by his former friend. He was the cruelest of the Thirty Tyrants, which the Spartans had placed over their defeated city: *the traitor, Critias.*

10

THE THIRTY TYRANTS

SOCRATES LISTENED TO THE CRIES spread throughout the streets of Athens, until it sounded as if panic gripped the entire city.[1] Word had arrived first at the harbor of Piraeus, where the state ship *Paralus* had docked, bearing news of their fleet's total annihilation. The citizens of Athens lay awake that night, their sleep disturbed by images of the punishment that now awaited them. Those old enough to have voted in the Assembly for the massacres committed, in their name, on Melos and elsewhere began to feel the painful bite of remorse. Any day the Spartans would come and, they feared, show them the same cruelty that they had inflicted upon others, and perhaps even worse.

After Lysander captured the Athenian fleet at Aegospotami, he sailed from one city to the next, securing Sparta's control of the region and tightening its stranglehold on Athens's crucial grain supply—the very danger Alcibiades had warned against. Lysander granted any Athenian he found in the region safe passage home—but this was no act of mercy. Athens would soon become overcrowded with refugees, and more mouths than they could hope to feed.

King Agis of Sparta already had troops stationed at Decelea, ten miles north of the Acropolis. Almost every Athenian ally had surrendered. Lysander now sailed to Athens with 150 ships to blockade Piraeus. Pausanias, the other king of Sparta, camped a huge army outside the city walls, in the grounds of the Academy park. Socrates had taken part in the siege of Potidaea during the outbreak of the war. Now, almost three decades later, he found himself trapped in Athens, a city besieged by, and about to fall to, the victorious Spartans.

Lysander waited three months for the Athenians to begin dying of starvation before allowing them to negotiate terms of surrender. Theramenes was sent to Sparta, as the envoy of Athens, where he found Corinth and Thebes, Sparta's most powerful allies, demanding that his city be destroyed. The Spartans, though, had long memories. They considered it prudent to show mercy to a city that had twice helped Greece defend itself against a Persian invasion.

Theramenes returned with the news that Athens would be spared if the Long Walls and fortifications of Piraeus were leveled and all but twelve of their ships given up. The Athenians, the terms read, must have the same friends and enemies as the Spartans, and be led by them in war, on land or sea. Finally, all exiles must be recalled, including aristocrats sympathetic to Sparta, who would form an oligarchic government. The Assembly was forced to accept. The Spartans proclaimed they had set all of Greece free from Athenian tyranny. While flute girls played in celebration, the defeated citizens of Athens were forced to tear down their precious defenses with their own hands.

The Assembly met, surrounded by soldiers, and appointed thirty Oligarchs to revise the constitution, modelling it on that of Sparta, whose Council of Elders, or *Gerousia*, had the same number of members. The leaders were to be Critias, the former student of Socrates and friend of Alcibiades; Charicles, a radical who had led prosecutions over the scandal of the herms; and Theramenes, the moderate who had served as a general under Alcibiades and had been the first to call for his return from exile following the Sicilian Expedition. The Spartans left this junta to govern Athens on their behalf—they would later become infamous as the "Thirty Tyrants." Before long, Samos, the last Athenian ally to hold out, surrendered, which finally brought the Peloponnesian War to a close, after twenty-seven years.

Critias soon became intoxicated by his newfound power and, still bitter over his recent exile, he claimed his revenge. The Oligarchs' first step was to appoint their own magistrates. In a move that earned praise from most of the citizens, they began prosecuting the paid informers used by Cleon and other demagogues. Before long, however, the Oligarchs also recruited three hundred lash-bearers to enforce their decrees. The citizens, too afraid to complain, watched powerless as the Thirty took the opportunity to settle old scores, putting to death anyone who had testified against them during the democracy, commencing with the most vulnerable citizens. Next, they asked Sparta to provide a garrison of soldiers, who acted as their bodyguards and emboldened Critias and the other Oligarchs to start arresting more prominent citizens, including not only their personal enemies but those whose wealth or reputation they saw as a threat to their regime.

When Theramenes saw his colleagues exploiting their power to seek revenge, he tried to counsel moderation. "What sense is there," he asked Critias, "in putting to death those men who supported the democracy but never harmed the aristocrats?" "Both you and I," he said, "did things in the past to curry favor with the people." That was how politics worked, after all, under the democracy—everyone, at times, had acted like a demagogue. Critias sighed. "You are being naive, my friend, if you think that just because there are thirty of us, we don't have to watch our backs as carefully as a tyrant does, who rules alone. We have no choice but to rid ourselves of those most likely to oppose our rule."

To prevent any attempts at resistance, Critias decreed the exiled Democrat leaders to be outlaws—any man could take their lives with impunity. Alcibiades, though once his friend, had been the first to be killed. Next on the list was Thrasybulus, the Democrat general, now exiled to Thebes, who had fought alongside Alcibiades and Theramenes. When news reached Thrasybulus of his friend Alcibiades's assassination and the worsening situation at Athens, he acted decisively. Braving the winter cold, he led a squadron of seventy handpicked men up the slopes of Mount Parnes, where they were able to take the Athenian fortress of Phyle by surprise. The rebels now controlled one of the most secure strongholds in the region, atop a steep rock overlooking the road between Thebes and Athens.

The Thirty responded by tightening their grip. More than fifteen hundred people, in all, would be summoned to a public building in the Agora called the *Stoa Poikile* and put to death for alleged crimes against the regime.[2] Theramenes urged restraint. "The oligarchy will not survive," he warned, "if we continue like this. We must share power with more citizens, otherwise the people will mistake us for tyrants." He wanted the hoplite class, at least, to have the vote.

"Our actions appear ridiculous to me because we are doing two inconsistent things," he said, "by organizing a government based on force, and the rule of the strong, while keeping it so small as to be weaker than its subjects." This made Critias's lip curl; it brought back the pain of having similar contradictions pointed out by Socrates. Afraid that Theramenes might create an opposition faction, he ordered the three thousand hoplites most loyal to the oligarchy to parade under arms in the Agora, as a show of strength. All other residents of Athens were disarmed and their weapons locked in the Parthenon temple on the Acropolis. Now the Thirty were free to do as they pleased. Critias passed a law allowing anyone not on his list of loyalists to be summarily executed. The Oligarchs exploited this not only to silence opposition but also to enrich themselves by seizing the property of victims.

The Thirty now marched against Thrasybulus, with their private army of three thousand hoplites. Unable to take the fortress of Phyle by storm, they prepared for a siege. The gods smiled on the rebels, however, when an unexpectedly heavy snowfall forced the Thirty to return to Athens. This gave Thrasybulus the time he needed to plan a full armed rebellion.

DIALOGUE WITH CRITIAS

AS THE THIRTY BECAME MORE oppressive, many left Athens for nearby Piraeus, a former Democrat stronghold. Chaerephon begged his friend to come with him, but Socrates remained in Athens, despite the danger. "You can see what sort of man Critias has become," said Chaerephon. "The same man he always was," shrugged Socrates, "albeit with more of those who appear willing to obey his orders."

"Do you remember how Critias responded to your debate with Gorgias, all those years ago, under the democracy, when he was still a young man?" asked Chaerephon, rolling his eyes. Socrates, who never forgot such things, was able to relate the whole conversation from memory:

"The words of a political orator," Socrates had said, "are made to twist this way and that, just to avoid displeasing the people by contradicting their changing mood.³ Philosophy never changes. Her statements may appear surprising and paradoxical, but they are consistent. She tells us that committing wrongdoing is a worse evil than suffering it at the hands of another. And I swear by the dog, Critias, that if you allow her assertion to go unrefuted, you will never be at peace with yourself. For my own part, I would rather be out of tune with a whole chorus, and have the rest of humankind contradict me, than be out of tune with a single individual, by contradicting myself."

"Socrates," replied Critias, "you sound like a demagogue yourself. Despite what you just said about disregarding the chorus of humankind, your whole argument depended upon an appeal to popular opinion. Our friend, Gorgias was too ashamed to admit that he doesn't teach justice. Alcibiades fell into the same trap when he agreed that doing injustice is more shameful than having it done to you. He was merely speaking of a popular convention in this regard, which tells us nothing. In nature, *real men* never become victims, because they are strong. Hence, being the victim of injustice is a greater evil than committing injustice.

"When wronged and insulted those who are weak and slavish can neither defend themselves nor anyone for whom they care. For this reason, the weak, who are many, have conspired against the strong, who are few, by making up moral conventions concerning what is just. For instance, the majority fabricated the idea that it is unjust and shameful for the strong to take a greater share. Throughout history, however, the strong have asserted their right to conquer the weak. They take what they like, in accord with the law of nature, and against the laws and conventions established by their inferiors." This was, of course, how the Athenians had behaved toward Melos and other cities weaker than them.

Critias continued: "In order to indoctrinate everyone in these rules, the Athenian people take the best and strongest men and, from an early age, tame them just as men tame lion cubs reared among them. They enslave them by teaching them that men ought to be equal and other unnatural nonsense. Whenever a man is born who is sufficiently strong, though, he shakes off these spells, breaks his chains, and tramples on their conventions. From time to time, a great man will dazzle the people by revealing himself to be their master rather than their slave. The law of nature, as Pindar says, rules over men and gods alike, and has set it down once and for all that *might is right*.

"You are only blinded to the truth of this by your love of philosophy, a pleasant game for children, perhaps, but one sure to ruin you if you keep it up much longer. Indeed, no matter how naturally talented a youth may be, if he wastes his time in your company studying philosophy, he will never become a real man. He will never be respected by his inferiors and will lack any influence in the courts and Assembly. That is what is shameful, Socrates. I feel toward your students as I do toward grown men who talk with a lisp like some little child—they deserve to be whipped for such unmanly behavior!

"Now, I like you, Socrates," said Critias, looking down his nose, "so let me give you some advice. You have neglected yourself when it comes to rhetoric and oratory. Your noble soul appears to others like that of a foolish child because of the unsophisticated manner in which you speak. You cannot contribute a single word of value to the deliberations of a court or persuade a single citizen in the Assembly of your cause. So do not take offense at my frankness. Are you not ashamed of the plight you find yourself in because of your philosophy? If someone were to have you arrested and dragged off to prison right now, you would be completely helpless. You would stand in court with your mouth gaping open, without the words to defend yourself. No matter how false and unjust the charges, if the prosecution uses rhetoric, and they *want* you to die, the jury will condemn you to die."

Socrates smiled. "Critias, I thank you," he said, "for I have come to believe that if I wish to test whether I am living well or badly, I require three qualities from a partner in conversation: *wisdom, goodwill, and frankness.* Gorgias and Alcibiades may be wise and well-intentioned but, as you observed, they did not speak freely enough. They were ashamed of contradicting social conventions but ended up contradicting themselves. I doubt, by contrast, that you would *ever* be inhibited by shame. So if I can convince you to agree with me, my friend, we shall know we have arrived at the truth.

"Let's start by clarifying how you define *natural justice.* Am I correct that you believe this consists in the stronger taking the property of the weaker by force, the better ruling over the worse, and nobles having more than the common people—that *might* is right?" Critias agreed. Socrates next asked if Critias was saying that "better" and "stronger" were the same. Critias explained that a larger city attacking a smaller one is both stronger and better, as it deserves to win. "Surely," said Socrates, "just as a large city is stronger than a small one, the common people, who are many, are stronger than the nobles, who are few?" Critias waited a moment, then nodded. "Then," said Socrates, "the laws imposed by the stronger are the same as those imposed by the majority. The majority, according to you, believe that justice consists in equality and that it is a more shameful thing to do what is unjust than to suffer injustice. Surely it follows that these beliefs are derived not only from convention but also, as you would have it, from nature? You said earlier that convention and nature are *opposed* in this regard but now you seem, do you not, to be contradicting yourself?"

"There is no end to this rubbish!" scoffed Critias. "Are *you* not ashamed, Socrates, to be playing word games? I told you that by stronger I meant better. Did you really think I meant that if you gathered together a heap of slaves and common rabble, with muscle but no brains, that whatever they say should have the force of law?" "Let me help," said Socrates. "Did you actually mean wiser, and better, rulers, when you said *stronger* men?" "Of course," said Critias. "So one wise man is superior to thousands of fools, and should rule them like a tyrant, and take the lion's share of everything they own?" "Exactly," said Critias, "natural justice consists in wiser and better men ruling over their inferiors."

"Suppose many of us gathered with a large amount of food, and someone present was a physician with expertise in the field of human nutrition. Would he be wise simply to claim the lion's share of the food and consume it all himself? Or would wisdom consist in distributing to each person, including himself, the most *appropriate* amount of food, for the benefit of each individual's health? Does wisdom consist in exercising rational moderation or indulging in excess?" "You're going on about food and drink, and other such nonsense, but that's not what I meant," complained Critias. "We are talking about expertise," he added, "in running the affairs of the whole city." "So what you intended to say is that the better men are wiser with regard to ruling cities?" asked Socrates. Critias agreed.

"Well, then, is there no need for self-mastery as long as one is master of others?" asked Socrates. "What do you mean?" said Critias. "Do your rulers rule *themselves* wisely?" asked Socrates. Critias frowned irritably, his head cocked to one side. "How can you be happy if you have to deny yourself pleasure?" he exclaimed. "Any man who wants to live like a man ought to go out and satisfy his appetites as much as he likes. The majority just lack the strength to do this. They may praise moderation but it is not a 'virtue' fit for free men. In all truth, Socrates, to those who wield absolute power, such as political tyrants, what could be more *disgraceful* than moderation and justice? No real man would voluntarily subjugate himself to the values of slaves. Your idea of self-mastery is contrary to nature. It is a lie invented by the naturally slavish and weak who joined forces in a conspiracy against their masters, the strong, in an attempt to shame them into submission."

"Many people share these opinions," said Socrates, "but are too ashamed to state them in public. So again, I am grateful to you, my friend, for your frankness. You are saying that the strong should indulge their passions and appetites as much as they like, are you not?" "Of course!" snorted Critias, as if what he said were common sense. "Answer me this," said Socrates, "does a man who has an itch, and the power to scratch it as often as he likes, live a good life in that regard?" "How bizarre of you, Socrates," replied Critias, "and how vulgar but, yes, let us say that even a man who scratches constantly would live a pleasant and happy life!"

Critias would not accept that moderation was a virtue because he wanted to insist that it was wrong for the strong to deny themselves anything that they desired. He believed that pleasure is good. Socrates pointed out several ways, however, in which we normally distinguish what is good for us from what is pleasurable. For instance, the pleasure of drinking water is over once our thirst has been quenched, and we rid ourselves of the pain or displeasure of craving water. The good that we obtain from becoming wise, by contrast, continues indefinitely after it has replaced the evil of folly. "So what?" exclaimed Critias. "It follows, my friend, that pleasure and pain, though opposites, are bound together in a way that wisdom and folly are not," said Socrates, "and therefore that good cannot be *identical* with pleasure nor evil with pain."

Critias wasn't convinced, so Socrates tried a different tack. "Did you imply earlier that you do not consider fools to be good men?" he asked. "Of course they are not," said Critias. "Have you ever seen a foolish man enjoying pleasure or a wise man suffering from pain?" asked Socrates. "I suppose so," said Critias, "but so what?" "Do wise men or fools experience greater pleasure?" asked Socrates. "I don't know," hissed Critias. "Are you therefore saying that there is no practical difference between good men and bad men in terms of their capacity for pleasure?" asked Socrates. Critias tentatively agreed. "You said earlier, though, that pain is bad and pleasure is good. So surely," said Socrates, "it follows that a man who is capable of feeling more pleasure is better than the man who is capable of feeling more pain?"

"I've been listening patiently to you, Socrates, talking nonsense, as if you don't realize that every normal person, myself included, distinguishes between pleasures that are good for us and ones that are bad for us," said Critias. "Are good pleasures the ones that benefit us and bad ones those that cause us harm?" asked Socrates. "Of course," sniffed Critias. "So we should endure certain pains insofar as they lead to what is good for us," asked Socrates, "and abstain from certain pleasures insofar as their consequences are bad for us?" Critias agreed. "Can any fool," asked Socrates, "tell healthy pleasures from unhealthy ones, and good pains from bad ones or does it require an expert?" "It may sometimes require an expert," admitted Critias hesitantly. "That's right," said Socrates, "a wise physician, for instance, could advise us that although some medicine tastes unpleasant it is good for our health, and that certain foods that taste pleasant are bad for our health." Critias agreed.

"Let us return to what I was talking to Gorgias and Alcibiades about," said Socrates. "There are occupations, such as that of confectioner, which pander to our appetites without distinguishing good pleasures from bad ones. Arts such as medicine, by contrast, study what is actually good for our health. These different occupations indicate different attitudes toward life." Critias sighed. "So, by the god of friendship, Critias, I beg you to take what we are discussing seriously," said Socrates, "and not to think of me as joking, but to recognize that we are, in fact, discussing one of the most important questions imaginable: *how a human being should live.*"

"Should one engage in what you and other politicians call 'manly' activities, such as pandering to the masses in the Assembly," said Socrates, "or should he live as we have been behaving just now, in this conversation, like philosophers who love wisdom?" Socrates explained that he considered political oratory to influence popular opinion by playing on our desire for pleasure and fear of pain rather than by appealing to what is actually good for us. "I disagree," grunted Critias, "but I'm going to go along with you, Socrates, so that we can finally end this foolish discussion." The philosopher smiled broadly. "Do you suppose," he asked, "that orators always speak with what is best for their fellow citizens in mind? Do they treat the assemblymen like children, by trying to please them, regardless of whether their speeches make the people better or worse?" "Some politicians are as you describe," said Critias, "but not all of them." "That answer will suffice," said Socrates.

"Let's suppose there are two kinds of oratory," continued Socrates, "one that panders shamefully to the masses, and a more noble sort that aims at improving their souls, whether it is pleasing to their ears or not. It is difficult to find a politician who has, in fact, improved the character of the citizens. Many politicians are praised for other achievements, such as constructing buildings or achieving victory in battle. A wise statesman would attempt to improve the people by giving speeches that praise justice and moderation and warn them against vices such as injustice and excess. He would encourage those desires that make someone better and persuade him to abandon those that make him worse. When someone is sick, doctors recommend that they abstain from eating certain food, and other activities. Likewise, when our soul is unhealthy, and ridden with vice and folly, we should practice moderation rather than excess. Indeed, to indulge our desires, without restraint, is far more dangerous when our mind is sick than when our body is."

"Don't you see that admitting your mistakes, for the health of your own soul, is like swallowing bitter medicine for the good of your body?" said Socrates. "I'm not remotely interested, Socrates," Critias scoffed. "They say you shouldn't leave a story half told," smiled the philosopher. "I'm not answering any more of these childish questions, Socrates," snapped Critias. "In that case," said Socrates, "I must take your place and answer my own questions if I want to finish our discussion. I do so, however, on condition that you all agree to challenge me if I say anything that appears false. If you prove me wrong, I will consider you among my greatest benefactors." Gorgias and the others agreed.

"Listen then as I recap. Critias and I agreed that pleasure cannot be identical with the good. A good man will be just and moderate, and he will therefore flourish. Such a person will be the opposite of the unrestrained tyrant whose freedom you earlier praised. The unjust and unrestrained man will not deserve and will never truly acquire the love and friendship of his fellow men. Wise men recognize, Critias, that the world is organized by the laws of nature, and humankind is organized by communities and bonds of friendship. So the law of nature is not really selfish as you claimed but rather embraces moderation, justice, and friendship toward others.

"What you accused Alcibiades of admitting out of shame turns out to be true after all: inflicting injustice is not only more shameful but also does us more harm than suffering injustice at another's hands. A good orator must therefore be wise and just himself, and understand what is right and wrong, before attempting to influence others. This is precisely what Alcibiades accused Gorgias of admitting only out of shame, despite not believing it himself. Only someone who has studied justice, such as a philosopher, would be qualified to employ oratory for good. Otherwise, a political orator, who is ignorant of what is *actually* good for the citizens, merely persuades them of what *appears* right to him.

"You reproach me for being unable to defend myself or any of my friends in court, and you compare me to an outlaw who is at the mercy of anyone who chooses to strike me in the face, steal my property, banish me from Athens, or even puts me to death. You call being in this position the worst form of disgrace. I believe, as I have consistently said, that it is not being struck undeservedly, or wounded in my purse or in my body, that is the ultimate disgrace. It is more harmful, I say, and more disgraceful, to be the person who strikes and wounds another wrongfully. To inflict any injustice on me, or anyone else, brings more disgrace upon the wrongdoer than upon we who suffer the wrong.

"These conclusions have already been shown to stand up to scrutiny in our preceding discussions. They have held fast, bound by a chain of argument as strong as adamantine, at least as far as I can judge at present. Unless you or someone else can break this chain, nobody can contradict me and maintain that he is telling the truth. For my part, I stick to my constant principle: I do not claim to *know* that this is true. However, I have never met anyone who produced a contrary opinion that was not shown to be absurd when examined by my method."

"I may be impressed by some of what you say," Critias admitted, through gritted teeth, "but, like most people, I am not persuaded that you are right." "Come now, Critias, do you say that I should, like a physician, try to improve the health of the Athenians, by guiding them toward the truth, or, like a servant, do and say only what pleases them?" asked Socrates. "I still think you would be advised to serve them," said Critias. "Like a panderer," said Socrates. "If you must keep using that offensive term, then so be it," replied Critias, before adding, rather darkly: "You seem very sure that you won't be dragged into court by someone who means you harm." "I would be foolish indeed," said Socrates, "if I did not realize that something like this could happen to anyone in the city and I would not be at all surprised if I were executed." "What do you mean?" said Critias.

"I believe that I am one of the few Athenians—perhaps the only one—who practices the true art of politics," replied Socrates, "precisely because what I say is not meant to please the citizens but to improve them. I shall therefore be judged as if I were a physician, brought before a jury of children, with a confectioner as my prosecutor. 'Children,' he will say, 'this man is harming you by prescribing you bitter medicine, and compelling you to abstain from the treats you enjoy so much. Look, though, at all the delicious sweets that I have given you.' If the physician claimed that he only caused them pain and deprived them of pleasure for the good of their health, despite it being true, there would be uproar among the children. Well, that is the situation in which I expect to find myself, if I ever come before a court of law. If they complain that I ruin the youths by reducing them to a state of helpless doubt or insult their elders by criticizing what they teach, I will be unable to defend myself by saying that I spoke only the truth and was acting in their interests."

"Do you really not think that it is better for a man to be able to defend his life and actions before his city?" asked Critias. Socrates replied, "I believe that the only defense a man requires is for his life to provide no evidence of wrongdoing. If I was unable to say this in my own defense, I would be ashamed whether the jury were large or small, or even one man. If I were to be deprived of my life for this reason, I would be ashamed, but I would *not* be ashamed if I lost my life solely because I lacked the knack of pandering to the jury.

The mere fact of one's death holds no terror for any man of wisdom and courage, although it terrifies the foolish and cowardly. It is our own wrongdoing that we should fear, for to depart from this life having one's character burdened by vice is the worst evil that can befall a man. A man is more likely to achieve this if he dedicates his life to the love of wisdom but abstains from meddling in public affairs, where the temptation to do wrong is great precisely because of the influence he will have over others. My original belief stands unrefuted, that doing wrong is even more to be avoided than being wronged and our supreme goal must be the reality rather than the appearance of goodness."

At first, Critias had followed Alcibiades in his association with Socrates, although he never liked being questioned by him. In the Assembly, he professed to be serving the people. Yet, in private, his conversation revealed him to be a *sham* Democrat. He looked down on the multitude and wanted Athens to be governed by an oligarchy modelled on the Spartan constitution, which he admired. Over time, he was drawn more toward Gorgias and other rhetoricians, believing that they held the keys to political power. Ultimately, however, it was Socrates's disapproval of Critias's lack of restraint that caused the final rift between them.

While Critias was still in Athens, Socrates noticed that he had become infatuated with Euthydemus, the adolescent boy with the extensive book collection, to whom Socrates had taught his philosophical method by means of a diagram. Socrates told Critias bluntly that his behavior was servile and unbecoming of a gentleman. It seemed hypocritical, he said, to claim to be in love with Euthydemus while pressuring the boy for favors that it would be wrong for him to grant. Critias ignored these warnings and kept pestering him. After a while, Socrates had enough and loudly exclaimed before Euthydemus, and many others, "Critias seems to have turned into a pig! He can no more keep away from Euthydemus than pigs can help rubbing themselves against stones."

This caused Critias so much embarrassment that he left Euthydemus alone. He never forgave Socrates, however, for humiliating him that day. The shame of being exposed in public as a predator festered within him. When he was later exiled, following the Battle of Ephesus, he went to Thessaly and reputedly indulged his vices without restraint. After being recalled by the Spartans and placed in control of Athens as one of the Thirty Tyrants, he finally had the power to exact revenge.

THE THIRTY AGAINST SOCRATES

ONE OF CRITIAS'S FIRST ACTS was, while drafting new laws, to insert a clause that made it illegal "to teach the art of argumentation," intended to outlaw philosophy. Theramenes, who had once, like Critias, been a student of Socrates, wanted no part of this. Critias felt he needed to silence Socrates, and he wanted to portray the philosopher's conversations as harming the youth. Once the Thirty began putting innocent people to death, most Athenians became too afraid to criticize them. Chaerephon, who was not known for holding his tongue, had been exiled by Critias, along with other alleged Democrat sympathizers. Nevertheless, once the Thirty began their purges, Socrates, in his typical fashion, was heard to say: "It seems odd to me that someone who lets his cattle grow sick or die would not admit that he is a bad herdsman. Is it not even stranger, then, if a statesman who either involves his citizens in crime or decreases their number feels no shame?"

As soon as Critias was informed of this, he summoned Socrates. He showed the law that he had recently penned to the philosopher and ordered him to cease his conversations with the young men. "May I question you," asked Socrates, "to ensure that I understand the new law?" Critias agreed. "Do you interpret it," asked Socrates, "as prohibiting both *sound* and *unsound* reasoning?" Critias was about to answer when Charicles, his fellow Oligarch, snapped: "Since you are ignorant of what the law means, Socrates, let us put it in language that you shall find easier to understand: you may not hold any conversations *whatsoever* with the young."

"In that case, if a young person asks me where Charicles or Critias are to be found, should I refuse to answer them?" asked Socrates. "Look," exclaimed Charicles in frustration, "you are being ordered to avoid your favorite topics, such as talking about shoemakers, physicians, and so on—I think we've heard enough of all that." As they were struggling to answer Socrates's questions, it became clear they had no idea how to interpret their new law. "Must I then avoid talking about the subjects these crafts are used to illustrate," said Socrates, "such as justice, moderation, and suchlike?" "Indeed," sneered Charicles, growing tired of the conversation, "and you must refrain from criticizing cowherds as well; otherwise, you may find the herd loses another one of its members!" Everyone who heard about this took it to mean that the Thirty were threatening to have Socrates put to death.

Socrates ignored the prohibition against doing philosophy because the Thirty could not state what it meant without contradiction. It would be preposterous for them to execute a man merely for anecdotes about cattle or for discussing justice in general terms. So Critias looked for another way to rid himself of the philosopher. Once the Thirty ran out of money with which to pay the Spartan garrison, they began executing wealthy foreign residents (*metics*), in order to confiscate their assets. They ordered prominent citizens to carry out the arrests, as a test of their loyalty. If they refused, they could be executed for treason themselves. If they agreed, they were no longer in a position to criticize the Thirty, having made themselves complicit in the regime's crimes.

Critias therefore called a group of five men before him, which included Socrates. They were to be deputized and ordered to go to the nearby island of Salamis, where they were to arrest a wealthy man named Leon and bring him back to Athens. Socrates knew that Leon was a man of good reputation and completely innocent of any wrongdoing. His only "crime" was to be wealthy and an ally of the Democrats. The philosopher therefore refused to take part in his arrest and said nothing, but instead turned away and walked quietly home to his family. He knew that his refusal to follow their direct order gave the Thirty the excuse they needed to have him executed. Leon was arrested and put to death anyway. Nevertheless, soon everyone in Athens was talking about Socrates's apparent act of civil disobedience. Critias had invited his nephew, a young aristocrat named Plato, to participate in the oligarchy, and at first he was optimistic about the change of regime. Plato, however, had become a follower of Socrates a few years earlier, and when he saw what was happening, his hopes were dashed. So young Plato joined his mentor in withholding his support from the regime.[4]

Soon, the Thirty began to distrust even one another. They agreed that each of them should carry out one of these arrests, to prove their loyalty. When this order was given to Theramenes, like Socrates, and doubtless inspired by his example, he refused. "It is dishonorable," he said, "for those who call themselves the 'best men' among us to act even worse than the wretched informers did under the democracy. They extorted money from their victims but at least allowed them to keep their lives. Are we really going to start killing innocent people?"

The more radical members of the Thirty turned on Theramenes, spreading rumors he was plotting against them. Critias called a council meeting at which he had a group of young men stand guard with daggers concealed under their robes. When Theramenes arrived, Critias rose and gave a speech about how executions had become necessary for the security of the state. "Now we find Theramenes here doing everything in his power to destroy us," he suddenly added, gesturing toward his former friend. "It is always he who opposes us whenever we want to get rid of some demagogue," he continued. Theramenes had supported the initial executions. By now distancing himself from the process, he was allegedly siding with the Democrat faction, and leaving the rest of the Thirty to take the blame. Critias called on the Thirty to punish him for treason. "If you are wise," he concluded, "you will show this man no mercy, as his destruction will cut short the hopes of your enemies."

Theramenes rose to speak. He said that after Leon of Salamis and other good men were executed, he began to question the actions of the regime. The banishment of Thrasybulus and Alcibiades, followed by the latter's assassination, merely fueled opposition to the Oligarchs. "It is you who, by confiscating property illegally and putting the innocent to death," he said, "behave as traitors and create unrest." "Do you not realize," he added, "that, because of Critias's actions, the city is now full of rebels who support Thrasybulus, and want nothing more than to see your government overthrown?"

The council applauded Theramenes and was ready to acquit him. Critias, though, ordered his armed henchmen to surround them, saying, "These friends of mine who are standing by the railing, say that they cannot allow anyone to go free who is doing harm to the oligarchy." As the guards dragged Theramenes away, through the Agora, he called out loud for his fellow citizens to witness the crime being committed. Socrates was among those in the marketplace; he and two friends intervened to try to stop the execution.[5] Theramenes begged them to step aside. Though he admired their courage, he said it would cause him grief to think that he might be the cause of their deaths. When the guards eventually gave him the hemlock cup, he downed its contents and then threw out the poison dregs, as he quipped, "And here's to that delightful fellow, Critias!" showing his defiance until the very end.

THE PRACTICE OF ANGER MANAGEMENT

THE HISTORY OF THE PELOPONNESIAN WAR can be viewed, to some extent, as a story about revenge. At first, under Pericles, the Athenians had negotiated treaties with other cities that at least tried to appear just. The expectation that promises would be honored formed a social contract that helped to hold together the many alliances on which the empire was founded. Pericles, in the eyes of many, exemplified what was best about Athenian democracy, as he brought out what was best in the citizens, by continually appealing to reason and justice. After his untimely death, though, cynical opportunistic demagogues like Cleon showed how easy it was to manipulate the Assembly, appealing to the citizens' worst tendencies and most irrational fears. Cleon was soon followed by a new generation of professionally trained political orators, who were experts in the art of persuasion or, as Socrates called it, the knack of pandering to the masses. The democracy became hopelessly corrupt as the political class became better at manipulating votes by exploiting weaknesses in the system their ancestors had created.

The threatened massacre at Mytilene, and the actual one at Melos, changed everything. The rhetoric of justice in foreign relations was replaced with the rhetoric of oppression and "might is right." Such aggression *is* pandering to the masses: it's exactly what angry mobs love to hear, but it is usually shortsighted and self-defeating. The Sicilian Expedition turned into the Athenians' greatest military disaster, mainly because much-needed allies in the region no longer trusted them. Athens had started treating neutral and allied states in the Aegean so badly that the Sicilians had become scared that they might face subjugation and enslavement if they threw open their doors to them.

We'll now recap some of the psychological techniques mentioned previously and show how they can be applied to the problem of *anger*. In Book Four of Plato's *Republic*, Socrates says that when a good man knows that he is in the wrong, and being punished justly, his spirit will not feel anger. On the other hand, when a man believes that he has been wronged, and is a victim of injustice, his spirit will "seethe and grow fierce." He will seek justice, says Socrates, and his anger, and desire for revenge, "will not let go until either it achieves its purpose, or death ends all, or as a dog is called back by a shepherd, it is called back by the reason within and calmed."[6] Someone has done something they should not have done, something unacceptable or unfair. You may even feel that they deserve to be punished. Not all anger takes that form, but a great deal of anger toward other people does. (For instance, you may become frustrated because you accidentally hit your thumb with a hammer and perhaps that leads to a *different* sort of anger, without any thoughts of injustice or revenge.) Anger, in other words, has long been associated with the belief that one has been wronged by another who has acted *unjustly*.

We don't normally think of the philosophy of justice as being a branch of psychotherapy. Our conception of *injustice*, however, may affect our emotional resilience. Over a century ago, Sigmund Freud observed: "Melancholics always seem as though they had been slighted or treated with great injustice."[7] Recent research has indeed found evidence that "perceived injustice" is linked with, and may help to cause, clinical depression.[8]

In the field of cognitive therapy, it has been proposed that anger is typically based on a belief that some rule has been broken or someone has acted unjustly.[9] This is usually associated with an initial sense of threat based on the perception that one or something one cares about might be harmed. That anxiety is quickly replaced with thoughts of retaliation or revenge, such as punishing the other person, when anger arises. Indeed, often anger can be interpreted as an attempt to *cope with* underlying anxiety by using another emotion to mask it.

Socrates couldn't be more emphatic in the dialogue above, as elsewhere, that *committing an injustice is worse than suffering one.* Critias finds this absurd: he believes that suffering injustice at the hands of others is worse, and more shameful. We may therefore expect that someone like Critias was more prone to anger than Socrates: Critias probably felt *ashamed* and *outraged* whenever he perceived others to be acting unjustly toward him. When the Assembly exiled him, he probably felt that they, the weak, were conspiring against him, the strong. Therapists often encounter rigid beliefs about the injustice or unfairness of certain events when treating patients for anger. If you find yourself unable to get past something that has made you angry, there are a few approaches that may prove useful.

First, you can try a version of the two-column technique introduced earlier. Begin by considering what you are angry about and, more importantly, the beliefs that justify your anger. You may find, as is often the case, that you believe the other person has acted unjustly or unacceptably—they've somehow violated an important rule or standard of behavior. Maybe it has to do with not respecting your time and that of other people, treating you rudely, or doing something else that seems unacceptable to you: "He *shouldn't* have done that!"

Draw two columns on a piece of paper, one headed "evidence for" and the other "evidence against." Let's say "People should always treat me with respect!" is one of your core beliefs. What if they don't, though, as will sometimes be the case? Having this rule violated may trigger feelings of anger. In fact, rigid attitudes toward perceived injustice are often a recipe for neurosis. Spend some time identifying any beliefs about injustice that may make you angry, therefore, and then list the evidence for and against each of them. Next, try to think of *alternative* beliefs about the same situation, ones that are rational and true but also more constructive. "I'd prefer people to treat me with respect, but if they don't, it's not the end of the world," might be one. Socrates would perhaps formulate his own belief as follows: "I'd prefer people not to punish me unjustly, but even if they do, what matters is that I respond with wisdom and justice."

One of the first steps, however, in tackling anger often consists in evaluating the pros and cons of the emotion itself, or associated patterns of thought and behavior. Socrates described a similar method of psychotherapy to Protagoras. First, you might want to ask yourself, generally, regarding your anger, "How has that been *working out* for you?" What are the *consequences* for you of getting angry? If you want to dig deeper, list the pros and cons, or costs and benefits of your anger. Think both in terms of the short-term and long-term consequences. It can be particularly helpful to compare the (perceived) *short-term benefits* of anger against its *long-term costs*.

Let's say you are angry at a friend for not returning a phone call. What are the *benefits* of getting angry with the person? Perhaps there are none in the long term. Maybe in the short term you feel as though you're temporarily getting something off your chest by expressing ("venting") your anger. Or maybe you feel that your anger might motivate you to do something constructive, like confronting the friend about how upset you believe he or she has made you feel. Are these *real* benefits? Answering the next question may help you decide: What are the *costs* of anger? Well, in the short term, although you may enjoy being angry in some ways, it probably also feels unpleasant and distressing in other ways. Longer term, though, it might affect different areas of your life such as your work, your relationships, and your personality in general, maybe also your physical health. In relation to the perceived benefits, are there *hidden* costs? Although venting can bring some short-term relief, in the long run, it might just encourage you to become angrier and angrier, and to alienate some of your friends. Anger spreads: those who are angry with their enemies end up also being angry toward others. Usually this is obvious to everyone except the person who is angry—it's a common blindspot. Perhaps being motivated by anger, likewise, can seem like a good idea at first, but in the long term it may lead you to be forceful and act while your judgment is clouded by strong feelings—and that can lead to disaster!

There's another aspect of anger, however, that may respond even better to this technique. In recent decades, cognitive therapists have become increasingly interested in a special type of cognition called *metacognition*. Metacognitions are *cognitions about cognitions*. They're basically beliefs about beliefs, or beliefs about your own thinking. For example, anger is often associated with a particular style of thinking called *rumination*. Rumination involves going over and over something in your mind, round in circles, asking yourself unhelpful questions. It's like worrying but in anger it tends to resemble an inner conversation about *why* someone did something that upset you or what it *means* and how you should *get back at them*.

Some people describe angry rumination as a *failed* attempt at problem-solving. It may also take the form of *revenge fantasies* and other aggressive thoughts. Although the initial thoughts that trigger periods of rumination may be automatic and not under your control, what happens next, your response to them, is often more voluntary than you may realize. Having noticed that you are ruminating, you can always choose to stop, even if the initial thoughts keep popping back into your mind. Accept them and then return your attention to the present moment in the real world. Wait until you're no longer feeling as angry, then ask yourself what the pros and cons are of your angry rumination. Repeat this exercise several times. Having a clear grasp of the negative consequences of rumination can help you to switch it off and will often tend to reduce your anger levels in the long term. Another way of approaching the same technique is by challenging the assumption that "my angry rumination is helpful" by listing the evidence for and against that statement and examining it rationally.

Another technique we mentioned earlier, *illeism* or referring to oneself in the third person, can also help us deal with our anger. In Plato's *Republic*, Socrates mentions a famous passage from Homer's *Odyssey*, in which Odysseus "smote his breast and chided thus his heart."[10] This is another way of saying that he told himself to be calm, in order to quell his anger. Socrates says, "Homer has clearly represented that in us which has reflected about the better and the worse as rebuking that which feels unreasoning anger as if it were a distinct and different thing."[11] The first step in using illeism here would be to gain cognitive distance from your angry thoughts by saying, for example, "Donald is feeling angry right now; he's telling himself 'What that guy did was totally unfair; I should teach him a lesson!'" Observing your angry thoughts from this detached perspective will have two main effects: reducing the *intensity* of emotion and increasing cognitive *flexibility*. Although the first thing you may notice is that you're feeling less angry, arguably the more lasting benefit will be that you're able to think about the problem in a more open-minded and creative way, which ultimately means you're more likely to figure out potential solutions.

Indeed, once you've managed to gain cognitive distance, you may want to talk yourself through possible solutions to the problem from a third-person perspective, in order to evaluate them by thinking through the consequences of responding in different ways. As we saw earlier, this psychological trick can help you access a greater capacity for wisdom. Think of illeism as a healthy replacement for angry rumination. When Critias became one of the Thirty Tyrants, he immediately set about exacting his revenge on everyone who had offended him in the past, including Socrates. Where did it get him? Take a step back and observe your life from a detached perspective: *Where does your anger get you?*

THE CIVIL WAR

AFTER KILLING THERAMENES, CRITIAS ONLY became more tyrannical and shameless. The Thirty issued a decree forbidding anyone who was not on their approved list from entering the city and evicted them from their estates. Some fled to Piraeus, but many were driven out completely and forced to seek refuge in neighboring Thebes and Megara. One of the first acts of the Thirty had been to have Alcibiades exiled and then killed. As Critias's hands became stained with the blood of one death after another, the people realized that the Thirty had acted quickly to destroy what they feared the most: a charismatic general to whom the disaffected could rally. Alcibiades had been taken from them but his exiled friend and ally, Thrasybulus, was still out there fighting under the banner of democracy.

As word spread of the rebel stronghold in Phyle, more men, furious at their treatment by the Thirty came to join Thrasybulus every day. As the size of his rebel army grew, he became emboldened. One night, he led seven hundred men down into the plains of Attica. They waited for the glint of dawn before grabbing their swords and charging into the Spartan encampment outside the city walls. The enemy were caught half-awake, some still in bed—over 120 of their hoplites were slain in the rout. Thrasybulus and his men returned to Phyle, laden with hoplite weapons and armor seized from the abandoned Spartan camp.

Critias and the Thirty now lived in fear. They had not expected that so many Athenians would be ready to fight for their city, and they were unprepared to face a general as daring as Thrasybulus. With each new crime committed by the Thirty, more exiled and disenfranchised Athenians walked into the rebel camp at Phyle, volunteering to bear arms against the Oligarchs. Within days, Thrasybulus commanded over a thousand men. As Socrates had observed, Alcibiades had the knack of turning apparent disasters into victory. The people now wanted to believe his friend could do the same.

Acting, once again, under cover of darkness, Thrasybulus marched them down into Piraeus, where the citizens welcomed them as liberators. Critias, incensed, marched against them at the head of his three thousand hoplites, supported by a number of Athenian cavalry loyal to the Oligarchs and the remainder of the Spartan garrison. The rebels lacked sufficient numbers to hold the port, which the Spartans had stripped of defenses. Nevertheless, Critias was surprised to see them abandon the city and fall back to a nearby hillock. The Thirty's hoplites, with the Spartans included, outnumbered them almost five to one, but many light troops from Piraeus, armed with slings, javelins, and whatever weapons they could improvise, had turned out to join the rebels.

As the enemy advanced up the hillside, Thrasybulus planted his shield firmly on the ground and raised his spear, in order to address his men:

Fellow citizens of Athens, look toward the enemy's right wing and you will see the same Spartans that we put to flight just four days ago. On their left are the Thirty Tyrants, who robbed us of our city, drove us from our homes, and, through their abuse of power, victimized our dearest friends. Today those hated men find themselves somewhere they always feared to be, and where we prayed, one day, to meet them. For we now face them with weapons in our hands. These men seized our friends from their beds and arrested them in the night. They exiled those who had committed no crimes, and had your former general put to death, simply because they feared his popularity. They have no regard for justice. You can be sure therefore that the gods are not on their side today, but on ours.

Now they march uphill toward us, in formation fifty ranks deep. Do not be afraid. Their generals, like novices, have made a grave tactical mistake. You will soon observe that they cannot throw their javelins over the heads of their front ranks. We, by contrast, cannot miss our marks, throwing our stones and javelins downhill. Remember also that we have defeated them each time we've met them in battle. We were ready to fight them on equal terms and win. Now, however, all you must do is let your weapons fly with force, and not one of you will miss his mark. While they struggle to march uphill, cowering under heavy shields from our ranged attack, you will thrust your spears downward with ease as though against blind men unable to defend themselves. So take heart because despite their greater numbers, they have already lost the battle.

Now, my friends, I want each and every one of you to fight in such a way that afterward you will truly believe you were the man who won victory today. For this, God willing, will give us back our country, our homes, our freedom, our honor, and, for those who have them, our wives and children. Blessed indeed will be those of you who, after this battle, see the light dawn on the gladdest day of your lives. Blessed too will be those who fall because no amount of wealth would ever buy you such a memorial.

When the time is right, I will strike up the paean, and we will call upon the God of War, and so let us all be of one mind, and give these men the punishment they deserve for the wrongs they have inflicted on our city.

As he predicted, the battle was over almost as soon as it began. Despite their superior numbers, the army of the Thirty struggled to advance uphill when faced with a shower of javelins. Critias's inexperience as a general showed. The rebels, in a stunning victory, broke the enemy's line and routed them, killing seventy of their hoplites. Critias was slain, along with other prominent members of his regime, less than one year after being handed control of the city by Sparta.

In the aftermath, as each side recovered the bodies of their dead, men began talking to one another, renewing old acquaintances. They soon agreed that it was against all religion for fellow citizens to fight one another in this way. Both sides blamed the Thirty for having caused more deaths through their political purges than were lost during any battle in the war.

Once they returned to Athens, the hoplites who had been fighting for the Thirty began to quarrel and became divided over their support for the regime. The Oligarchs, after promising so much to their loyal supporters, appeared to be bringing Athens even closer to ruin. Meanwhile, the rebels, who now controlled Piraeus, continued to arm themselves and recruit more soldiers. The remaining members of the Thirty soon fled to Eleusis, which they had prepared as a stronghold. They sent envoys to Sparta requesting help. Lysander, the Spartan general who had defeated the Athenian navy, came with reinforcements, and blockaded Piraeus by sea with his fleet. It appeared the Democrat uprising might come to nothing after all.

The Spartan king, Pausanias, surrounded Piraeus with an army. Although there were some skirmishes, he preferred to negotiate terms of peace. The remnants of the oligarchy were soon defeated, and democracy was restored. Thrasybulus, like Alcibiades before him, encouraged the Assembly to set aside factional bickering and personal animosities for the sake of Athens. Exhausted by the civil war, the citizens took oaths that there should be an amnesty for past conflicts, so that they may live in peace and rebuild their city.

Among them were Socrates and Chaerephon, best friends and companions since their youth. They had studied philosophy side by side, read Anaxagoras, argued with the natural philosophers, and debated with the Sophists, including Protagoras and Gorgias. It was Chaerephon who asked the Pythia if any man was wiser than Socrates, the question that had launched him on his philosophical mission. After living through the worst plague and longest war in Greek history, they had watched the rise to power first of Alcibiades and then of Critias, who had exiled Chaerephon along with other Democrats. Although some poked fun at him for being a misfit, Socrates considered Chaerephon to be one of the best men he knew. He was approaching seventy when he passed away peacefully in his home. After watching his old friend die, Socrates seemed to become more resigned to his own demise. His age was starting to catch up with him. He felt his quickness of mind and ability to benefit the young through questioning had diminished. He reached the conclusion that he could do Athens more good by standing up for philosophy more publicly, and more assertively, than ever before.

Socrates, who survived the plague and several major battles of the Peloponnesian War, had only narrowly avoided execution under the oligarchy. Their regime fell before Critias had a chance to have him condemned. When Socrates was later prosecuted under the democracy, he faced the threat of execution for the third or fourth time.[12] He had always spoken freely, but on this occasion, as we have seen, he gave a full-throated defense of his life and philosophy, for which the jury sentenced him to death.

II

THE SWAN SONG

THERE ARE TINY CREATURES THAT can bite or sting us, without even being noticed. We feel nothing, and no wound is visible. Only much later do we discover, to our surprise, an itch or swelling where it seems we must have been bitten. You once warned me, Socrates, that this may be my experience when dealing with the wise. You said, "Phaedo, my young friend, do you think that we are always aware precisely where and when and how wisdom has gotten its teeth into us? Or do we sometimes only realize afterward that we have been affected by a conversation when some little thing that was said, or perhaps a question that was asked, begins to trouble us?"[1]

As a youth, after I was taken captive and sold into slavery, I believed that I should be better off dead. Once they brought me to Athens, and I discovered how I would be used, my misfortunes seemed to double. One day I heard there was a man in the marketplace who, like an enchanter, could turn bad fortune into good. There were many other people who said you corrupted the young, but I felt that I had nothing to lose. I stealthily closed my door and came to find you, risking a beating each time, so that I could listen to you ask questions and tell stories about how a man may live well rather than badly.

Because you asked Alcibiades and Crito to rescue me, and they would do anything for you, they set me free and, in effect, gave me another chance to live my life. I was so moved that I said to you, "Socrates, I am a poor slave and have nothing else to give in return for your kindness, so I offer you myself," and you answered, "My dear Phaedo, do you not understand that merely by giving me your friendship you are offering me the greatest gift of all?" From that day forward, I never left you alone. I followed wherever you went and listened to you talk about philosophy with everyone you met. I began to write down some of the most remarkable things I heard. You told me, for instance, to make good use of a mirror. You said that contemplating our own reflections should remind the young to make themselves beautiful within, either to live up to our good looks, if we are handsome, or to make up for them, if we are not. I also learned from you that, although it is hard to know ourselves, by carefully examining the reasoning of others we may glimpse a mirror image of our own minds.

Nothing gives me more pleasure now than to call you to mind, Socrates, whether talking about you myself or listening to someone else do so. To me you seemed to be everything that a truly good and happy man must be. If anyone doubts this, let him set the character of other men beside yours; then let him judge. In my opinion, you deserved not to be executed but to be highly honored by the state. Indeed, we, your friends, all felt as if we had lost a father when you died, and that we would pass the rest of our lives as orphans.

The day before your trial, a priest of Apollo garlanded the prow of the sacred ship of Theseus, in preparation for its annual voyage to Delos. The city must be kept pure, in accord with tradition, until its return. So for thirty days you sat, the man who freed me, clapped in irons like a slave himself, inside the prison house on the edge of the Agora. The eleven officers in charge have mostly public debtors in their custody and a few convicted criminals awaiting execution: men such as temple robbers, kidnappers, brigands, and traitors. They had never known a prisoner like you. Until that time, you had spent most of your mornings walking on the streets outside the courtyard wall, where you discussed philosophy with anyone who was willing, rich and poor, Athenian and foreigner alike. Now you sat and listened to the sounds of the market from inside your cell, but you were not alone.

We gathered at the courthouse every day, just after dawn, and walked to the prison as soon as the turnkey opened the door. We stayed and talked with you about philosophy, until the sun began to set and visitors were required to leave: Crito, Antisthenes, Aeschines, myself, and many of your other friends. The last time I set eyes upon you, about fifteen or twenty of us had gathered in the prison courtyard outside your cell. We found you released from your chains, with your wife, Xanthippe, already sat beside you. In her arms, she held your youngest son, who was named after your father: Sophroniscus. Throughout your time in prison, despite your circumstances, you continued to live exactly as before: the most serene and cheerful man whom any of us had ever known. You were barefoot and dressed in a threadbare cloak, in your typical fashion, when I saw you. I had brought you a beautiful new robe to wear, but you smiled and said, "Come now, Phaedo, is my own good enough to live in but not to die in?" Silver plates and purple robes, as you liked to say, are useful if you're an actor on the stage but they're of little value in real life—and of no value at all when the time comes to face one's death.

When Xanthippe saw us, she cried aloud: "Socrates, this is

the last time your friends will ever see you!" She was so overcome with grief that she cried aloud and beat her breast with
her hands. You said, "Let someone take her home for now,"
and Crito's servants led her away. I felt that even though you
were going down to the underworld, you were doing so with
the blessing of the gods. You had lived such a life that I had no
doubt that you of all men would fare well when you got there.
Although sorrow would seem natural, given the circumstances,
I felt none, as long as we continued to talk about philosophy, in
our usual manner.

I did, however, experience a strange feeling, to which I was
unaccustomed: a mixture of pleasure and pain, as I found myself
enjoying your company as much as ever, while nevertheless knowing that you were soon to die. Everyone present, in fact, was affected in the same way, sometimes laughing, then weeping. Your
voice, though, sounded the same on the day of your execution as
it had done during your trial, and on every previous occasion that
we had spoken—you had the same look in your eyes and on your
face as always.

Being with you during your final hours was an astonishing experience. Although witnessing the death of a man who had been
my good friend, I had no feelings of pity. You were happy, both
in your words and actions, and your death appeared beautiful
and without fear. As soon as we began talking, the conversation
turned to philosophy once again. You sat up on the bed, bent your
leg and rubbed it where the iron fetters had been removed, saying,
"What a strange thing pleasure is and how remarkable its relation is with pain, which people call its opposite! A man cannot
have both at the same time. Yet once he gets a hold of one, he is
almost always bound to end up with the other, as if hunting two
creatures with one head. This seems to be happening to me right

now. Those chains hurt my leg. Now they have been removed, I feel relieved, and pleasure follows."

You had already become quite absorbed in our discussion of this idea when Crito reminded you that you were supposed to avoid overtalking. The guard had warned him that those who get heated up by conversation sometimes require two or three doses for the poison to take effect. You said to take no notice, as you didn't mind whether they had to poison you twice, and that you would prefer to continue our conversation regardless. As you sat up and put your feet on the ground, you explained that it was appropriate for one who was about to leave life to examine what we believe that journey to be like. How could our time be better spent, you said, than by discussing the topic of death while we waited for the sun to go down?

Throughout your incarceration, when your friends kept offering to bribe the guards so that you could escape, you smiled and asked them whether they knew anywhere outside of Attica that was inaccessible to death. A man who has spent his life engaged in philosophy, you said, should be cheerful when facing his own demise, and hopeful that afterward he will be blessed.

Most people fail to realize that the goal of all true philosophers is to rehearse dying and to prepare themselves for death. It would therefore be strange if they resented it when the time came. We could even say that, in a sense, philosophers are already half-dead. By this, I took you to mean that philosophers constantly seek to grasp the truth through reason rather than being misled about reality by their bodily senses and about what is good or bad by their feelings of pleasure and pain. You described your method as a kind of purification of the mind, or soul, through which it is freed from the prison of the body and becomes capable of wisdom. Whereas men who chase one pleasure after another are never satisfied, and constantly fear death, no man whose life has been full of virtue feels regret when it eventually comes to an end.

Philosophers, therefore, having trained themselves for dying, fear death least of all men. Such men are lovers of wisdom rather than the body and do not fear pain, love, pleasure, or hanker after wealth and reputation. They must, therefore, excel in the true virtues of courage and moderation. You helped us to realize that to the wise, what other men call courage and moderation, appear primitive and strange. The majority of people consider death to be a great evil. Those they call brave only face death from fear of other evils. They risk their lives in battle, for instance, but only because they are scared of being captured and enslaved. Fear and cowardice can make us appear brave when we are not. In the same way, it is our own excess that often causes us to exercise moderation. We desire some pleasures so much that we are willing to abstain from others, like a man who goes without food or sleep, waiting at the door of his beloved. We master some of our desires because we ourselves are mastered by others.

It is therefore false courage, you said, to endure one fear in order to avoid another, and it is false discipline to renounce one desire in order to indulge another. Wisdom is the only valid currency for which we should exchange our actions, by exercising courage and moderation in its name. When one desire is exchanged for another, without reference to wisdom, we have only the illusion or *appearance* of virtue rather than real virtue. This is the mark of a truly slavish character, you said, in the sense that it causes us to become enthralled by our own desires. Wisdom requires purifying the soul of such attachments. Those who love wisdom, therefore, do not travel the same road as others, who do not know where they are going. Philosophers follow where philosophy leads them, and are not led astray by fear and desire.

You told us that the founders of the mystery religions had glimpsed this truth, which they expressed symbolically, when they said that those who arrived in the underworld uninitiated would wallow in the mire, whereas those who arrived purified would dwell with the gods in the afterlife. We talked for many hours about this and what awaits us after death. Are souls dispersed like smoke when the body dies, no longer existing anywhere? Or do the souls of those who die live on in the underworld? Or is the ancient theory true that claims our souls come back from the dead to be born again, repeatedly, in new bodies?

There was a long pause, while you appeared to contemplate in silence something we had been discussing. We wanted to ask you more questions but said we were hesitant to bother you in your current misfortune. You laughed and told us that it would be hard to persuade others not to think of your present fate as a misfortune, if you couldn't even persuade your friends. Suddenly you said: "You seem to think me inferior to the swans! They sing most beautifully when they realize that they are about to die. Most men, because of their own fear of death, tell lies about the swans, and claim that their song is a lament. I believe, on the contrary, that as these birds are sacred to the god Apollo, they are prophetic. Having a knowledge of the future that awaits them after death, they sing with great joy of the blessings of the afterlife and their eagerness to depart from this world in order to join the god whom they serve."

Your friends were left puzzled by this talk of swans until, after a long pause, you added: "I have been detained here this length of time, awaiting my death, because of the festival of Delian Apollo. I consider myself to be, like the swans, his servant, and I have received from him a gift of prophecy not inferior to theirs. So I am no more sorrowful at leaving life than they are. You should, therefore, speak with me and ask me whatever you want, while there is still time remaining."

I could hold back no longer and tearfully exclaimed, "What I find hardest to bear, Socrates, is that we know you are being put to death unjustly!" I was sitting by your right on a low stool beside the couch. You placed your hand gently on my head, smiled, and asked, "Would you prefer that I was put to death justly?" I said that I would not. I blushed to think that you were consoling me when you were the one about to die. "If I am to be executed unjustly," you said, "the ones who prosecuted me will bear the shame of it. For if to do injustice is shameful, what shame is it of mine that others have decided to act unjustly toward me?"

You stroked the hair on the back of my head, as you were in the habit of doing. "Tomorrow, Phaedo," you said, "you will probably cut this beautiful hair of yours." "Yes, most likely I will do so in mourning for you," I said. "Not if you take my advice," you replied. "We would be better advised, both of us, to cut our hair today to mourn this discussion if we cannot find the courage to continue it any further." You were laughing.

I have often admired you, Socrates, but never more than on this occasion. It came as no surprise to me that, even as you discussed death with us on the eve of your execution, you had a reply to every question. What impressed me, though, was the patience and kindness with which you listened to your young companions' arguments, and how keenly you were aware of the effect the conversation was having on us. I marveled at how you healed our sorrow and instilled courage in us, as though recalling us from defeat and flight, and turning us around to face the enemy once again with confidence.

You joked that we, your friends, seemed to have a childish fear that when we die a breeze might come and blow away our souls, scattering them as they leave our bodies. Were we so superstitious that we worried what might happen if we were to die in a high wind rather than calm weather? We laughed and said that perhaps there was a child within us who had such fears and that you should try to persuade him not to be so afraid of death, as if it were a terrifying bogeyman. You said we should sing a magic charm to the child within us every day until we dispel his fears.

Where will we find someone who can cast good charms, we asked, now that you are leaving us? You suddenly looked at us very intently, as I remember, and said that we should spare no trouble or expense to search all of Greece or even the barbarian lands, until we find someone. There is nothing, you said, that we could spend our money on to greater advantage. We should look first among ourselves our group of friends, however, as we may not find others who could help us as easily as we could help ourselves.

When you noticed that we were all becoming tearful once again, you laughed. "Why are you only now beginning to weep? Have you not always known that from the day of my birth, nature had condemned me to death? Do you think it strange," you said, "if God has decided that I should die now? Don't you see that to this day, in my estimation, no man has lived a better or a more enjoyable life than I? For those men surely live best who strive the hardest to become as good as possible, and the most rewarding life is theirs who are aware of making progress in the right direction.

"If I were to live much longer, I would be forced to pay the old man's forfeit: to become half-blind and half-deaf, dull-witted, slow to learn, and quicker to forget. No, I believe that God in his kindness is taking my side and providing me with the opportunity of ending my life not only at the right moment but also in the easiest way."

When it was nearing sunset, you said it was time for you to take a bath. You wanted to save the women the trouble of washing your corpse. Crito asked about your final instructions concerning your sons and what little property you owned. After listening to you, he also asked, "What can we do that would please you the most?" You said the same thing as always: We would please you, and ourselves, by always taking good care of our own souls. "You will do yourselves the most good," you explained, "if you put your philosophy into practice, because even if you agree with every word I say today, you will achieve nothing if you neglect to take care of yourselves tomorrow, and every day thereafter."

"We will be eager to follow your advice," said Crito, "but how shall we bury you?" "Any way you like," you joked, "assuming that you can catch me!" Turning to the rest of us, smiling, you said, "Crito has not yet been persuaded that I am Socrates talking to you right now, but he still believes that Socrates is the body that will soon become a corpse. After I have drunk the poison, I shall no longer be with you but shall go and enjoy good fortune with the blessed. You know well enough already, Crito, that to express yourself badly is not only a fault of speech but also of *thought*, and therefore does harm to the soul. So please, my old friend, do not say at the funeral that you are laying out and burying Socrates. You must be of good cheer, and loudly proclaim that you are burying *the body* of Socrates. You may do so in whatever way you find most appropriate, according to our customs."

It was now growing late, and Xanthippe returned, bringing your sons to say goodbye to their father for the last time—Lamprocles was already a young man, but the other two were still children. You spoke to your wife and your eldest boy quietly for a while, and Crito passed on your final instructions. Once your family had left, you joined us again. The sun was beginning to slip behind the Hill of the Muses outside.

You talked for only a short while longer before the room fell silent as we saw a burly shaven-headed guard walk through the door. He stood directly before you, but his eyes were downcast as he spoke: "I know that I shall have no need to reproach you as I do other condemned men, Socrates. They are angry with me and curse me when, following the orders I have been given, I tell them to drink the poison. During the weeks you have been here, I have come to know you as the noblest and gentlest man who has ever come to this place. I already know that you will not argue with me, and that you do not blame me. You already know what message I bring: farewell, and try to endure what you must as easily as possible." I noticed, as the man turned to leave, that he, too, had tears in his eyes.

You called after him and said, "Farewell to you too, my friend; we shall do as you bid." Once he had left, you turned to us and said, "Since I was sent here, that man has come in and conversed with me regularly, and I have found him to be a most pleasant fellow. Come, Crito, let us do what he instructed. Ask them to bring me the poison if it is ready; if not, let the man prepare it." "But wait, Socrates," stammered Crito, "I think the sun still shines upon the hills outside and has not yet set. I know that others have drunk the poison quite a long time after they have received the order to do so. They are permitted to eat a last meal and to spend time with their loved ones. Do not hurry; there is still some time remaining." "It is natural, Crito, for others to do this," you replied, "for they assume that it is in their interests to delay the inevitable, but it is not appropriate for me to do the same. I do not expect to gain anything by drinking the poison a little later, except to become ridiculous in my own eyes for clinging desperately to life, when there is none left. So please do as I request, my friend, and do not refuse me."

Crito sent for the slave whose role it was to administer the hemlock, and he arrived carrying it ready-mixed in a wine cup. When you saw him, you said, "Well, my good man, you are an expert in this. What must one do?" The man told you to drink the poison and walk around until your legs felt heavy, then to lie down and wait for it to take effect. He offered the cup to you, his hands trembling. You took it quite cheerfully, without the slightest change in your expression, but looked up at the man from under your eyebrows, as you often did, and asked, "Am I allowed to pour a libation to the gods from this drink?" The man said they had only mixed as much as they believed was necessary for one dose. "I understand," you said, holding the cup in your hands, "but I must nevertheless utter a prayer that my journey from here to there may be a good one. This is my prayer and may it be so."

You raised the hemlock cup to your lips, and drank. We felt as though all of us, indeed all of Athens, swallowed the poison along with you. Most of us had held back our sorrow until this point, but we could hold it back no longer. My own tears flooded down my cheeks against my will, so much that I felt the need to cover my face. In truth, I wept for myself rather than for you, Socrates. I could see that you were unafraid of dying but I was afraid, because I was about to lose my dearest friend. I was surprised to see, though, that Crito was already in tears. He stood up quickly, turned away, and walked across the room. "What is this," you said, "you strange fellows! The priests tell me that it is preferable to die in silence. So keep quiet, good friends, please, and no more tears."

You stood up and walked around until your legs felt heavy, then you lay on your back as you had been advised to do. The man who gave you the poison checked your body. After a short while, he pressed hard on your foot and asked you if you could feel anything there. You said no. Your legs were becoming cold and stiff, as the poison spread, and we were told that when the cold reached your heart, it would stop beating.[2] You looked toward Crito and said your last words: "We owe a cock to Asclepius, make this offering to him, my friend, and do not forget." As you covered your face with your cloak, Crito whispered: "It shall be done." Then he paused for a moment before adding, "Tell us if there is anything else," but there was no answer from you, just silence followed by a slight shudder.

A moment later, the man uncovered your face, and we saw that your gaze had become fixed. Crito, your oldest friend, leaned forward and closed your mouth and eyes. Some said you meant that death had cured you of the ills of life, such as old age and sickness. Asclepius, of course, is the god of medicine, to whom a cock is sacrificed in exchange for a remedy. He is the son of Apollo, the god of healing, to whose service you had dedicated your life. You often told us that even death could be seen as a kind of medicine if we faced it like philosophers, who improve themselves by contemplating its nature, and I think this is what you meant.

Such was your end. You were the first philosopher ever to examine, by means of reason, the moral conduct of our lives, and the first to be executed by the state.[3] I, Phaedo, do not believe that there exists a record anywhere of a more noble death. I find it impossible to forget you or, in remembering you, to hold back my praise.

Who among us was more temperate and less enslaved by his bodily desires than Socrates? What man has ever lived with more freedom? For you accepted neither gifts nor payment from anyone. Who could be deemed more just than you, content with so little, wanting nothing from anyone else? And who could surpass your wisdom, Socrates, who from your first words, ceaselessly pursued and learned about every virtue?

Anyone who knows what manner of man you were, and who seeks wisdom, continues to this day to miss you beyond all measure. For you alone proved to be our foremost guide on that journey. And, what is more, you were, of all the men whom I have known, the best, the wisest, and the most just.

ACKNOWLEDGMENTS

I would like to thank Stephen Hanselman, my agent, for giving me the opportunity to write this book, and Tim Bartlett, my editor, for his help with the manuscript. Special thanks are due to my good friend, Lalya Lloyd, for her help editing the initial draft. I'm also grateful to my wife, Kasey, for her support and understanding throughout a period of our lives during which a great deal of my time was dedicated to writing something that I had, at one time, considered almost impossible to write.

NOTES

FRONT MATTER GENERAL

1. K. Jaspers, 1962, 13, italics added.
2. Waterfield, 2023, xxxviii.
3. See, for example, Waterfield, 2023, 47.

INTRODUCTION

1. Cicero, *De Finibus*, 5.1.
2. Byron, 1839, 193.
3. Epictetus, *Enchiridion*, 5.
4. For instance, in Book 1 of Plato's *Republic* where Cephalus refers to the role of attitude in determining our experience of old age; and in Xenophon's *Memorabilia*, where Socrates tells Chaerecrates (2.3) that his perspective causes his anger toward his brother and shows Lamprocles (2.2) that his way of thinking about his mother makes him irritated with her.
5. Jules Evans, "RIP Aaron Beck, founder of CBT and reviver of the Stoics' cognitive approach to therapy."
6. Xenophon, *Memorabilia*, 2.2.
7. Apuleius, *On the God of Socrates*, 19.6, slightly modified.
8. For instance, it's been noted that the character of Callicles in Plato's *Gorgias*, who is otherwise unknown, may have been perceived by ancient audiences as standing in for a specific individual or class of individuals recognizable to them, such as Critias, a notorious former student of Socrates and uncle of Plato. I have therefore put some of Callicles's words into the mouth of Critias and taken similar liberties with other dialogues and characters.
9. We must be cautious about attributing ideas from Plato's later works, such as the *Republic*, to Socrates, but I think this basic aspect of the Allegory of the Cave, aside from the Theory of Forms, broadly expresses the philosophical role that Socrates saw himself as fulfilling.

10. Plutarch, "Whether an Old Man Should Engage in Public Affairs," 796d.

11. Socrates in Phaedo 91c.

1. THE TRIAL

1. The main source for this account of Socrates's trial is, of course, Plato's *Apology*, although I have also drawn upon material from Xenophon's *Apology* and other sources.

2. Aristophanes, *Clouds. Wasps. Peace.*

3. The text of the charges against Socrates is quoted, credibly, by Diogenes Laertius in *Lives and Opinions*, 2.5.

4. Aristotle asserts that Socrates had been to Delphi, although he does not specify whether it was on the same occasion that Chaerephon obtained the oracle, as we have presumed for the sake of our story.

5. There was also a third maxim, less well known today because it is harder to translate, that said, "Surety brings ruin," which Plutarch interpreted as a warning against intellectual conceit and a potential slogan of Greek Skepticism.

6. This is how Plutarch, who was both a philosopher and a priest at Delphi, interprets its significance in *The E at Delphi*, 15.

7. There was no formal process of cross-examination in ancient Athenian law courts, although it was possible for defendants to question witnesses directly and attempt to refute their testimony, as Socrates is shown doing, albeit in his own idiosyncratic way, in Plato's *Apology*.

8. Plato leaves this individual unnamed, and it's possible that Socrates, out of respect, avoided naming someone who was deceased. The most obvious candidate would be Pericles, although Protagoras, his advisor, was also a statesman of sorts, and I believe it's *possible* that Socrates could be referring here to the famous Sophist.

9. At least this is a popular theory, although some question the truth of the story.

2. THE FIRST PHILOSOPHER

1. We depend on a handful of scattered references and some inference for the claim that Socrates initially worked in his father's sculptor's workshop (e.g., Diogenes Laertius; 2.5.18, 2.5.20).

2. Pericles's building program on the Acropolis is believed to have started around 447 BCE and the work on the propylaea is dated to the 430s, when Socrates was in his thirties. So Diogenes Laertius's claim that "the draped

figures of the Graces on the Acropolis have by some been attributed to him" (2.5.19) does not readily square with my assumption that he abandoned being a sculptor somewhat earlier in life.

3. Phaedo 96a-c describes how Socrates, as a young man, was interested in such questions from natural philosophy.

4. Modern scholars doubt that the philosopher created this sculpture so it is probably best regarded as an interesting fiction, although we're told that Plato's successor put up statues of the Graces in the shrine of the Muses at the Academy, the symbolism of which was surely of interest to early students of philosophy.

5. Diogenes Laertius (2.3.7) implies that Anaxagoras was born in 500 BCE, and states that he lived in Athens for thirty years. Most scholars date the arrival of Anaxagoras in Athens to around 456 BCE but Taylor (1917) provides a persuasive argument for dating this to 480 BCE, when Pericles was aged around fifteen. Taylor believed that the issue of the date was conclusively settled by the fact that several ancient authors refer to Pericles as the "student" (*mathetes*) of Anaxagoras, which he takes to mean that the philosopher was responsible for Pericles' early eduction. Taylor also notes that as Plato's *Phaedo* portrays Socrates being dissatisfied with Anaxagoras's book but not seeking clarification from the man himself, despite being shown elsewhere conversing with most of the other great thinkers of Periclean Athens, Plato must be taken to imply that Anaxagoras had written his book and departed from Athens "when Socrates was still quite young," which Taylor therefore dates to around 450 BCE.

6. It is mainly from Plato that we learn of Socrates's early interest in Ionian philosophy, although no dates are specified, forcing us to speculate. We're also forced to explain why there is no reference to Socrates having spoken to Anaxagoras, despite the fact we're told he devoured the Ionian philosopher's writings.

7. Most of our information on Anaxagoras is derived from Diogenes Laertius 2.3.

8. At least, Socrates is mocked by the Syracusan in Xenophon's *Memorabilia* for being nicknamed "the Thinker" (*Phrontistes*) perhaps because Aristophanes in the *Clouds* had harshly satirized him as the head of "the Thinkery" (*Phrontisterion*)—giving us a clear example of a nickname not unlike *Nous* being employed sarcastically in Athens.

9. Maps of this kind were introduced by previous Ionian philosophers, so we're probably justified in imagining that Anaxagoras could have employed such aids in his teaching.

10. This was clearly an important event. We don't know for certain that the attention it brought to Anaxagoras's philosophy propelled him into

the limelight and heightened the controversy around his teachings, but it's a reasonable supposition for our story to make.

11. Assuming Taylor (1917) is correct to date the arrival of Anaxagoras in Athens to 480 BCE, when Pericles was about fifteen, and that the young noble therefore became his student (*mathetes*) early on. In Plato's *Phaedrus* (269e–270a), for instance, Socrates attributes Pericles's acclaimed oratorial style, primarily, to the influence of Anaxagoras, which only makes sense if the two men were acquainted prior to, or early on in, Pericles's political career.

12. Thucydides, 2.28.

13. Anaxagoras was, likewise, able to infer that the earth must be spherical because he realized that during *lunar* eclipses, the earth casts its shadow across the moon, and we can see that it is always round.

14. The details of Anaxagoras's trial are fragmentary and quite problematic. Some scholars, such as Waterfield (2010), believe that the Athenians wanted to place him on trial but probably did not do so. Others, such as Taylor (1917) and Mansfield (1979) believe that the trial at Athens did take place, but disagree with each other over the date.

15. It's implied by Diogenes Laertius that he later killed himself voluntarily, out of grief. Despite being sentenced to death *in absentia*, it would have been difficult for Athens to enforce the sentence against him while he resided far away in Lampsacus. Although our sources for Anaxagoras's fate are problematic, the image of Athens's first philosopher as a tragic victim of political infighting, which we find, albeit slightly garbled, in the ancient sources, offers an interesting contrast to the fate of Socrates, which I've chosen to develop slightly further for our story.

16. Diogenes Laertius, 2.3.

17. The first trial may have taken place in Athens around 450 BCE, when Socrates was aged about twenty. We do not know for certain that he witnessed the trial, but he must surely have been interested in the outcome, so it seems likely he may have been present, or at least have listened to detailed reports from others who were. It would undoubtedly have been a key event in his life.

18. We're told that Socrates was a student of Archelaus, which makes it puzzling that he appears not to have met Anaxagoras, the latter's teacher. I've tried to resolve this in our story by assuming that Archelaus and Socrates only became friends after Anaxagoras was exiled, although there's some evidence that, in fact, they may have known each other earlier.

19. Diogenes Laertius (e.g., describes a philosophical succession passing from Anaxagoras, through Archelaus, to Socrates; 1.1).

20. Ancient Athenians are seldom described as nodding to show agree-

ment in the way that we do today. They probably did *not* typically shake their heads to express disagreement. However, for the sake of convenience, I have sometimes referred to nodding in these dialogues.

21. In Plato's *Phaedo* (97b), Socrates says, "One day I heard a man reading from a book, as he said, by Anaxagoras," and I have agreed with Taylor (1917) who comments that this meant "presumably his successor Archelaus," before Socrates later acquired and read the book himself.

22. Plato's *Apology* has Socrates say that Anaxagoras's book was freely available in the marketplace, yet he does not appear to have lectured in public. For the sake of our story, we assume therefore that Anaxagoras's students published his book following his exile.

23. Some may question whether familiarity with philosophical doctrines could become so widespread in Athens, even among the illiterate masses. However, in Plato's *Apology* (26d), Socrates is depicted saying in court that it would be ridiculous for his accusers to pretend that the five hundred jurors before them are so illiterate that they do not recognize the doctrines of Anaxagoras, and that, moreover, the doctrines of natural philosophy were frequently described in the theatre, presumably in satires, where he says anyone can hear them for a single drachma.

24. One of our few tantalizing references to Socrates's early influences comes in this brief passage of Plato's *Phaedo*, where he recounts his reasons for growing disillusioned, as a young man, with the writings of Anaxagoras.

25. Both these excerpts from poems attributed to Socrates are found in Diogenes Laertius (2.5.42), although he mentions one earlier author having cast doubt on the authenticity of the hymn to Apollo.

26. Epictetus, *Discourses*, 2.1.

27. We will explore this dialogue, which was with Euthydemus, in chapter 4.

28. See, for instance, Martell et al., 2013.

3. THE FEMALE SOCRATES

1. Socrates was nearer the truth than Anaxagoras. Although the sun *appears* to glow like a fire, it does not burn like a fire but rather emits heat and light due to nuclear fusion, consuming hydrogen atoms rather than oxygen.

2. Xenophon attributes these remarkably astute criticisms of natural philosophy to Socrates in *Memorabilia* 4.7.

3. We learn what little we know of Phaenarete from Plato's *Theaetetus*, assuming we can take what he says about her occupation literally.

4. The French term *sage-femme* would be a better translation, as it means both midwife and wisewoman.

5. We have no evidence that Phaenarete knew Aspasia. However, they were both experts on matchmaking and Socrates was later part of Aspasia's circle. It seems reasonable to imagine that his mother, known as a local *maia,* would have been interested in what Aspasia said about matchmaking and love, and if they met, it's plausible that Socrates came to know of Aspasia in this way.

6. In this dialogue, I've taken the liberty of taking simple ideas about matchmaking attributed to Socrates in Xenophon's *Memorabilia* and transferring them instead to Phaenarete. It's possible that Socrates and his mother would have discussed similar ideas, given her expertise in this area.

7. Several sources link Socrates to Aspasia, including Plato's *Menexenus*, where she is portrayed as one of his teachers. We do not know when their friendship began, although it seems reasonable to speculate that it probably came after his interest in natural philosophy.

8. The content if this dialogue is derived from the words of Diotima in Plato's *Symposium*. Some scholars have argued that Plato was, indeed, using Diotima as a pseudonym for Aspasia. For example, see D'Angour (2020).

9. We're told that "being convinced that the study of nature is no concern of ours"; Socrates instead "claimed that his inquiries embraced" whatever is good or evil in our house or halls, quoting *Odyssey* 4.392, according to Diogenes Laertius (2.5).

10. This conversation is based on Xenophon's *Memorabilia* 2.6, which Socrates does in fact link to advice on matchmaking he received from Aspasia.

11. This theme in the Socratic dialogues inspired the Latin saying *Esse quam videri* derived from Cicero's *On Friendship*, 98.

12. Matthew, 7.12.

13. J. Beck, 1995, 160.

4. THE ORACLE OF APOLLO

1. We don't know that this was Chaerephon's reason for consulting the oracle, but it seems plausible. Why ask if any man is wiser than Socrates unless you're troubled by the more general question: Which man is wisest?

2. We are not explicitly told that Socrates was present on the occasion when Chaerephon questioned the Oracle, although Aristotle mentions

that at some point Socrates did visit Delphi. There is no evidence, as far as I know, that speaks against this having been the case. D'Angour (2020) therefore also believes that Socrates was at Delphi with Chaerephon when the Pythia gave her famous pronouncement.

3. The date of Chaerephon's visit to Delphi is one of the most problematic aspects of Socrates's biography. Some scholars, such as Waterfield (2010), believe it to be a complete fiction, although I'm not so sure. It is, in any case, integral to the *literary character* of Socrates constructed by Plato and Xenophon, and further developed by later authors, and for that reason I have also made it central to the narrative presented in this book. If it did happen, it seems likely to have been before Socrates left for Potidaea. I have also placed it before Socrates's conversation with Protagoras, whom we can then view as one of those questioned by him in order to test the pronouncement.

4. This short dialogue is based on *Memorabilia* 2.3. We do not know when it took place, but by assuming it was immediately prior to Chaerephon's visit to Delphi, we can interpret his surprising question as having been influenced by such examples of his friend Socrates's wisdom, which surely had a profound effect upon him.

5. Epictetus goes so far as to claim that one of the most important qualities Socrates exhibited was his ability to tolerate others without irritation and put an end to quarrels (*Discourses*, 2.12).

6. *Memorabilia* 4.2.

7. Of course, as it's Greek, he writes the letters delta for *dikaiosune* and alpha for *adikia*.

8. In some ways, this aspect of the Socratic method resembles what we call "brainstorming" today, as Socrates must think creatively each time and come up with a variety of good examples that challenge his interlocutor's definition.

9. Persius, *Satire 5*, 105–110.

10. Borkovec and Sharpless (2004) review several research studies that support their hypothesis that the symptom of pathological worrying in generalized anxiety disorder is linked to inflexibility across various psychological response systems, including cognitive rigidity, which they treat by training clients to brainstorm multiple alternative ways of interpreting the events about which they are worried.

11. E.g., Hayes et al., 1986.

12. This scene is largely my invention, although I think we can imagine Socrates was probably quite taken aback by the question Chaerephon chose to ask the Pythia.

5. THE WISEST MAN ALIVE

1. Based on Plutarch, *Lives*, Alcibiades 2.3, but we're not told Socrates witnessed this. Knucklebones was forerunner of jacks, which usually consisted of five small bones (the anklebones of a sheep or goat) being tossed in the air and caught on the back of the hand, although other variations of existed.

2. Two of Socrates's most influential students, Aeschines and Antisthenes, wrote lost dialogues called *Aspasia* and *Alcibiades*, and two dialogues named after Alcibiades are attributed to Plato (though the attribution is doubtful for the second one)—he also features prominently in Plato's *Symposium*. Both Aspasia and Alcibiades, therefore, seem to have been regarded as important characters in portraying Socrates's life and thought by those who knew him personally.

3. As Waterfield (2010) puts it, in terms of status, Alcibiades could be compared to a high-ranking British peer or lord.

4. Plutarch, *Lives*, Alcibiades, 2.2.

5. *Iliad*, 6.208; 11.784.

6. The dialogue in this chapter is, of course, closely based on Plato's *Protagoras*.

7. Protagoras quoted in Diogenes Laertius, 9.8.51.

8. The claim that Protogaras was exiled comes from later sources and is often considered unlikely to be true.

9. This speech is paraphrased in Plato's *Protagoras*, and I have paraphrased it again for modern readers. Some have seen it as foreshadowing aspects of Darwinism—e.g., the development of a sense of moral justice is here explained as necessary for the survival of the human species.

10. Protagoras's famous doctrine that "Man is the measure of all things" might be taken to support, among other things, the view that we should measure how good or bad something is based on our experience of pleasure rather than, for instance, by reference to the will of the gods.

11. See Nezu et al., 2013.

6. THE LION OF ATHENS

1. This brief account of Socrates's response to the oracle is based on that given in Plato's *Apology*.

2. This dialogue is based on Plato's *Alcibiades I*.

3. As far as we know, the ancient Greeks may have nodded in agree-

ment but did not shake their heads in disagreement. So I refer in less specific terms to them gesturing no, or expressing disagreement nonverbally through frowning, etc.

4. Galen, on the *Passions and Errors of the Soul*, 2.

5. Matthew, 7.3.

6. Freaks, 2015.

7. Wisdom was defined by the researchers in terms of measures of intellectual humility, such as being willing to search for additional information; open-mindedness, such as being more likely to look at the situation from the perspectives of others; and compromise, or being willing to combine alternative perspectives to find a solution.

8. Diogenes Laertius (2.5.33), and elsewhere in the same book, Plato and Zeno the Stoic both recommend the use, literally, of mirrors to increase self-awareness of our moral character.

9. Antisthenes quoted in Diogenes Laertius, 6.1.6.

10. In Plato's *Crito*, Socrates also imagines himself engaging in a dialogue with the Laws, who refer to him in the second person, allowing him to imagine conversing with himself in a detached manner.

11. Grossmann et al., 2021.

12. Beck, Emery, and Greenberg, 2005, 323.

13. Beck, Emery, and Greenberg, 2005, 194.

14. Hayes et al., 2012.

15. Plato's *Symposium*, 215e.

16. We learn of Socrates having fought at Potidaea from several sources, most notable Plato's *Symposium* 220d-e. Here I have chosen to construct the scene using our fragmentary knowledge of the battle and some inference.

17. The Athenians used foreign cavalry instead of shipping their own horses such a long distance, which may help to explain why Alcibiades seems to have been fighting in the infantry during this battle.

18. Our knowledge of the Battle of Potidaea and subsequent Peloponnesian War depends almost entirely upon the history written by Thucydides.

19. Alcibiades, in Plato's *Symposium*, does not specify what Socrates was contemplating, so for the sake of our story I have speculated that it may have been something relating to the pronouncement of the Delphic Oracle, drawing upon Plato's *Apology* 22d-e.

20. This anecdote is based upon Cicero, *De Fato* 10–11, and *Tusculanae Disputationes* 4.80.

21. Aristophanes, *Frogs*, 1431–1433.

7. THE PELOPONNESIAN WAR

1. Our main source regarding the plague of Athens is the seventh chapter of Thucydides. Modern scholars believe it may have been a form of typhus.

2. The dialogue that follows is, of course, based on the first part of Plato's *Gorgias*.

3. I've incorporated this anecdote from Diogenes Laertius (2.5.21) because I think it provides some helpful context for the *Gorgias* dialogue. Socrates seems to have had a reputation for taking risks by provoking others with his questions, and some Athenians found it odd that he didn't learn to speak up for himself in court.

4. This anecdote is based mainly on Alcibiades's account of the battle in Plato's *Symposium*.

5. *Cognitive Therapy and the Emotions*, 1976.

6. Beck et al., 1976.

7. Beck et al., 1976, 243.

8. See Plato's *Phaedrus*.

9. Perhaps we can say that because of his knowledge and experience, the officer class came to view Socrates as we would a sergeant major, or as Romans would a centurion.

10. Plato says Xanthippe held Socrates's youngest child in her arms while he was awaiting execution. If we assume the child was no older than two, and she gave birth to him aged no more than forty, she would be forty-two or younger in 399 BCE, making her fourteen or younger in 427 BCE, which would give approximately the earliest date she could have married. However, no wife of Socrates is mentioned by Aristophanes's satire *The Clouds* (423), although she seems to have provided perfect satirical material for later authors. That suggests Socrates may have married her in 423 at the earliest. By some accounts, Socrates had a first wife called Myrto, who may have still been alive when he also married Xanthippe, but she probably died before Socrates, as we hear little about her.

11. We do not know the year, but Hipparete's father, Hipponicus III, was alive at the time, and he is believed to have died in 422, so that is the latest plausible date.

12. The notorious Milesian Dialogue is described in Thucydides, 5.84–116.

13. Thucydides, frustratingly, does not tell us who proposed the Siege of Melos to the Assembly or who was responsible for ordering the massacre. Perhaps we can appeal to the "argument from silence" to infer that Thucydides's *failure* to mention Alcibiades, in this instance, implies that he probably did not play a significant role.

14. Hesiod, *Works and Days*, 202.

8. THE SICILIAN EXPEDITION

1. The Attic talent was a measure of weight, approximating to 26 kg, so this would equate to around 1,560 kg of uncoined silver.

2. The dramatic date of Plato's *Symposium* is 416 BCE, the year before Alcibiades set sail, and he portrays Alcibiades as still in love with Socrates, although over time he'd increasingly found himself drawn away and spending time engaged in Athenian politics.

3. The dialogue that follows is based on the conversation with Polus in Plato's *Gorgias*, but I have taken the liberty of putting his words into the mouth of Alcibiades. Polus is otherwise unknown, but some scholars believe Plato's audience would have naturally identified him with the class of young nobles, including Alcibiades or Critias.

4. We do not know the name of Alcibiades's ship, but *Eleutheria* is attested as the name of an Athenian warship, which I have adopted for the sake of our narrative.

5. Beck, 1976, 2, italics added.

6. Beck et al., 2005, 195.

7. There was talk that Alcibiades could obtain funds from his friend Tissaphernes to pay the Athenian navy, on condition that the democracy was replaced with an oligarchy. Years later, his son would deny these rumors, insisting that Alcibiades had always opposed oligarchy and pointing out that his father only ever served Athens under a democratic regime.

8. Thucydides, 8.86.4.

9. Plutarch, *Lives*, Alcibiades, 26.4.

9. THE FALL OF ATHENS

1. We have no record of Alcibiades meeting Socrates on his return to Athens, but given how close they were, and the fact that they had saved each other's lives, it seems almost certain that Alcibiades would have missed seeing his old friend and mentor.

2. This dialogue is mostly conjecture on my part, very loosely based on remarks found in ancient sources, but it helps, I think, to bridge a gap in our narrative.

3. This dialogue is based on the *Axiochus* of pseudo-Plato.

4. The anecdote about Phaedo is based on a few scraps of information in Diogenes Laertius 2.5.31; 2.9.105.

5. Isocrates, *On the Team of Horses*, 16.45–46, although Hipparete is not

named as Alcibiades the Younger's mother, it's implied she died not long after he was born, while his father was again in exile.

6. In this chapter, we've put some of Axiochus's words into the mouth of his nephew, Alcibiades, as we can imagine him having similar concerns, and his character is more central to our narrative.

7. Seneca, *On Tranquility of Mind*, 11.6.

8. Epictetus, *Enchiridion*, 5.

9. Isocrates, *On the Team of Horses*, 16.45–46.

10. Alcibiades had one son who survived but he was stripped of his property, which he never recovered in full.

11. Plutarch and our other sources say only that he was killed by ranged weapons, possibly meaning darts, javelins, or arrows.

12. "This man, defamed by most writers, three historians of very high authority have extolled with the greatest praises; Thucydides, who was of the same age with him; Theopompus, who was born some time after; and Timaeus; the two latter, though much addicted to censure, have, I know not how, concurred in praising him only; for they have related of him what we have stated above, and this besides, that . . . with whatever people he was, he was regarded as a leading man, and held in the utmost esteem." (Cornelius Nepos, 7.11)

10. THE THIRTY TYRANTS

1. Our main source for this period in Athenian history is Book 2 of Xenophon's *Hellenica*, chapters 3–4.

2. This would, of course, later become the home of Stoic philosophy.

3. Here I have taken the words of Callicles from Plato's *Gorgias* and put them in the mouth of Critias.

4. Plato recounts these events in his *Seventh Letter*.

5. Waterfield (2010, 172) believes that Theramenes was not a hero but a hardcore Oligarch and that the story about Socrates trying to save him from execution is absurd.

6. *Republic*, 440c-d.

7. Freud, *Mourning and Melancholia*, 1917, in Freud et al., 2001, 243–258.

8. Sullivan et al., 2020. Similarly, in standard tools used to measure clinical depression, we find references to perceived injustice such as "I feel I am being punished" in the Beck Depression Inventory (BDI-II, item 6).

9. Beck, 1976, 64–72.

10. Homer's *Odyssey*, 20.17–18 quoted in Plato's *Republic* 3.390d, and in the *Phaedo* 94d-e.

11. Plato, *Republic*, 4.441b-c.

12. Under the democracy, the mob at the trial of the generals following the Battle of Arginusae threatened to have him put to death. Then under the oligarchy, the Thirty appear first to have threatened his life for breaking their new law against philosophy and then again when he refused to arrest Leon of Salamis. Under the restored democracy, the court finally sentenced him to death. He therefore faced threats of execution, perhaps twice under each regime.

11. THE SWAN SONG

1. Most of this dialogue is based on excerpts from Plato's *Phaedo*, although the opening anecdote is from a fragment of a dialogue attributed to Phaedo in Seneca's *Letters* (94.41).

2. Some authors, such as Waterfield (2010, 29) object that Plato's *Phaedo* does not appear to describe the known effects of hemlock poisoning. Others, such as Bloch (2001), have made the case that certain varieties of hemlock could have caused precisely the effects described by Plato.

3. If this is correct, it implies that Anaxagoras was not executed by the state, although we are told he was sentenced to death *in absentia* and that he later took his own life.

REFERENCES

Ahbel-Rappe, Sara. *Socrates: A Guide for the Perplexed.* London: Continuum, 2009.

Apuleius, and Christopher P. Jones. *Apologia. Florida. De Deo Socratis.* Loeb Classical Library. Vol. 534. Cambridge, MA: Harvard University Press, 2017.

Aristophanes. *Clouds. Wasps. Peace.* Translated by Jeffrey Henderson. Loeb Classical Library. Vol. 488. Cambridge, MA: Harvard University Press, 1998.

————. *Frogs. Assemblywomen. Wealth.* Translated by Jeffrey Henderson. Loeb Classical Library. Vol. 180. Cambridge, MA: Harvard University Press, 2002.

Beck, Aaron T. *Cognitive Therapy and the Emotional Disorders.* 1976. Reprint, New York: Meridian Book, 1979.

Beck, Aaron T., Gary Emery, and Ruth L. Greenberg. *Anxiety Disorders and Phobias: A Cognitive Perspective.* 2nd ed. 1985. Reprint, New York: Basic Books, 2005.

Beck, Aaron T., A. J. Rush, Brian F. Shaw, and Gary Emery. *Cognitive Therapy of Depression.* New York: Guilford Press, 1979.

Beck, Judith S. *Cognitive Behavior Therapy: Basics and Beyond.* 2nd ed. 1995. Reprint, New York: Guilford Press, 2021.

Bloch, Enid. "Hemlock Poisoning and the Death of Socrates: Did Plato Tell the Truth?" *Plato Journal* 1, no. 1 (2001). https://doi.org/10.14195/2183-4105_1_1.

Borkovec, Thomas, and Brian Sharpless. "Generalized Anxiety Disorder: Bringing Cognitive-Behavioral Therapy into the Valued Present." In *Mindfulness and Acceptance: Expanding the Cognitive-Behavioral Tradition*, edited by Steven C. Hayes, Victoria M. Follette, and Marsha Linehan, 209–42. New York: Guilford Press, 2004.

Cicero. *On Ends.* Translated by H. Rackham. Loeb Classical Library. Vol. 40. Cambridge, MA: Harvard University Press, 1914.

————. *On the Orator: Book 3. On Fate. Stoic Paradoxes. Divisions of Oratory.* Translated by H. Rackham. Loeb Classical Library. Vol. 349. Cambridge, MA: Harvard University Press, 1942.

————. *Tusculan Disputations*. Translated by J. E. King. Loeb Classical Library. Vol. 141. Cambridge, MA: Harvard University Press, 1927.

Cooper, John M., and D. S. Hutchinson. *Plato: Complete Works*. Indianapolis: Hackett Publishing Company, 1997.

Cornelius Nepos. *On Great Generals. On Historians*. Translated by J. C. Rolfe. Loeb Classical Library. Vol. 467. Cambridge, MA: Harvard University Press, 1929.

D'angour, Armand. *Socrates in Love: The Making of a Philosopher*. London: Bloomsbury Publishing, 2020.

Diogenes Laertius. *Lives of Eminent Philosophers, Volume I: Books 1–5*. Translated by R. D. Hicks. Loeb Classical Library. Vol. 184. Harvard University Press, 1925.

————. *Lives of Eminent Philosophers, Volume II: Books 6–10*. Translated by R. D. Hicks. Loeb Classical Library. Vol. 185. Harvard University Press, 1925.

Ellis, Walter M. *The Athenian*. San Jose: Writers Club Press, 2001.

Epictetus. *Discourses, Books 1–2*. Translated by William Abbott Oldfather. Loeb Classical Library. Vol. 131. Cambridge, MA: Harvard University Press, 1925.

————. *Discourses, Books 3–4. Fragments. The Encheiridion*. Translated by William Abbott Oldfather. Loeb Classical Library. Vol. 131. Cambridge, MA: Harvard University Press, 1928.

Evans, Jules. "RIP Aaron Beck, Founder of CBT and Reviver of the Stoics' Cognitive Approach to Therapy." Medium, November 1, 2021. https://julesevans.medium.com/rip-aaron-beck-founder-of-cbt-and-reviver-of-the-stoics-cognitive-approach-to-therapy-da055ba45cbf.

Farnsworth, Ward. *The Socratic Method: A Practitioner's Handbook*. Boston: Godine, 2021.

Freaks, Data. "Why We Give Great Advice to Others but Can't Take It Ourselves." Forbes, April 7, 2015. https://www.forbes.com/sites/datafreaks/2015/04/07/why-we-give-great-advice-to-others-but-cant-take-it-ourselves/.

Freud, Sigmund. "Mourning and Melancholia." In *The Standard Edition of the Complete Psychological Works of Sigmund Freud. Volume XIV, (1914–1916), on the History of the Psycho-Analytic Movement, Papers on Metapsychology and Other Works*, edited by Anna Freud, translated by James Strachey, 243–58. London: Hogarth Press, 1957.

Galen. *Galen on the Passions and Errors of the Soul*. Translated by Paul W. Harkins. Columbus, OH: Ohio State University Press, 1963.

Gordon, George. *Lord Byron: The Complete Poetical Works*. Edited by Jerome J. McGann. Vol. 3. Oxford: Clarendon Press, 1981.

Grossmann, Igor, Anna Dorfman, Harrison Oakes, Henri C. Santos, Kathleen D. Vohs, and Abigail A. Scholer. "Training for Wisdom: The Distanced-Self-Reflection Diary Method." *Psychological Science* 32, no. 3 (February 4, 2021): 381–94. https://doi.org/10.1177/0956797620969170.

Grote, George. *Plato, and the Other Companions of Sokrates.* Vol. 1–4. 1865. Reprint, e-artnow, 2021.

Hadot, Pierre, Arnold I. Davidson, and Michael Chase. *Philosophy as a Way of Life : Spiritual Exercises from Socrates to Foucault.* Malden, MA: Blackwell Publishing, 2017.

Hanson, Victor Davis. *A War like No Other: How the Athenians and Spartans Fought the Peloponnesian War.* New York: Random House, 2006.

Hayes, Steven C., Aaron J. Brownstein, Robert D. Zettle, Irwin Rosenfarb, and Zamir Korn. "Rule-Governed Behavior and Sensitivity to Changing Consequences of Responding." *Journal of the Experimental Analysis of Behavior* 45, no. 3 (May 1986): 237–56. https://doi.org/10.1901/jeab.1986.45-237.

Hayes, Steven C., Kirk D. Strosahl, and Kelly G. Wilson. *Acceptance and Commitment Therapy: The Process and Practice of Mindful Change.* 2nd ed. New York: Guilford Press, 2012.

Hesiod. *Theogony. Works and Days. Testimonia.* Translated by Glenn W. Most. Loeb Classical Library. Vol. 57. Cambridge, MA: Harvard University Press, 2018.

Hughes, Bettany. *The Hemlock Cup.* London: Vintage Books, 2011.

Isocrates. *Evagoras. Helen. Busiris. Plataicus. Concerning the Team of Horses. Trapeziticus. Against Callimachus. Aegineticus. Against Lochites. Against Euthynus. Letters.* Translated by La Rue Van Hook. Loeb Classical Library. Vol. 373. Cambridge, MA: Harvard University Press, 1945.

Jaspers, Karl. *Socrates, Buddha, Confucius, Jesus: The Paradigmatic Individuals.* Edited by Hannah Arendt. New York: Harcourt, Brace World, 1962.

Johnson, David. *Socrates and Alcibiades: Four Texts.* Indianapolis: Hackett, 2003.

Johnson, Paul. *Socrates: A Man for Our Times.* New York: Viking, 2011.

Juvenal, and Persius. *Juvenal and Persius.* Translated by Susanna Morton Braund. Loeb Classical Library. Vol. 91. Cambridge, MA: Harvard University Press, 2004.

Kagan, Donald. *The Fall of the Athenian Empire.* Ithaca: Cornell University Press, 1992.

———. *The Peace of Nicias and Sicilian Expedition.* Ithaca: Cornell University Press, 1991.

Kaligas, Paulos, ed. *Plato's Academy: Its Workings and Its History.* Cambridge: Cambridge University Press, 2020.

Macdonald Cornford, Francis. *Before and after Socrates*. 1932. Reprint, Cambridge: Cambridge University Press, 1999.

Mansfeld, J. "The Chronology of Anaxagoras' Athenian Period and the Date of His Trial." *Mnemosyne* 32, no. 1/2 (1979): 39–69. https://www.jstor.org/stable/4430850.

———. "The Chronology of Anaxagoras' Athenian Period and the Date of His Trial. Part II. The Plot against Pericles and His Associates." *Mnemosyne* 33, no. 1/2 (1980): 17–95. https://www.jstor.org/stable/4430931.

Martell, Christopher, Sona Dimidjian, Ruth Herman-Dunn, and Peter Lewinsohn. *Behavioral Activation for Depression: A Clinician's Guide*. New York: Guilford Press, 2013.

Massimo Pigliucci. *The Quest for Character*. New York: Basic Books, 2022.

Navia, Luis E. *Socrates: A Life Examined*. Amherst, NY: Prometheus Books, 2007.

Nezu, Arthur M., Thomas J. D'zurilla, and Christine M. Nezu. *Problem-Solving Therapy: A Treatment Manual*. New York: Springer Publishing Company, 2013.

Plutarch. *Lives, Volume IV: Alcibiades and Coriolanus. Lysander and Sulla*. Translated by Bernadotte Perrin. Loeb Classical Library. Vol. 80. Cambridge, MA: Harvard University Press, 1916.

———. "The E at Delphi." In *Moralia, Volume V,* translated by Frank Cole Babbitt. Cambridge, MA: Harvard University Press, 1936.

———. "Whether an Old Man Should Engage in Public Affairs." In *Moralia, Volume X,* translated by Harold North Fowler. Cambridge, MA: Harvard University Press, 1936.

Pressfield, Steven. *Tides of War: A Novel of Alcibiades and the Peloponnesian War*. New York: Bantam, 2001.

Renault, Mary. *The Last of the Wine*. London: Virago, 2015.

Romilly, Jacqueline de. *The Life of Alcibiades*. Ithaca: Cornell University Press, 2019.

Seneca. *Epistles, Volume III: Epistles 93-124*. Translated by Richard M. Gummere. Loeb Classical Library. Vol. 77. Cambridge, MA: Harvard University Press, 1925.

———. "On Tranquility." In *Moral Essays, Volume II,* translated by John W. Basore. Cambridge, MA: Harvard University Press, 1932.

Stone, I. F. *Trial of Socrates*. Boston: Little, Brown and Co., 1988.

Stuttard, David. *Nemesis: Alcibiades and the Fall of Athens*. Cambridge, MA: Harvard University Press, 2018.

Sullivan, Michael J. L., Heather Adams, Keiko Yamada, Yasuhiko Kubota, Tamra Ellis, and Pascal Thibault. "The Relation between Perceived Injustice and Symptom Severity in Individuals with Major Depression: A

Cross-Lagged Panel Study." *Journal of Affective Disorders* 274 (September 2020): 289–97. https://doi.org/10.1016/j.jad.2020.05.129.

Taylor, A. E. "On the Date of the Trial of Anaxagoras." *The Classical Quarterly* 11, no. 2 (April 1, 1917): 81–87. https://doi.org/10.1017/s0009838800013094.

———. *Socrates: The Man and His Thought.* New York: Doubleday, 1952.

Taylor, C. C. W. *Socrates : A Very Short Introduction.* Oxford: Oxford University Press, 2019.

Thucydides. *History of the Peloponnesian War, Volume I: Books 1–2.* Translated by C. F. Smith. Cambridge, MA: Harvard University Press, 1919.

———. *History of the Peloponnesian War, Volume II: Books 3–4.* Translated by C. F. Smith. Cambridge, MA: Harvard University Press, 1920.

———. *History of the Peloponnesian War, Volume III: Books 5–6.* Translated by C. F. Smith. Cambridge, MA: Harvard University Press, 1921.

———. *History of the Peloponnesian War, Volume IV: Books 7–8.* Translated by C. F. Smith. Cambridge, MA: Harvard University Press, 1923.

———. *The Landmark Thucydides : A Comprehensive Guide to the Peloponnesian War.* Edited by Robert B. Strassler. New York: Free Press, 1996.

Vlastos, Gregory. *Socrates Ironist and Moral Philosopher.* Ithaca, NY: Cornell Uniersity Press, 1991.

Waterfield, Robin. *Plato of Athens.* Oxford: Oxford University Press, 2023.

———. *Why Socrates Died.* Faber, 2010.

Wilson, Emily R. *The Death of Socrates.* Cambridge, MA: Harvard University Press, 2007.

Xenophon. *Conversations of Socrates.* Translated by Robin Waterfield. London: Penguin, 1990.

———. *Hellenica, Volume I: Books 1–4.* Translated by Carleton L. Brownson. Loeb Classical Library. Vol. 88. Cambridge, MA: Harvard University Press, 1918.

———. *Memorabilia. Oeconomicus. Symposium. Apology.* Translated by Jeffrey Henderson. Loeb Classical Library. Vol. 168. Cambridge, MA: Harvard University Press, 2013.

———. *The Landmark Xenophon's Hellenika.* Edited by Robert B. Strassler. New York: Free Press, 2009.

INDEX

ABOUT THE AUTHOR

DONALD J. ROBERTSON is a cognitive-behavioral psychotherapist, trainer, and writer. He was born in Ayrshire, Scotland, and after living in England and working in London for many years, he emigrated to Canada, and now resides in Quebec. Robertson has been researching Stoicism and applying it in his work for over twenty years. He is one of the founding members of the nonprofit organization Modern Stoicism. He is also the founder and president of the Plato's Academy Centre nonprofit in Greece. Robertson is the author of *Verissimus* and *How to Think Like a Roman Emperor.*